an outline history of

MUSIC

BROWN

MUSIC SERIES

Edited by

FREDERICK W. WESTPHAL, PH.D.
Sacramento State College
Sacramento, California

The autograph first page of Johann Sebastian Bach's *b minor Mass*. Courtesy Baerenreiter-Bild-Archiv.

an outline history of

MUSIC

ᕼᕮᕼ

MILO WOLD
Linfield College

EDMUND CYKLER
University of Oregon

Revised Edition

WM. C. BROWN COMPANY PUBLISHERS

DUBUQUE, IOWA

Manufactured by WM. C. BROWN CO. INC., Dubuque, Iowa
Printed in U. S. A.

Introduction

An Outline History of Music has been planned and organized to be used in a variety of ways. (1) It can be used as a basic text in music history with collateral readings in the many authoritative studies in the specialized periods and styles in the history of music that are readily available to the student. In this manner the text will serve as a practical core from which the student can expand his studies to include the vast amount of source material that has been edited and published in recent years. (2) It is designed to be used as an outline and review for any standard text on the subject. The student can utilize its plan and material to focus attention on the most important developments and still have the benefit of the complete discussion usually found in such texts. (3) The present volume will prove valuable to the student who wishes to embark on a study of the literature and history of music on his own without the guidance of an instructor. Its information on scores, recordings and collateral readings can be a guide to unlimited reading and to a selected list of musical examples that will serve as a basis for the understanding of musical styles.

The authors are of the strong opinion that the primary source material of music history is the music itself. Consequently the present volume is designed as a guide to musical examples that explain and illustrate the historical development of music. Obviously it would be impossible to include actual scores of all the music necessary for such a study in a single volume. Therefore, it has been indicated where both the music and the recordings are to be found in each case. In the earlier periods especially, anthologies that are accompanied by recordings are listed. This makes it possible to use actual music as source material with a minimum of library facilities. Great care has been taken to use only music and records that are currently in print, and recordings of anthologies that give strong evidence of continuation have been the basis of much of the selection rather than outstanding performance. The student is urged to study the music, listen to the recordings and, whenever possible, to perform selected examples as a part of the classroom experience. Examples need not be confined to those listed. Other music that the instructor might suggest or the student might seek out will serve to broaden the student's acquaintance with forms and styles.

The authors have avoided the temptation to divide music history in a series of short, specialized periods of time. On the contrary, only the rather large, but generally accepted, designation of periods of history such as Gothic, Renaissance, Baroque, etc., are specified. While the music of every composer is different from that of his contemporaries in specific details and the earliest music in a style differs from the later music in the same style, it is the opinion of the authors that a general adherence to a basic stylistic pattern is rather consistent over a long period of time. For example, the principal characteristics, patronage, function, performing practice and musical style in the Renaissance are fairly uniform for a period of about 200 years. Moreover, in spite of the widely publicized "isms" of twentieth century music, there is still a constancy of style in modern music that has already lasted over fifty years.

The present volume subjects each major period of music history to analysis by means of an outline of important movements that influence the patronage and function of music, musical devices, forms, composers, etc. No claim is made to exhaustiveness of the categories or of the items in each category.

Only those facts that seem pertinent to a basic understanding of the development of music have been included. No doubt teachers and others who use this outline will wish to supplement it with additional material. The following is a brief survey of the plan of each chapter:

I. Sociocultural Influences on Music

Under this heading any important trends and movements in such areas as religion, economics, government, social and cultural life that seem to have a bearing on the patronage, types and style of music are set forth. Because such influences are usually subjective and vague in nature, only generalizations as to their relationships can be suggested.

II. Function of Music

Because composers usually write with a purpose in mind and because the various cultural conditions call for different types of music, the functions of music in a historical period are significant. Moreover, the economic conditions under which a composer lives are partially determined by the demand for, and support of, music with a specific function. Needless to say, function has a great deal to do with the style and expressiveness of music.

III. Characteristics of Style

Each basic element of music is examined from the point of view of its general stylistic qualities and also any special devices or techniques that are prominent in the music itself. The subdivisions of the basic elements are:

1. Formal Organization
2. Melody
3. Rhythm
4. Harmony
5. Texture
6. Media

IV. Practice and Performance

Each important device or practice that enables performers to realize the composer's purpose is defined and explained. Such techniques as notation, dynamics, instrumentation, etc., are included under this heading.

V. Vocal Forms

Each important vocal form is defined and the general characteristics of its musical substance is commented upon. In addition, a specific example which is representative of the form is suggested, together with an available score and recording. In the case of more important forms more than one example is given. The instructor, or student, may substitute or use additional examples as further illustrations. It is realized that no one form can be fully represented by one or two examples.

VI. Instrumental Forms

The same procedure is applied to instrumental forms. In those periods of music history where instrumental forms predominate, this item in the outline will appear before the vocal forms.

VII. Important Composers

Composers are listed as being of major importance not only because of the permanency and quality of their works but also because of their innovations and influence. These composers are listed in the chronological order of their dates of birth, together with brief biographies. Important works and suggested examples with scores and recordings are also given. From the Classic period on, specific scores and recordings are omitted, due to the fact that there are numerous editions and recordings from which to choose.

VIII. Other Composers

Composers of lesser importance are listed in the chronological order of their dates of birth and according to countries. The authors are aware that the classification of composers into the foregoing two lists is an arbitrary one, and that it is often only an opinion that places one in the list of major composers and another in the list of minor composers.

IX. Important Writers on Music

Writers on music often give an illuminating account of the musical scene in which they live. They are also important sources for the practices and interpretations of a musical style. With few exceptions, only those writers whose works serve these purposes have been included. Information as to title, place and date of publication of the important writings is given. In addition, a brief statement regarding the contents of the writings is made where pertinent.

X. Manuscript Sources

In the earlier periods especially, the only sources of the music itself are the collections of manuscripts, usually preserved in monasteries or universities, which are of great value to the scholar. This item is dropped from the outline after the Renaissance because from then on widespread publication of music made authoritative editions accessible. It is realized that for scholarly research it is still necessary to examine original manuscripts whenever possible, even of present-day composers.

XI. Suggested Readings

Collateral readings from current major texts on music history, as well as specialized studies in the various periods, are listed together with specific page numbers at the end of each chapter. The following are the abbreviations used for these readings:

Austin	Austin, William W. *Music in the 20th Century.* New York: W. W. Norton, 1966.
Bukofzer	Bukofzer, Manfred F. *Music in the Baroque Era.* New York: W. W. Norton, 1947.
Cannon-Johnson-Waite	Cannon, Beekman C., Johnson, Alvin H., & Waite, William C. *The Art of Music.* New York: Crowell, 1960.
Einstein	Einstein, Alfred. *Music in the Romantic Era.* New York: W. W. Norton, 1947.
Ferguson	Ferguson, Donald. *A History of Musical Thought.* New York: Appleton-Century-Croft, 3rd. Ed., 1959.

Grout	Grout, Donald Jay. *A History of Western Music.* New York: W. W. Norton, 1960.
Hansen	Hansen, Peter, *Introduction to Twentieth Century Music.* New York: Allyn & Bacon, 1961.
Lang	Lang, Paul Henry. *Music in Western Civilization.* New York: W. W. Norton, 1941.
Machlis	Machlis, Joseph. *Introduction to Contemporary Music.* New York: W. W. Norton, 1961.
Harman & Mellers	Harman, Alec, & Mellers, Wilfrid. *Man and His Music.* London: Oxford, 1962.
Oxford	*New Oxford History of Music.* London: Oxford, 1954.
Reese-MA	Reese, Gustave. *Music in the Middle Ages.* New York: W. W. Norton, 1940.
Reese-R	Reese, Gustave. *Music in the Renaissance.* New York: W. W. Norton, 1959.
Sachs-RMA	Sachs, Curt. *Rise of Music in the Ancient World, East and West.* New York: W. W. Norton, 1943.
Sachs-HER	Sachs, Curt. *Our Musical Heritage.* New York: Prentice Hall, 2nd. ed., 1955.
Ulrich-Pisk	Ulrich, Homer, and Pisk, Paul A., *A History of Music and Musical Style.* New York: Harcourt, Brace & World, 1963.
Wold-Cykler	Wold, Milo, and Cykler, Edmund. *An Introduction to Music and Art in the Western World.* Dubuque: Wm. C. Brown Company Publishers, 3rd ed., 1967.

XII. Further References:

Reference for more detailed and independent study will be given under this heading. Because of their great numbers, biographical studies will not be listed except in those instances where a work is of major significance. The student can easily seek out biographies of those composers in whom he is most interested.

Bibliography

Only basic reference works and anthologies are included in the following list. Comprehensive bibliographies will be found in every standard music history and other scholarly studies.

Reference Works

Baker's Biographical Dictionary of Musicians. 5th ed., revised by N. Slonimsky. New York: G. Schirmer, 1958, Supplement, 1965. Dates and spellings in the present volume are according to Baker's Dictionary.

Die Musik in Geschichte und Gegenwart. Kassel: Bärenreiter, 1945.

Grove's Dictionary of Music and Musicians. 5th ed., 10 vols., London: Macmillan, 1954.

Harvard Dictionary of Music. Edited by Apel, Willi. Cambridge: Harvard University Press, 1950.

New Oxford History of Music. 11 vols., (3 to date). London: Oxford, 1954.

Oscar Thompson's International Cyclopedia of Music and Musicians. 9th ed., edited N. Slonimsky. New York: W. W. Dodd, 1964.

Source Readings in Music History. Selected and Annotated by Oliver Strunk. New York: W. W. Norton, 1950.

Anthologies and Recordings

Anthology of Music. Edited by Fellerer, Karl Gustav. 28 vols. Cologne: Arno Volk, 1959.

Examples of Music Before 1400. Gleason, Harold. New York: Crofts, 1946.

Geschichte der Musik in Beispielen. Schering, Arnold. Leipzig: Breitkopf and Härtel, 1931.

Historical Anthology of Music. Davison, Archibald T. and Apel, Willi. 2 vols. Cambridge: Harvard University Press, 1946.

History of Music in Sound. 10 vols. London: Oxford, 1953. Recorded by RCA. (This Anthology contains only partial scores, but the recordings are complete.)

Masterpieces of Music Before 1750. Parrish, Carl and Ohl, John F. New York: W. W. Norton, 1951. Recorded by Haydn Society.

Treasury of Early Music. Parrish, Carl. New York: W. W. Norton, 1958. Recorded by Haydn Society.

Recordings of a number of examples of early music are to be found in the *Archive Productions of the Deutsche Grammaphon Gesellschaft.*

All recordings are designated according to the *Schwann Record Catalog.*

The following are the abbreviations for the foregoing anthologies as used for examples:

AM	*Anthology of Music*
EM	*Examples of Music before 1400*
GMB	*Geschichte der Musik in Beispielen*
HAM	*Historical Anthology of Music*
HMS	*History of Music in Sound*
MM	*Masterpieces of Music Before 1750*
TEM	*Treasury of Early Music*

Contents

Chinese Musicians. A wall painting from the caves of Tung-
Chuang in the province of Kan-su from the time of the T'ang-
Dynasty (618-907 A.D.). Courtesy of Baerenreiter-Bild-Archiv.

1

༄༅

Nonwestern
Musical Systems

I. Sociocultural Influences on Music

The knowledge of the music of the cultures that preceded the present Western European one is at best very sketchy and piecemeal. The perishable nature of music limits all real knowledge of it to those systems which had devised some adequate method of notation. At no time previous to the Romanesque has a system of notation existed that enables scholars to reconstruct more than a mere handful of melodic fragments with any degree of certainty. Music among primitive as well as civilized peoples existed in practice principally as a form of free improvisation.

The best sources of study of music's pre-western history, and these can be only partially adequate, are:

1. The musical practices of primitive groups such as the various African, North and South American Indian, and Oceanic tribes. Through a study of the music of such primitive groups, scholars are able to reconstruct in part, at least, the music of early historical civilizations.

2. The musical practices of ancient civilized peoples whose cultural institutions are in some measure still in existence

today, such as the Chinese, Indian, Siamese, Japanese and other Oriental groups.

3. The reconstruction of musical systems by the study of pictorial descriptions of instruments, fragments of notation, writings about music and some few examples of ancient instruments still intact. Such material has been used particularly in the study of music of the Mediterranean area, the Egyptian, Hebrew and Greek.

It is doubtful that any culture previous to our own used music as an independent art form. Music as an expressive medium is, however, as old as man himself. Evidence of its use is to be found among all peoples, primitive and civilized, though emphasis varied from culture to culture. Since music lacked any artistic independence it was most probably associated exclusively with overt emotional expression. Most references to music, whether in written or pictorial form, lead us to believe that the practice of music was particularly dependent on the strength and attitudes of the dominant religious organizations of each culture. The attitude of the dominant religious body determined not only whether music was to be used, banned or merely tolerated, but also the kind of music that was permissible, its manner of presentation, the instruments to be used and many other factors dealing with musical expression.

Among the Chinese, for example, certain types of instruments were closely related to seasonal and geographical considerations, and their use was dictated by these considerations rather than aesthetic ones. Such influences are to be found on the music of all the early cultures and some remnants of these socio-cultural forces still determine the use of music in the western world. Some religious sects today forbid the use of certain music and certain instruments. The Greek Orthodox Church allows no instruments whatsoever in its services. The Roman Catholic Church generally forbids all instruments but the organ, and at one time allowed only male voices in the sung liturgy.

The Greeks ascribed certain ethical values to their music, depending on the tonal relationships within the scales or modes on which the melodies were built. Melodies built in one mode were considered effeminate and damaging to the morals of the youth, while melodies in another mode might be stimulating to warlike action, etc.

In India the melodic patterns called ragas, that act as basic elements for improvisation, are divided into those that are appropriate for certain periods of the day. Ragas designed for use in the morning must not be used in the afternoon, and vice versa. In Oriental cultures magical powers are attributed to scale patterns, pitch levels, and intervals themselves. These powers are interpreted in accordance with the religious, economic and political institutions of the various cultures.

II. Function of Music

1. The more primitive the society the more closely tied to ritual was the musical expression. Monotonous incantations and instrumental rhythms accompanied religious rites and festivals to achieve a kind of magic hypnosis. In highly civilized societies too, the use of music was mainly for religious ritualistic purposes, but other uses of music are also to be found.

2. An outgrowth of the combination of music and religious ritual was the musical drama and the incidental use of music in spoken drama. The musical dramas of the Chinese represent a highly developed relationship of music and dramatic presentation. In Greece there was a definite use of music in the performance of the great dramatic works of the classic Greek theater. Unfortunately there is little or no knowledge of what the music was like or precisely how it was used.

3. From the paintings, reliefs, and the writings of ancient peoples it also is obvious that forms of secular music existed. Folk dances and songs, as well as a highly organized kind of secular music, were used for festive occasions. Songs of love and work are found among all peoples, past and present.

III. Characteristics of Style

Three general characteristics prevailed in all nonwestern music: (1) It was predominately vocal, (2) it was predominately melodic, (3) it was predominately improvisatory.

1. *Formal Organization.* Generally speaking, the music was based upon melodic and/or rhythmic patterns which constituted a point of departure for the performer, and upon which he improvised rather freely. The formal organization was one of repetition and rhapsodic variation.

2. *Melody.* Melody was one of the two dominant elements of music. Although often based on traditional fragments or patterns, the art of the singer consisted of spinning out variations that used arabesque-like decorations characteristic of all nonwestern music. Trills, turns, rapid and florid scale passages were the main features of the melodic line.

All pre-western melodic invention was based on the recognition of the octave as a closed system. As far as can be determined most pre-western societies seem to have constructed their melodic patterns on a selection of five tones within the octave, a basic system of melodic construction known as pentatonic. The music of the present day Oriental cultures, Chinese, Japanese, Siamese, Indonesian, etc., is built on a five tone division of the octave closely resembling the relationships represented by the 1st, 2nd, 3rd, 5th and 6th tones of the modern major scale. There are no intervals corresponding to the half steps found between the 3rd and 4th and the 7th and 8th tones in the modern major scale. However, many Oriental systems divided this basic pentatonic scale into very small intervals representing one-fourth, one-eighth and even one-sixteenth of a modern whole step. Writings of the Greeks indicate a vast knowledge of musical theory. They had available, through scientific discovery, the actual twelve tones of the octave which constitute the modern chromatic scale. Their melodies were based on a system of tetrachords which, when placed side by side, resulted in an octave scale of seven tones similar to those in the modern major scale. Since each of the seven tones might be used as the basic tone, a series of seven different modal scales was theoretically possible for the construction of a melody. These were the scales or modes to which the Greeks ascribed ethical values.

3. *Rhythm.* The second important element of nonwestern music was rhythm. In many respects rhythmic patterns among

primitive as well as civilized groups achieved a complexity that western civilization did not cultivate until the present century. Rhythm is generally quantitative — long and short beats, rather than qualitative — strong and weak beats. Irregular rhythmic patterns of seven, ten and fourteen, for example, are not uncommon, especially in India.

4. *Harmony.* Harmony in the modern sense of the term was nonexistent. However, the use of drone bass and ostinato accompanying patterns was probably more widely spread than heretofore realized. This is particularly true of the music of the southeastern Asiatic societies such as Java and Bali.

5. *Texture.* Texture was achieved through multiple playing and singing of the same basic melodic line by various voices and instruments. Accounts and pictures of large groups numbering into the hundreds of instrumentalists and singers would indicate that there was appreciation for tonal texture achieved through duplication of the same melodic patterns at the unison or octave, or even at other intervals, by various media.

6. *Media*

   a. Since music and word were so closely connected in early musical performance it is obvious that the voice was by far the most important medium of expression.

   b. Instruments consisting of wind, string and percussion families were widely used to accompany the voice, generally at the unison or octave. The development of the percussion instruments was very advanced with all types of material used. Percussion instruments were made of wood, metal, stone and even of vegetable fibre such as gourds. They were divided into groups which were accurately pitched according to scale divisions and those which were merely used for sound effects with no pitch accuracy. Division of the octave system into smaller intervals than the half step of our western system was exploited in many of the tuned instruments.

c. Both bowed and plucked string instruments were used. The bowed strings were not perfected in either workmanship or performance, but the plucked strings reached a high state of perfection second only to the percussion instruments in make and performance.

d. The least developed of the pre-western instruments were the wind instruments corresponding to our present brasses and woodwind types. The brasses never advanced beyond the simple natural form and were made of various materials, metal, bone and wood, the primitive mouthpieces being part of the horns themselves. Woodwind instruments were only fitted with open holes, if indeed such were even used. There was a great variety of both flute and reed type instruments, however, ranging from simply made folk instruments to those elaborately constructed.

IV. Practice and Performance

1. Lacking a fixed notation, all practices were a matter of tradition within the culture. The selection of instruments, voices, dynamics and tempi was undoubtedly the result of traditional usage. References to musical performance indicate that certain instruments, for example, were used only for certain occasions due to the association of their timbre with moral and ethical values.

2. Judging from practices now in use in cultures other than those of western Europe, it is probable that the voice also was used in a different fashion from the European tradition. Various tonal qualities were cultivated by such practices as tightening of the throat passage, falsetto, guttural grunts, etc.

3. Again from the evidence of other contemporary cultures it is probable that a strikingly high perfection of performance skill was achieved in the use of percussion instruments. This is especially evident in the present day performance of African, Indian, and western Oriental peoples.

V. Vocal Forms

It is impossible to speak about vocal forms beyond the fact that vocal music, both spiritual and secular, was employed. The improvisational character precluded most set formal structure, and lack of notated examples gives us no basis for reconstruction of formal designs if any existed.

VI. Instrumental Forms

As in vocal music there were no set forms as such. In fact there was a minimum of purely instrumental music. Little mention is made of use of instruments except in combination with voices or for dance purposes.

VII. and VIII. Composers

There are no records of any composers or their works which have come down to us. Accounts of performers such as David in the Old Testament are the only records which would give any indication of composers as such, since every performer was in fact a composer.

While there are no specific composers to whom compositions can be attributed, examples of ancient music do exist. Volume I of *The History of Music in Sound* gives fifty-two short examples of the music of pre-western cultures from early music of China to that of Greece and Islam.

> Ex. 52 works of nonwestern cultures
> HMS. Vol. I pp. 13-38
> Rec. RCA LM - 6057 HMS Vol. 1

Innumerable recorded examples of primitive people outside of western culture are also available.

IX. Important Writers on Music

Early writers deal either with music in a mathematical-theoretical way or in a philosophical-ethical manner. Among the former the most important are those who base their theories on the work of Pythagoras, the early Greek mathematician and speculator of the harmony of the spheres. Among the latter the most extensive writings are those of the Greek philosophers, although references to music can be found in the works of many ancient writers, Chinese, Indian, Hebrew and others.

1. Pythagoras (c. 582 B. C.–c. 500 B. C.) was a Greek philosopher and mathematician to whom is ascribed the discovery of musical ratios of which only the octave and fifth were considered pure consonances. There is no record of any of Pythagoras' writings and his theories are known only as they were developed by his followers.

2. Plato (427 B. C.–347 B. C.) was the great Greek philosopher whose concern with music was almost entirely that of ethical values. Passages in the *Timaeus* and the *Republic* state his concepts of music and its place in society.

3. Aristotle (384 B. C.–322 B. C.), a pupil of Plato, also was concerned with the ethical values of music as evidenced in several of his writings, notably in the *Politics*.

4. Aristoxenus (354 B. C.–?) was the most important of the Greek writers on music. Two works, *Harmonic Elements* and *Elements of Rhythmics*, have come down to us, the first complete the second in fragmentary form. An English edition of these two works by H. S. Macran was published in 1902.

5. Cleonides (first half of the second century A. D.) was a Greek writer. *Harmonic Introduction* was an early source of information for the Renaissance musicians on classic Greek music, having been published in Venice in 1497.

6. Aristedes Quintillianus (flourished c. 200 A. D.) was a Greek theorist whose treatise, *De Musica Libri VII*, provides a basic source for knowledge of the music of ancient Greece. A German translation by Schafke was published in 1937.

7. Athenaeus (flourished c. 200 A. D.) was a Greek writer who lived in Rome. While he was not a musician his descriptions of musical performance in his books, *Sophists at Dinner*, are a valuable source in giving an insight into the regard for and place of music in Roman life.

Excerpts from most of the foregoing are to be found in Strunk, *Source Readings in Music History,* New York: W. W. Norton, 1950.

Plato	p. 3
Aristotle	p. 13
Aristoxenus	p. 25
Cleonides	p. 34
Athenaeus	p. 47

X. Manuscript Sources

Again the lack of notation and the fact that music was not an independent art form precludes any large manuscript collections of early music. What few examples of Greek music there are have been deciphered from inscriptions on stone. Music of the Orient was handed down orally until recent centuries when it was recorded in writing.

XI. Suggested Readings

Cannon-Johnson-Waite	pp.	5-25
Ferguson	pp.	8-40
Grout	pp.	3-19
Lang	pp.	1-36
Oxford V. 1	pp.	1-464
Sachs, HER	pp.	1-48
Sachs, RMA	pp.	57-290
Ulrich-Pisk	pp.	3-25
Wold-Cykler	ch.	3

XII. Further References

Idelsohn, Abraham. *Jewish Music in its Historical Development.* New York: H. H. Holt, 1929.

Kunst, Jaap. *Ethno-Musicology.* The Hague: M. Nijhoff, 1959.

Nettl, Bruno. *Music in Primitive Culture.* Cambridge: Harvard University Press, 1956.

Winnington-Ingram, R. P. *Mode in Ancient Greek Music,* Cambridge: Cambridge University Press, 1936.

Portrayal of singing at the choral service (left), and at the Mass (right), from an antiphonary dating from the turn of the tenth to the eleventh century. The work of J. Reichenauer. Courtesy of Baerenreiter-Bild-Archiv.

2

꙲

Romanesque
500-1100

I. Sociocultural Influences on Music

The term Romanesque is generally used to describe the medieval style of art that was influenced by the Roman Empire. While the term is more accurately used to designate architecture, it is also commonly used to refer to that period of music that was dominated by monophony. While the monophonic chant continued its development beyond 1100, it lost its importance as a style after the introduction of harmony and the development of polyphony in the Gothic period. Sacred monophony is generally referred to as plainsong, or chant.

It must be noted that our knowledge of Romanesque music in general is based upon rather meager evidence. While we have examples of early sacred music which have been preserved by the Catholic Church, its interpretation is open to question. This is due to the fact that there was an inadequate system of notation, particularly in relation to time values. We have even fewer authentic examples of secular monophony because of the lack of a systematic preservation of tradition.

1. Under the patronage of early Catholicism, music was organized according to the specification of the church service and in keeping with a simple ascetic faith.

2. The many monastic orders that flourished during this period were mainly responsible for the development and organi-

zation of sacred music. In keeping with liturgical practice, this music was always set to an ecclesiastical Latin text.

3. The medieval denial of physical matter was partly responsible for the apparent lack of instrumental music in the Church. Another reason was that the Church fathers could sanction only music with a religious text.

4. In general, the music of the early Church took its forms and liturgical order from the Byzantine Church and the Jewish Service, but modern scholarship is in doubt as to the exact details of such connections.

5. Feudalism gave rise to a society with a well-developed social consciousness. Consequently, a large body of secular music and poetry in the vernacular was derived from its entertainments and its desire for self-expression outside the confines of the Church.

II. Function of Music

1. The function of sacred plainsong was to express a simple faith in God in keeping with the other-worldly spirit of early Christianity. This function was achieved by the musical setting of portions of all rituals of the Church, of which the most important was the Mass. Other rituals that also used music were the so-called Divine Offices or Canonical hours, such as Matins, Lauds and Vespers.

2. The liturgy of the Catholic Mass called for the musical setting of eleven texts. These were divided into two sections. The first section, the *Ordinary*, consisting of the Kyrie, Gloria, Credo, Sanctus (Benedictus), Agnus Dei and Ite missa est, used the same text for each service. The second section, the *Proper*, changed texts from service to service according to the church calendar. It consisted of the Introit, Gradual, Alleluia, Offertory, and Communion.

3. In addition to the Mass and the Divine Offices, plainsong was used extensively in musical settings of hymns, psalms,

and some nonliturgical texts inserted between words of liturgical texts. These latter were called tropes.

III. Characteristics of Style

1. *Formal Organization*

   a. The organization and forms of sacred plainsong were
   determined by the Latin text of the particular portion
   of the liturgy.

   b. In a few instances, mainly the trope and sequence,
   the organization was based on melodic configuration,
   with syllables being only incidental.

   c. The forms of secular monophony were also determined
   by the text, but these texts were most often poetic
   in form and consequently the music reveals such patterns as verse with refrain, repeated melodic phrases,
   etc.

2. *Melody*

   a. Sacred melody, plainsong, is monophonic, without
   accompaniment.

   b. Plainsong melody has a narrow range that rarely exceeds the interval of a fifth.

   c. Plainsong melody is modal and is based on the eight
   church modes. Each mode is a different octave segment of the diatonic scale. The octaves D-d, E-e, F-f,
   and G-g became the basis of the eight church modes.
   Each octave was used for two modes, one authentic,
   the other plagal. The authentic modes were numbered
   I, III, V, VII, the plagal, II, IV, VI, VIII. The principal
   tone in each mode was called the *final*. The secondary
   principal tone was called the *dominant*. The *range* was
   that segment of the mode within which the melody
   was sung. Greek names were given to the modes in
   the latter part of the Romanesque and we refer to
   them in this manner today.

(CHART OF MODES)

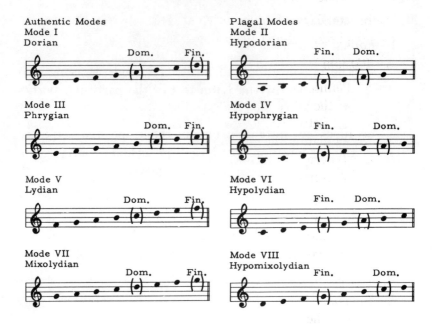

Figure 1

d. Some plainsong chants, especially those used in the psalm settings, made use of a reciting tone. This is a tone upon which most of the syllables of the chant are executed and is usually the dominant of the mode.

e. There are four types of plainsong melody: (1) syllabic, in which each note is set against a syllable of the text; (2) neumatic, in which a small group of notes are sung to one syllable; (3) psalmodic, using many syllables to one pitch, and (4) florid, or melismatic, in which extended groups of notes are set to one syllable.

f. Melody in secular monophony often uses a wider range of notes than plainsong.

g. Secular monophony is not restricted by the church modes and often approaches tonality.

h. Secular monophony is also usually cast in regular phrases, while plainsong is more irregular.

3. *Rhythm*

a. Plainsong rhythm was determined by the poetic flow of the prose and the quantitative quality of ecclesiastical Latin. The long and short syllabic structure of Latin regulated the rhythm. As a consequence, rhythmic patterns of stressed and nonstressed accent are absent in sacred monophony.

b. Because secular monophony used the vernacular in which there is a more qualitative accent, its rhythm is most often metric and shows more symmetric organization than plainsong.

4. *Harmony*

a. There was no systematic harmonic development during the Romanesque. However, both sacred and secular monophony were accompanied on occasion by instruments and consequently some harmonic practices, such as drone bass and ostinato figures, were probably present.

b. As early as 850 the practice of singing in parallel fourths and fifths began and was called *organum.* There were two types: Strict organum which involved singing in parallel fourths and fifths and free organum which permitted the singers to start and end in unison. This led ultimately to the use of contrary motion.

5. *Texture*

a. Since sacred plainsong was monophonic, there was no texture in the sense of a combination of lines or tonal coloring of later music. However, the austere line of plainsong sung by the priest, or the chant sung in unison or organum by a choir, created a mystic simplicity of linear sound that complemented the stark simplicity of the Romanesque cathedral itself.

b. Secular monophony, because of its wider range, more definite rhythmic patterns and frequent use of instruments, together with its vernacular text reveals a fuller texture that expresses human feelings and emotions.

6. *Media*

a. Sacred plainsong is always vocal. While there is some evidence that instruments were occasionally used as accompaniment, as a rule instruments were prohibited in the Romanesque Church.

b. Secular monophony was mainly vocal, but was often accompanied by instruments, especially when used as dance music.

c. Instruments used in secular music were the stringed instruments, both plucked and bowed, and a variety of wind and percussion instruments.

IV. Practice and Performance

1. There were five important types of sacred plainsong, or chants as they were called when in collections. Each of these collections formed the basis of musical practice in the particular area of its origin. (1) Byzantine Chant is the earliest collection and came as the result of the establishment of the Eastern Church by Constantine. It is still used in the Greek Orthodox Church. (2) The Ambrosian Chant is a collection organized by Ambrose, Bishop of Milan during the fourth century. (3) Gallic Chant was used in France until about 800. (4) Mozarabic Chant was prominent in Spain and first appeared about 900. (5) Gregorian Chant is still the most often used, and is so named because it was collected and organized under the leadership of Pope Gregory (c. 540-604). Its continued wide use is due to the fact that it was the collection used in Rome. When Rome became the center of Catholicism the Gregorian Chant spread throughout the whole Catholic world.

Ex: *Byzantine Music*
    HMS Vol. II p. 2
    Rec. RCA LM-6015 HMS Vol. II

Ex: Ambrosian psalmellus for Quadragesima: *Redde mihi*
    TEM p. 3
    Rec. HSE-9100 Side 1

Ex: Gallican *Improperia* for Good Friday: *Popule meus*
    TEM p. 8
    Rec. HSE-9100 Side 1

Ex: Mozarabic Antiphon for Easter; *Gaudete populi*
    TEM p. 12
    Rec. HSE-9100 Side 1

Ex: Gregorian hymn for Whitsunday; *Veni Creator Spiritus*
    TEM p. 16
    Rec. HSE-9100 Side 1

2. The musical setting of psalms provided the most important body of plainsong literature for both the Mass and the Office Hours. There are three types of psalm settings, defined according to the practice of performance:

(1) responsorial in which a soloist sings the verse and is answered by a choir; (2) antiphonal where the choir is divided into two groups, singing alternately; (3) direct psalmody in which the psalm is sung by a soloist or single choir with no refrain.

3. It is probable that sacred plainsong was sung with a nasal quality of voice, without vibrato and with the use of the falsetto voice. Only male singers were permitted to participate in the liturgy.

4. Chants of the Mass and Office hours were sung by the clergy, but the congregation joined in the hymns and some processional chants.

5. A device to aid in sight-singing, called the hexachord system, was perfected by Guido d' Arezzo in the eleventh century. The six tones of the hexachord were designated by six syllables in order, from the lowest to the highest, ut, re, mi, fa, sol, la, corresponding to the first syllables of successive lines of a hymn to St. John the Baptist. A system of mutation was de-

vised that enabled the singer to sing melodies that lay outside the range of a single hexachord.

6. The practice of singing in parallel 5ths and 4ths, called organum, appeared about the ninth century and was probably improvised. While it is generally associated with sacred music, there is evidence that it was also practiced in secular music as well. In its simplest form a second voice, vox organalis, sang a melody at the interval of a 5th or 4th below the principal voice, vox principalis. Later developments brought the practice of contrary motion and the use of non-perfect intervals. By the end of the 11th century organum was so well established that it was referred to in theoretical treatises. Rules were established for avoiding the tritone, for arriving at unison cadences, and identifying those parts of the liturgical chant that were permitted to be used in this manner. The practice of organum led directly to the development of polyphonic forms in the Gothic.

V. Vocal Forms

With few exceptions, the musical form and organization of specific plainsong chants were based solely on the form of the text. Any suggestion of A-B-A or similar formula was the result of textual considerations. There were some traditions that placed specific texts in certain of the Church modes and naturally those chants set to the same texts show a degree of similarity. However, there are few distinguishable forms as such. For example, there is nothing about the formal organization of an Introit to distinguish it from a Sanctus, other than the difference in text. The Monophonic Mass is not a true musical form but is a collection of appropriate chant settings of the Ordinary and Proper of the Mass.

> Ex. *Mass for Easter Sunday*
> EM   p. 3
> Rec.   DGG   ARC-3090

The following are forms of plainsong used in the Mass or Office hours that do have some formal characteristics.

1. *Antiphon.* A short sentence of scripture, or other verse, sung both before and after the psalm in syllabic style. The formal effect was that of a refrain to the psalm.

 Ex: *Laus Deo Patri* and *Psalm 113, Laudate Pueri*
   MM p. 3
   Rec. HS-9038 MM r. 1

2. *Alleluia.* The alleluia is added at the end of sections of many chants. It consists of a refrain on the word "alleluia" and is then followed by a verse, or section, with the refrain repeated. The final vowel, the jubilus, of the word alleluia provides a strong basis for musical form.

 Ex: *Vidimus stellam*
   MM p. 6
   Rec. HS-9038 MM r. 1

3. *Trope.* A trope is music with a text inserted between phrases of the liturgical text. The words provided a commentary on the liturgy. The trope is one of the first forms to provide opportunity for creative expression on purely musical terms. Because tropes had a tendency towards secularism, they were abolished by the Council of Trent. The following example is in organum.

 Ex: *Agnus Dei*
   MM p. 18
   Rec. HS-9038 MM r. 1
 Ex. Polyphonic trope; *Kyrie Jhesu dulcissime,* Fronciaco
   TEM p. 66
   Rec. HSE-9101 Side 1

4. *Sequence.* The sequence evolved from the practice of troping, and consisted of added poetic words to the final melisma of the alleluia, replacing the verse that followed the alleluia. The texts that provided the musical incentive were usually long and in a free style with repeated sections. Such formulas as A, BB, CC, DD, E, etc., were common and represented independent

compositions. Like the trope, the sequence inclined toward secularism. Only five were eventually retained in the body of Church music.

>   Ex: Sequence: *Victimae Paschali*
>   MM   p. 8
>   Rec.   HS-9038   MM   r. 1
>   Ex: Sequence: *Rex caeli, Domine*
>   MM   p. 16
>   Rec.   HS-9038   MM   r. 1

5. Secular monophony of the period to 1100 has not been preserved as well as that of sacred music. No doubt this was partly due to the fact that no adequate notation had been devised, and that there was no institution whose duty it was to maintain the traditions, as was the case in sacred music.

It is known that secular monophony flourished during the Romanesque through the songs of the Goliards, Jongleurs and Minstrels. Some of the most important of these songs were those of the Goliards who were wandering ecclesiastical students. The most noted collection of Goliard poems is the *Carmina Burana*, made famous in modern times by Carl Orff. Only one of the Goliard songs has been deciphered into modern notation to date, *O Admirable Veneris* dating from the tenth century. Its melody also appears as *O Roma Nobilis*. It is metric and in strophic form with a refrain.

>   Ex: *O Admirable Veneris*
>   HMS   Vol. II   p. 25
>   Rec.   RCA   LM-6015   HMS   Vol. II

The Jongleurs and Minstrels were itinerant performers and entertained with song, dance, tricks, juggling, etc. While they cannot be considered either poets or composers, they sang verses in the vernacular. One of the early types of Jongleur song was the *Chanson de Geste,* a narrative song telling of heroic deeds. The most famous of these is the *Song of Roland* which became a national epic of France. Unfortunately no authentic music to this has survived.

6. *Conductus*. The monophonic conductus was probably first sung while a participant in the Mass or liturgical drama was "conducted" from one place to another in the Church. The text was nonliturgical and metric. The melody was always freely composed, not taken from a chant collection. While this form first appeared in the Church, it soon became a secular form and the title was applied to almost any Latin song of a serious nature.

> Ex: *Conductus, anon*
> HAM No. 17
> Rec. (No recording available)

VI. Instrumental Forms

While instrumental music was generally banned in the Church, it is known that organs existed in the churches as early as 800. We do not know, however, how they were used, or what music was played.

It is evident from manuscripts and pictorial representations that instruments were used in secular music both as accompaniment to song and independently as dance music. As is the case with all Romanesque secular music, we have no information about specific forms, as none of the music has survived in decipherable notation.

VII. and VIII. Composers

Because of the improvisatory nature of early music, almost every performer was a composer. This was especially true in secular music and no doubt the same procedure was responsible for the origin of most of the chants that later became traditional. It is known, however, that the following were composers of some stature and influence during the Romanesque.

1. Notker Balbulus (c. 840-912) was one of the earliest identified composers and was especially known for his sequences.

> Ex: Sequence; *Sancti Spiritu avidit nobis gratia*
> HMS Vol. II p. 21
> Rec. RCA LM-6015-2 HMS Vol. II

2. King Robert the Pious (995-1031).
3. Rodulphe of St. Trond (d. 1136).
4. Wipo of Burgundy (d. 1048).

> Ex: Sequence; *Victimae paschali laudes*
> GMB No. 6
> Rec. (no recording available)

5. Hermannus Contractus (1013-1054), also known as Herman the Cripple, was a theorist as well as a composer. His *Alma Redemptoris Mater* achieved a great popularity and became the basis for numerous works in both monophony and polyphony.

> Ex: *Versus*
> GMB No. 7
> Rec. (no recording available)

6. Abelard (1079-1142) is known to have made a collection of hymns that were used by the monks and nuns. One of these nuns was the famous Heloise.

IX. Important Writers on Music

Most of the early theoretical writings on music were not derived from the current musical practices of the times. They were, in effect, either interpretations of the music theory of the ancients and the subsequent concept of music as a science or attempts to link music and religion by means of allegorical writings.

1. Boethius (c. 480-524) was one of the earliest theorists. He was also a philosopher and mathematician. His chief work is *De Institutione Musica,* in which he relates the music of his time to the theories of the Greek philosophers.

2. Cassiodorus (c. 485-c. 580) was an historian, philosopher, statesman, and the founder of a monastery. Like Boethius, his important work is *Institutiones musicae,* written between 550 and 562.

3. Isidore of Seville (d. 636) was a Spanish scholar. His *Etymologiarum sive originum libri xx* is an encyclopedia of the arts with an account of liturgical music.

4. Odo of Cluny (d. 942) was a theorist of the tenth century. The *Dialogus de Musica* contains an account of modes and medieval notation. He was the first to use letters to indicate pitches.

5. Guido d'Arrezo (c. 990-1050) was a Benedictine monk. He was the most important writer to be concerned with the actual practices of music. He dealt with the problems of notation and especially with the technique of singing. His numerous writings have been an important source for modern scholars on the musical practices of medieval times.

6. *Musica enchiriadis* (c. 900). The authorship of this collection has never been established. For a long time it was thought to have been written by Hucbald (c. 840-930) but recent scholarship has denied his authorship. *Musica enchiriadis* covers the whole range of musical knowledge. Most of its material was borrowed from the ancients, including the concept of music as mathematics and the acceptance of Pythagorean theory of numbers and the division of the scale according to intervallic ratios.

The writings of the foregoing theorists are not readily available in English. Important excerpts from each can be found in Strunk, *Source Readings in Music History*. New York: W. W. Norton, 1950.

Boethius	p. 79
Cassidorus	p. 87
Isidore	p. 93
Odo	p. 103
Guido	p. 117
Musica enchiriadis	p. 126

X. Manuscript Sources

1. There is only one important collection of original manuscripts prior to 1100. This is called the *Winchester Troper*, a liturgical book containing tropes.

2. The great literature of plainsong melody has been in the process of being collected, edited and published by the Benedictines of Solesmes since 1889. To date sixteen volumes have been published in the *Paleographie Musicale*.

XI. Suggested Readings

Cannon-Johnson-Waite	pp.	26-72
Ferguson	pp.	32-57
Grout	pp.	19-57
Harman and Meller	pp.	1-39
Lang	pp.	37-121
Oxford Vol. II	pp.	171-213
Reese-MA	pp.	57-272
Sachs-HER	pp.	41-68
Ulrich-Pisk	pp.	26-55
Wold-Cykler	ch.	5

XII. Further References

Apel, Willi. *Gregorian Chant.* Bloomington: University of Indiana Press, 1958.

Fortescue, A. *The Ceremonies of the Roman Rite Described.* London: Burns and Oates, 1930.

Young, Karl. *Drama of the Medieval Church.* Oxford: Clarendon Press, 1933.

King David playing the rota. Eighth century miniature from the Canterbury Psalterium. Courtesy Baerenreiter Bild-Archiv.

Chapter

3

༆

Gothic
1100-1400

I. Sociocultural Influences on Music

The period from 1100 to about 1400 has been designated as Gothic mainly to describe a type of architecture that is characterized by the pointed arch, ribbed vaulting, and flying buttresses. The term was introduced by seventeenth century writers who looked upon this style as unclassical and vulgar, associating it with the medieval Goths of northern Europe. In its present connotation the term merely identifies the artistic style of this period without derogatory implications.

The rise and development of polyphonic forms and the merging of secular and sacred musical styles were the major musical contributions of the Gothic. In fact, many of the forms, as well as musical practices, that have come down to modern times were Gothic in their origin. We have a fairly adequate knowledge of Gothic music, due to the fact that a system of notation was devised during this period that makes it possible for modern scholars to re-create much of the music with authority and accuracy. The development of Gothic music was accelerated by a number of varied sociocultural movements that took place between 1100 and 1400.

1. Scholasticism was a medieval philosophy that systematized every area of intellectual and religious experience according to rigid rules of medieval logic. Its effect on religious music

was twofold. First, it regulated the theory and practice of music according to canons of acceptable practice in the Church. For example, triple rhythm was held to be more perfect than duple rhythm and perfect intervals were ruled necessary on all strong beats while dissonant intervals were generally avoided whenever possible. Second, scholasticism also controlled and codified the emotional content of sacred music. Church officials frowned upon ornate melodies because they felt such melodies obscured the meaning of the texts. Any move to make music more emotionally expressive was to be avoided because it appealed to the senses and not to the soul. Expressive qualities were finally to appear in sacred music, but only after a long period of development. Although scholasticism had little direct effect on secular music, there was an indirect influence inasmuch as church composers who rebelled against strict control found freedom in the secular style.

2. Western man was becoming more and more independent economically, intellectually, and artistically. He was becoming skeptical of the authority of the Church to order and control all of the activities of life. Communication with the East, the result of the Crusades (eleventh to the thirteenth centuries) opened new channels of trade, brought new wealth, new ideas, and new incentives for living. New social customs and cultural practices were eventually integrated into western civilization. As a consequence, a favorable climate for artistic development existed during the Gothic in contrast to the rather severe asceticism of earlier times. Entertainment outside the Church became widely cultivated and even religious music was infused with this new humanism.

3. The rise of towns stimulated centers of learning in newly established universities. This was especially true in England, The Netherlands, and France. Music became an integral part of education, first as a science and eventually as an art. The real leaders and innovators of Gothic music either were at the universities or associated with the courts where music was given great importance. It is interesting to note that beginning with the Gothic

period musical leadership came from northern Europe instead of Italy where musical activity had been centered up to this time.

4. The Gothic period also saw the beginning of the struggle between Church and State which, in effect, was a struggle between asceticism and humanism. In music it took the form of a conflict between the sacred and the secular, a conflict in which each reached new heights of musical expressiveness.

II. Function of Music

1. Gothic sacred music served the same function for religion as Romanesque music. The same liturgical texts were set to music as previously, but in polyphony instead of monophony. An important addition to sacred music was the motet, a form that was later to become one of the most important vocal polyphonic forms. The Gothic spirit precipitated a great program of church building, an activity that in turn led to an increased demand for church musicians. This led to the establishment of a number of schools such as St. Martial and Notre Dame where sacred music was especially cultivated.

2. Music also took on increased importance in the social fabric of the Gothic. The rise in the social status of secular music, as is evidenced by the nobility of the Troubadours and Trouvères, shows the wide interest in secular song in the vernacular. The establishment of courts and the growing power of non-church institutions encouraged strong centers of secular culture in many medieval cities. For the first time in music history, individual composers achieved recognition for their creative efforts. Moreover, the most significant developments in music have been traced to many of these secular composers.

III. Characteristics of Style

Although both sacred plainsong and secular monophony continued in the Gothic, the growth and refinement of the polyphonic style was the major concern of Gothic composers. This concern for devices of polyphony marked the beginning of the emancipation of music from its dependence on plainsong and pre-existing materials, a process that was to continue through the Renaissance.

1. *Formal Organization*

   a. All vocal music was organized according to the text, but poetic and syllabic considerations were frequently submerged in favor of rhythmic and harmonic structure.

   b. Composers of sacred polyphony were able to organize sections of text into complete units by means of short repeated rhythmic patterns called rhythmic modes. In the fourteenth century longer sections were combined on the basis of the isorhythmic principle, a repetition of longer and more complicated rhythmic patterns.

   c. Both monophonic and polyphonic secular forms, like the rondeau, virelai, and ballads were organized on the basis of two musical phrases combined in repeated patterns such as AbAbaA, etc. A number of secular forms also contain a two-line refrain both at the beginning and at the end of each stanza.

   d. Secular polyphony made extensive use of canonic imitation as a means of formal organization. The most obvious example of this is the rondelus.

   e. All characteristics of vocal forms were also present in instrumental music.

2. *Melody*

   a. All Gothic melody was vocal in style with a limited range. Melodies from the secular literature and the fourteenth century sacred forms sometimes use more than an octave range.

b. Sacred melody in polyphonic forms, other than plain-song, usually consisted of short phrases in repeated metric patterns. Secular melody both monophonic and polyphonic was often cast in longer phrases and was more lyric in character.

c. There was no attempt to express the meaning of the text in sacred melody, but secular melody often captured the mood of the text.

d. All Gothic melodies, both monophonic and polyphonic, were modal. However, secular song had a tendency toward intervals that suggested tonality.

e. A common melodic practice of many Gothic composers was to move from the leading tone to the sixth tone before proceeding to the tonic. This has been referred to as the Landini cadence, but it is known that the composer Landini did not initiate the practice (Fig. 2).

Figure 2

3. *Rhythm.* The problem of rhythm held the attention of all Gothic composers who were concerned with extending the expressiveness of music. To emancipate musical form from the rhythm of text and to gain some agreement of accent between the voices of polyphonic forms, it was necessary to invent some sort of rhythmic system that was independent of poetic rhythm.

a. Composers devised a system by which rhythmic cohesion could be brought to a melody by means of repeated patterns called rhythmic modes, a rigidly repeated rhythmic sequence. These patterns were usually separated by a rest before repetition. There were six rhythmic modes, each identified by number.

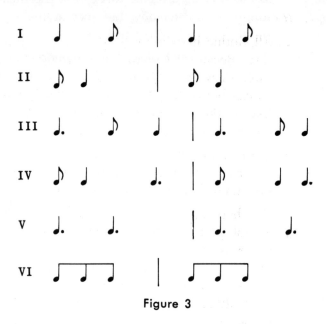

Figure 3

It was not uncommon for each line of a melody in a polyphonic form to have its own separate rhythmic mode. In the late Gothic these modes were extended to longer patterns which formed the basis of isorhythmic compositions. While the principle of rhythmic modes involved a series of exact repetitions, the practice was to introduce a degree of flexibility by varying the patterns.

b. Rhythmic patterns in triple meter were used extensively in sacred music, while secular forms had the privilege of using either triple or duple meter.

    c. Subdivision of beats of many kinds appeared in the fourteenth century to give the rhythmic flow more freedom and subtlety.

    d. Alternate interruption, between the voices, of the rhythmic flow by means of pauses called "hockets" was introduced in early polyphony.

4. *Harmony*

    a. All Gothic harmony was the result of polyphonic texture. Because there was no systematic chordal structure, there often were sharp and unresolved dissonances between voices. This was partly due to the fact that, in the early Gothic, each of the upper voices was related to the lowest voice and not to one another.

    b. Because melodies were composed in modes, harmony was also modal, although secular polyphony on occasion tended toward major and minor tonality.

    c. The harmonic vocabulary was largely limited to the use of perfect fourths, fifths and octaves. All other intervals were considered dissonant and were the result of voice leading. In the later Gothic, thirds and sixths were considered imperfect consonances and were utilized, first in secular forms and then in sacred music.

    d. Chromaticisms were generally avoided as expressive devices. Chromatic alterations were introduced in cadences to avoid the whole-step between the leading-tone and the final. Chromatics were used to avoid the augmented fourth above the root of a chord and also to avoid the tri-tone interval in a melody.

5. *Texture*

    a. A polyphonic texture prevailed in almost all Gothic music after 1300. Prior to this secular music was monophonic, while religious music used primitive polyphony in the form of organum in addition to the traditional plainsong.

b. Three voice polyphony was the most common, but four voices were in frequent use by the end of the fourteenth century.

c. In three voice polyphony the lower voice contained the cantus firmus and the two upper voices usually moved more rapidly and were often ornamented. In four voice polyphony the lowest part was the contra-tenor. It had the same range as the tenor and frequently crossed the tenor line.

d. There was no distinction between the texture of sacred and secular polyphony.

e. There was frequent crossing of voices but the different voices retained their melodic independence.

f. There was an openness about the sound of early polyphony. This was due to the extensive use of the intervals of the fourth, fifth and octave which lack the harmonic direction of dissonant intervals.

6. *Media*

a. Vocal performance was still the most important in both sacred and secular music.

b. Instruments of all kinds, both winds and strings, were sometimes substituted for the cantus firmus in polyphonic forms. No doubt instruments also doubled vocal parts, especially in secular polyphony.

c. Secular monophony was usually accompanied by instruments. The lute, viol and harp were the most commonly used for this purpose.

d. Combinations of instruments were also used for dances and out-of-doors music, but because this kind of music was either improvised or played from memory, we have few actual examples.

IV. Practice and Performance

1. The most vital innovation in the practice of Gothic music was the development of a system of notation. After the emer-

gence of a system of lines and spaces in the twelfth century, pitch designation was fairly accurate. The next pressing need was for the notation of duration and stress. By the thirteenth century a kind of notation called mensural (measured) had been developed. A system of black notes was used which, according to modern usage, is best translated as follows in Figure 4.

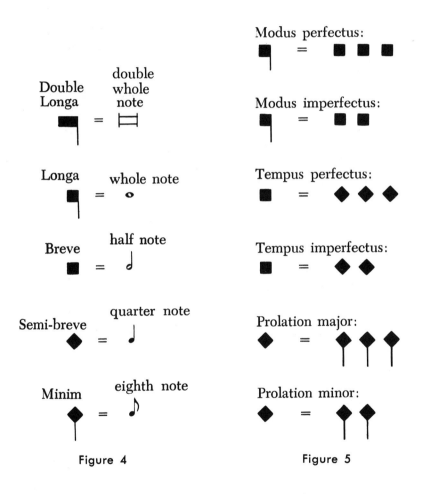

Figure 4

Figure 5

Each of the time units shown in Figure 5 had the possibility of being divided into either two or three smaller units.

Symbols were finally devised to indicate whether the division called tempus was perfect or imperfect, and the division called prolation was major or minor.

A circle indicated tempus perfectus, a broken circle, tempus imperfectus. A period within the circle indicated prolation major, and its absence, prolation minor. Figure 6 illustrates this practice.

Tempus perfectus—prolation major

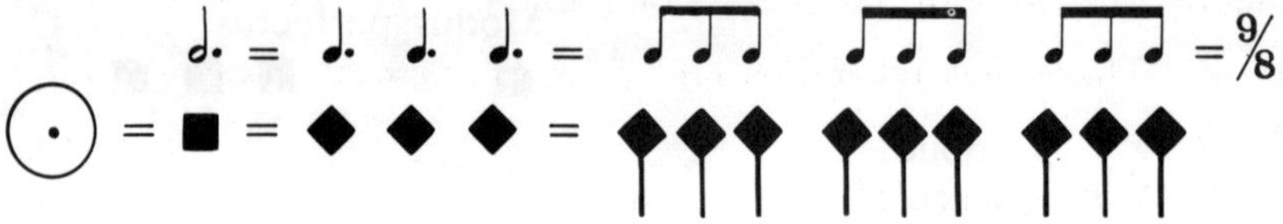

Tempus imperfectus—prolation major

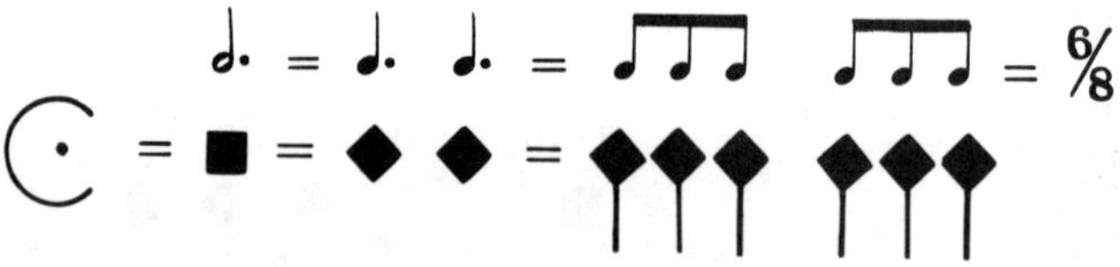

Tempus perfectus—prolation minor

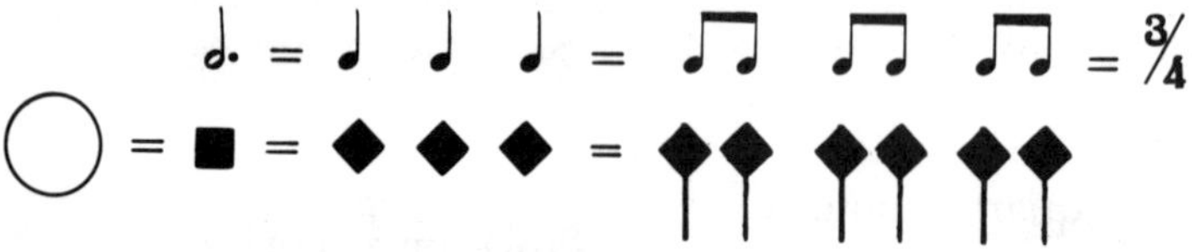

Tempus imperfectus—prolation minor

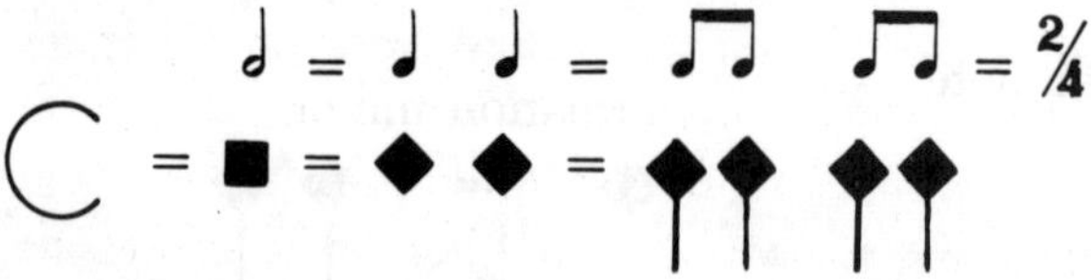

Figure 6

2. The practice of musica ficta, or false music, enabled performers to introduce flats or sharps into the modes in order to

avoid certain intervals, to modify the church modes, or to make intervallic adjustments for the sake of beauty.

3. While secular polyphony was notated for voices, there is evidence that a common manner of performance was by a small vocal and instrumental group in which instruments doubled the voices. Another favorite method was to use instruments on all parts except the upper or solo line. The entire composition could also be played rather than sung. It is probable that secular polyphony was seldom sung unaccompanied.

4. There was no indication of tempo or dynamics in Gothic music.

5. Instruments often substituted for or doubled the vocal parts in sacred polyphony. The cantus firmus was usually played rather than sung. However, the practice of using instruments was probably not as widespread in sacred as it was in secular music.

6. When instruments played the vocal line in secular polyphony it was the general practice to embellish the melody with ornaments, usually in an improvisatory manner.

7. Music for out-of-doors used the "high" or loud instruments, notably the brass and winds. When the same music was performed indoors the "low" instruments such as lutes and viols were used.

V. Vocal Forms

1. *Secular monophony.* There are a great many forms of secular monophony in the music of the Troubadours, Trouvères and Minnesingers. However, individual songs were poetic types designated according to subject matter. So far as musical form and organization is concerned there are only four types, each derived from a well-known form that was already in existence: (1) the hymn or stanza type; (2) the litany type; (3) the rondel type; (4) the sequence type.

    a. Canso. The canso is an example of the hymn type. Each stanza has six or seven lines with the melody of the first two lines repeated for the second two. The last two or three lines use a different melody. For example, AB AB CD. The German version found in the literature of the Minnesingers is called a bar.

> Ex: *Nu al' erst,* Walther von der Volgelweide
> HAM p. 18
> Rec. Lyrichord LL 85
>
> Ex: *Be m' an perdut,* Bernart de Ventadorn
> TEM p. 27
> Rec. HSE-9100 Side 1

b. Rotrouenge. The rotrouenge, an example of the litany type, is a form in which the same melody is used for all the lines of the poem except for the last two. The pattern would be A A A A B B etc.

> Ex: *Pour mon coeur*
> HAM p. 17
> Rec. (no recording available)

c. Virelai. The virelai is a rondel-type form with a refrain and stanza principle. The general pattern is: AB CC AB AB, etc.

> Ex: *Le jeu de Robin et de Marion,* Adam de la Hale
> Edward Marks, Ed.
> Rec. DGG ARC-3002
>
> Ex: *Or la Truix*
> MM p. 11
> Rec. HS-9038 MM r. 1
>
> Ex: Cantiga: *Gran dereit',* Alfonso El Sabio
> TEM p. 33
> Rec. HSE-9100 Side 1
>
> Ex: Lauda: *Ogne homo*
> TEM p. 37
> Rec. HSE-9100 Side 1

d. Lai. The lai is derived from the sequence with one melody to every two lines of poetry. The lai text is usually addressed to the Virgin Mary and is cast in irregular stanzas of from six to sixteen or more lines. The musical form consists of AA BB CC DD, etc. In Germany it was called a leich.

Ex: *Ey ich sach in dem trone*
      HMS   Vol. II   p. 32
            Rec. RCA LM-6015-2   HMS   Vol. II

Ex: Minnelied: *Willekommen Mayenschein*, Neidhart von Reuenthal
      MM   p. 13
      Rec. HS-9038   MM   r. 1

2. *Polyphonic Conductus.* The conductus is a two, three, or four voice form in which the lowest voice is a freely invented melody on a Latin text. An important feature is the syllabic and rhythmic unity between the voices, giving the effect of chords.

Ex: *De castitatis thalamo*
      MM   p. 31
      Rec. HS-9038   MM   r. 1

3. *Notre Dame Organum.* In the thirteenth century there was developed a type of polyphony called Notre Dame Organum. It can be considered a form because the principle of organum was restricted to those portions of the chant which were normally sung by a solo voice. Other sections were sung in plainsong. In the organum the tenor sang the plainsong melody in long pedal tones while the upper voices, or voice, sang rhapsodic melodies above it, usually in a metric manner.

Ex: *Alleluya (Nativitas)*, Perotin
      MM   p. 22
      Rec. HS-9038 MM r. 1.

4. *Clausula.* A polyphonic form which used a melismatic section of a chant as a cantus firmus was called clausula. It was often only a section of an organum. The upper voices move in a quick but measured rhythm against the tenor which moves in even length notes. Because the melisma used only a few syllables, or at the most two or three words, there was no meaningful text to the clausula. All parts vocalized on the vowel sounds of the tenor line.

Ex: *Viderunt Omes*, Leonin
      TEM   p. 41
      Rec. HSE-9100   Side 2.

5. *Motet.* The motet was the most important vocal form of the thirteenth and fourteenth centuries. In the earlier motet the lowest voice, the tenor (cantus firmus), is a plainsong melody in a slow moving rhythmic mode. The two upper voices, the duplum (motetus) and triplum respectively, move more quickly each with its own text. At times even the language of each text was different. Due to the fact that the tenor notes were an elongation of the original plainsong, its text was unimportant and it was a common practice to play the tenor line on an instrument. Note that the title of the following example includes the text of each part — tenor, duplum (motetus) and triplum.

> Ex: *En Non Diu! Quant voi; Eius in Oriente*
>   MM   p. 27
>   Rec. HS-9038   MM   r. 1
> Ex: *Ave gloriosa mater-Ave Virgo-Domino*
>   TEM   p. 46
>   Rec. HSE-9100   Side 2
> Ex: *Je n'amerai autre-In seculum*
>   TEM   p. 56
>   Rec. HSE-9100   Side 2

6. *Isorhythmic Motet.* The isorhythmic motet was developed in the fourteenth century and had much the same characteristics as the earliest motet already described. The basic difference was that the rhythmic modes were extended to larger phrases called talea that were repeated. Moreover, each of the upper voices frequently had its own repeated talea that could be the same as that of the tenor.

> Ex: *O Maria Virgo Davidica*
>   HMS   Vol. II   p. 53
>   Rec. RCA   LM-6015-1   HMS   Vol. II
> Ex: *Veni Sancte Spiritus,* John Dunstable
>   TEM   p. 87
>   Rec. HSE-9101   Side 1

7. *Polyphonic Mass.* The Mass was not a musical form in itself. However, the late Gothic composers began the practice of setting the liturgical texts of the Ordinary of the Mass with some semblance of unity among the various sections. This unity

is achieved by means of motives common to each section, by similarity of mood, and by similarity of imitative devices. As yet composers did not use the same plainsong as cantus firmus for each section.

>   Ex: *Agnus Dei* from Messe de Nostre Dame, Machaut
>   MM   p. 36
>   Rec.   HS-9038   MM   r. 1

>   Ex: *Agnus Dei* from the Mass of Tournai
>   TEM   p. 62
>   Rec.   HSE-9101   Side 1

8. *Rota.* The rota is a medieval round, or canon, in which each singer returns from the end of the melody to the beginning. The phrases of the melody are so composed that each one makes acceptable harmony with the others. This enables all voices to end on a cadence at the finish of any phrase. The rota was usually a secular form.

>   Ex: *Sumer Is Icumen In*
>   HAM   p. 44
>   Rec.   RCA   LM-6015-2   HMS   Vol. II

9. *Ballata.* The ballata is an Italian secular form that was derived from the virelai. It was written for two or three voices. The ballata has a chain of six line stanzas with a two line refrain before and after each stanza. It has two melodies, one for the refrain and one for each of the two first pair of lines of each stanza. The third pair of stanza lines use the refrain melody. The pattern is A b b a A.

>   Ex: *Chi piu' la vuol sapers,* Francesco Landini
>   MM   p. 40
>   Rec.   HS-9038   MM   r. 1

>   Ex: *Notes pour moi,* Anthonello de Caserta
>   TEM   p. 83
>   Rec.   HSE-9101   Side 1

Ex: *Soy Conteno y vos servido,* Juan del Encina
TEM p. 94
Rec. HSE-9101 Side 1

10. *Caccia.* The caccia is a hunting song that appeared in the fourteenth century. It often has three voices with the two upper voices moving in strict canonic imitation when three voices were used. The lower part is independent and was probably performed on an instrument. The example is the French version of the form called chace.

Ex: *Se Je Chante Main*
HMS Vol. III p. 13
Rec. RCA LM-6016-1 HMS Vol. III
Ex: *Con Brachi assai,* Giovanni da Firenze
TEM p. 76
Rec. HSE-9101 Side 1

11. *Madrigal.* The fourteenth century madrigal is a lyric poem with two or three stanzas of three lines each. There is a different melody for each stanza and it ends with a ritornello of two lines with a new melody in a contrasting rhythmic pattern. The upper voice usually contains coloraturas, while the lower voices move in a chordal fashion and were often played rather than sung.

Ex: *Nel Mezzo a Sei Paon,* Ciaverri du Carcia
HMS Vol. III p. 19
Rec. RCA LM-6016-1 HMS Vol. III

VI. Instrumental Forms

1. Notated instrumental forms were very slow to develop. Most dances during the Gothic were still improvised as they had been earlier. Many medieval dances were cast in pairs — dance and after-dance. There was usually a slow moving section in duple time followed by a faster movement in triple time. Sometimes the section in triple time used the same melody as the first part. Because of the improvisatory nature of these dances, very few have come to us in notation.

Ex: *Four Dances*
HMS Vol. II p. 43
Rec. RCA LM-6015-1 HMS Vol. II

2. It was a common practice to perform almost all the vocal forms on instruments and it must be remembered that many vocal forms were dance melodies. In addition to dance songs, conducti, motets and even polyphonic sections of the Mass were sometimes performed instead of sung.

Ex: *Instrumental Motet, In Seculum Longum*
TEM p. 54
Rec. HSE-9100 Side 2
Ex: *Organ paraphase of a Kyrie*
TEM p. 72
Rec. HSE-9101 Side 1

3. *Estampie.* The dance form most commonly notated in the thirteenth and fourteenth century was the estampie. It is similar to the vocal sequence and consists of a number of sections called punta which were repeated. Its form is: A A: B B: C C: etc.

Ex: *Estampie*
MM p. 33
Rec. HS-9038 MM r. 1

VII. Important Composers

1. Leonin (12th cent.) was the first of the great masters of the Notre Dame School. He is noted for his style of organum. He made extensive use of the syllabic technique, but also foreshadowed the motet principle by lengthening the notes of the plainsong solo as a cantus firmus with a freely moving voice above it. He wrote a cycle of two-part liturgical settings for the church calendar.

Ex: *Judaea et Jerusalem.* Zeitshrift für Muskwissenschaft Vol. 1
Breitkopf & Härtel Ed.
Rec. DGG ARC-3051

2. Perotin (12th cent.) was the successor to Leonin at Notre Dame. He developed organum from the Leonin style by instilling a greater rhythmic accuracy. His tenor was cast in a

series of rhythmic motives that were the predecessors of the rhythmic modes. He expanded two-voice organum to three-voice and four-voice. In addition, his music shows evidence of canonic imitation. His most famous work is *Sederunt Principis*, a quadruple organum.

Ex: *Sederunt Principis.*
      Universal Ed.
      Rec. DGG ARC-3051

3. Adam de la Hale (c. 1240-1287) is one of the best known trouvères. He was both a poet and a composer. Many examples of both his monodic as well as polyphonic compositions survive. Besides many rondeaux and virelais, his musical play *Le jeu de Robin et de Marion* written for the entertainment of the Arogonese court at Naples is still performed.

Ex: *Le jeu de Robin et de Marion*
      Edward Marks, Ed.
      Rec. DGG ARC-3002

4. Machaut, Guillaume de (c. 1300-1377) was the most important composer of the fourteenth century. Born in France, Machaut was more than just a musician. He was a theologian, holding many important ecclesiastical posts, including that of Canon of Rheims. He was also secretary to King John of Bohemia. Among Machaut's musical innovations was the development of a more lyric style of melody and a more suave harmonic texture using thirds and sixths to soften the dissonance of earlier organum. He was the first to compose a complete polyphonic setting of the Ordinary of the Mass with some degree of unity between the sections. He wrote in all the forms of his time, both sacred and secular. Among the secular forms, he excelled in the ballade form, bringing to it an ingenuity of imitation, a sonorous harmony and an expressive melody that foreshadowed the Renaissance style.

Ex: *Ten Secular Works.*
      Guillaume de Machaut, Musikalische Werke
      Breitkopf & Härtel, Vol. I and III
      Rec. DGG ARC-3032

5. Landini, Francesco (1325-1397) had the distinction of being the most famous Italian composer of the fourteenth century. Blinded in his youth, he managed to become a virtuoso performer on a number of instruments, but was best known as an organist. His skill as a performer and as a composer won him legendary fame in the annals of Italian music. Landini's compositions number over 150 works that have been preserved and include every form of secular music, although the greater portion are two-part and three-part ballate. His melodies are very expressive and the harmonies are exceedingly smooth and fluid.

> Ex: *Amar Si Le Alto Tue Gentil Costumi.*
> HMS Vol. III p. 21
> Rec. RCA LM-6016-1 HMS Vol. III

VIII. Other Composers

1. *France*
   Franco of Cologne (active 1250-1280)
   Pierre de la Croix (active 1270-1300)
   Philippe de Vitry (1291-1361)
2. *Italy*
   Giovanni da Cascia (Giovanni da Firenze) (14th cent.)

IX. Important Writers on Music

The Gothic writers still considered music the servant of the Church and their philosophy is mainly a repetition of the earlier authors. However, the major portions of their writings are concerned with practical problems of music, mainly those of rhythm and notation. An especially important subject was the interpretation of rhythmic notation. The first writer to theorize on the "new art" was Philippe de Vitry (1291-1361) who was also known as a composer. His *Ars Nova* is a treatise in which he describes the new way of measuring time.

The conflict between the more conservative style of the early medieval with that of the fourteenth century "new art" was made articulate by Gothic writers. This controversy is made especially clear in the writings of Jacques de Liege and Jean de Muris. The former was an ardent foe of the new style and a champion of the more traditional manner.

1. Franco of Cologne (active 1250-1280) was a medieval theorist and a practical musician. A number of medieval writings were attributed to Franco, but only one work has been definitely authenticated as genuine, *Ars Cantus Mensurabilis*. Franco made a great contribution to notation and in its earlier stages it was called "Franconian." In other areas of musical knowledge his writing is based on the earlier theorists.

2. Marchetto da Padua (14th cent.) was an Italian who wrote an account of the musical practices in Italy. He was also the author of a theoretical treatise, *Pomerium*, which was a justification of duple time in music.

3. Jacques de Liege (Jacob of Liege) (c. 1270-c. 1330) was a Belgian and the author of *Speculum Musicae*, written about 1325, which was an attack on the modern musical practices and more particularly an attack on the writings of Jean de Muris. In addition to its controversial nature, the *Speculum* is a compendium of all medieval knowledge about music.

4. Jean de Muris (c. 1290–c. 1351) was a writer on music, astronomy and mathematics. He was the author of *Musica Speculativa* and the important treatise, *Ars le novas musica*. He championed the cause of the "new style" and also dealt with the interpretation of rhythmic notation.

The writings of the foregoing Gothic theorists and historians are not readily available in English. Important excerpts from each can be found in Strunk, *Source Readings in Music History*, New York: W. W. Norton, 1950.

<table>
<tr><td>Franco of Cologne</td><td>p. 139</td></tr>
<tr><td>Marchetto da Padua</td><td>p. 160</td></tr>
<tr><td>Jacques de Liege</td><td>p. 180</td></tr>
<tr><td>Jean de Muris</td><td>p. 172</td></tr>
</table>

X. Manuscript Sources

There are a large number of collections of manuscripts from the twelfth to the fourteenth centuries. However, the following are generally recognized as the most important:

1. *St. Martial MSS* of the twelfth century is a collection of early organum.

2. Two important collections of motets from the thirteenth century are the *Codex Montpellier* and the *Codex Bamberg*.

3. Fourteenth century Italian secular music is adequately represented by the *Codex Squarcialupi*. It contains works by Francesco Landini and other Italian composers. Forms included are madrigals, ballatas and caccias.

XI. Suggested Readings

Cannon-Johnson-Waite	pp.	73-141
Ferguson	pp.	58-121
Grout	pp.	57-129
Harman-Mellers	pp.	40-184
Lang	pp.	122-167
Oxford Vol. I.	pp.	220-477
Vol. II.	pp.	1-101
Reese-MA	pp.	272-424
Sachs-HER	pp.	69- 99
Ulrich-Pisk	pp.	56-101
Wold-Cykler	ch.	6

XII. Further References

Parrish, Carl. *The Notation of Medieval Music.* New York: W. W. Norton, 1957.

Apel, Willi. *The Notation of Polyphonic Music.* Cambridge: Medieval Academy of America, 1949.

Apel, Willi. *French Secular Music of the Late Fourteenth Century.* Cambridge: Medieval Academy of America, 1950.

Johannes Ockeghem with his chapel singers. Courtesy of Baerenreiter-Bild-Archiv.

Chapter

4

ॐ

Renaissance
1400-1600

I. Sociocultural Influences on Music

In its narrowest sense the term Renaissance means a rebirth of interest in the ideals and forms of classic antiquity as applied to the artistic and cultural life of Italy during the fifteenth and sixteenth centuries. In its wider sense, however, the Renaissance implies a general renewal or rebirth of interest in the dignity and inherent value of man, a trend already indicated in the Gothic period. This attitude is reflected in all the political, religious, and social institutions of the period as well as in the several arts, and is most adequately expressed in the philosophy of humanism. Music partook of the movement only in the broader sense, and found its greatest expression in the works of the Burgundian and Netherland composers until the final half of the sixteenth century. At that time the Italians, educated in the style of the period by the long influx of northern composers, blossomed into a dominating school. With the contributions of these greater schools of composition the Renaissance witnessed the birth of music as an art.

Institutions arising out of humanism and phenomena manifesting its spirit which often exercised a direct influence on music were:

1. *The Roman Catholic Church.* Although there was a growing tendency toward secularization, as evidenced by the actions

of the Council of Trent (1543-63), the Church retained its important position as the leading patron of musical production throughout the world. The abolition of tropes and sequences (except for four), as well as the secular canti firmi for the composition of motets and masses by the Council, was evidence of its deep concern in counteracting the increasing secularization of religious music. Moreover, the Council's determination to stem the great wave of secularization almost resulted in the banning of all polyphonic settings of liturgical music and a return to the exclusive use of the traditional plainsong.

2. *The Protestant Reformation.* The Reformation exercised a greater influence upon the historical course of religious music specifically, and European music generally, than any other movement initiated in the Renaissance.

Both the Huguenot and the English Reformations gave rise to musical expression appropriate to these movements. It was, however, the positive inclusion of music by Luther as a vital and important part of the religious ceremony in the form of congregational chorale singing that sowed the seeds of a musical renaissance in the German speaking lands. It was this movement that ultimately led to the supremacy of German and Austrian music from the middle of the seventeenth to the end of the nineteenth century.

3. The rise of wealthy and powerful aristocratic patrons in the ruling courts of Burgundy in the fifteenth century, the Holy Roman Empire of Charles the Fifth and Phillip the Second, and the princely courts such as those of Florence, Mantua, and Venice were powerful influences on music. Usually these aristocratic rulers were as influential in religious as in secular affairs, since they maintained important chapels within the courts and patronized composers for their religious as well as secular compositions.

4. The invention of printing in the fifteenth century led to devices for printing music, and the first successful music printing from moveable type took place at the beginning of the sixteenth century. Ottaviano Petrucci (1466-1539), an Italian, was the

first to print an edition of part music, *The Harmonice Odheca-ton*, in 1501. Pierre Attaignant, a Frenchman, published the first collection of French chansons with moveable type in Paris in 1528. Thomas Tallis (1505-1585) and William Byrd (1542-1623) published the first English collection of motets in 1575. By the end of the sixteenth century large numbers of printed musical works were available, particularly editions of considerable magnitude in the area of secular music such as madrigals, airs, chansons, etc. While the aristocracy and wealthy upper middle class were the principal purchasers of such works, the multiplicity of printed copies tended to spread the musical literature of important composers over a wider area than was heretofore possible through limited manuscript examples.

II. Function of Music

1. The primary purpose of Renaissance sacred music was liturgical. It served both the traditional Roman Catholic service and the newly founded Protestant church, particularly the Lutheran sect. The Roman Catholic Church had the more highly organized musical service. The greater body of religious music will therefore be found in Catholicism during this period.

2. Secular music provided a highly cultivated group of amateur performers among the aristocracy and upper middle class with appropriate music for singing and playing. The cultivated lady and gentleman of the Renaissance were capable performers in either singing or playing, if not in both.

3. During the last half of the sixteenth century, instrumental music was employed to provide a select society with entertainment performed by professional and skilled amateur players. These performances took place in the salons of the nobility and the homes of wealthy burghers.

4. Dances were written by serious composers in response to the demand for formal court functions.

5. Popular songs and dances of folk-like character supplied the great mass of people with music that was appropriate to festivals and other social occasions, both religious and secular.

III. Characteristics of Style

All music of the Renaissance was based on polyphonic practices. Consequently there was a unity of style in both secular and religious music. This unity applied to vocal and instrumental compositions as well. It may be said that the Renaissance represents the last period of musical history in which there is such unity of style in all forms and in all media.

1. *Formal Organization.* Except in the case of small poetic and dance forms of a secular nature, Renaissance music shows a unity of formal organization.

   a. The technique of employing a cantus firmus derived primarily from plainsong literature or from folk song sources gave rise to works which were basically polyphonic elaborations of a pre-existing melodic idea. The cantus firmus was generally placed in the tenor voice which in the early Renaissance was the lowest pitched voice.

   b. The imitative use of melodic material became an increasingly important organizational device. In order to give variety to such practice, various forms of imitation were used, such as:

      (1) canonic imitation. By this device all voices use the same melodic material, but each voice begins at a different time. Canonic imitations vary from strict to free imitation of the original melodic ideas, and can be constructed so that the pitches of each voice are at the same or at different intervals.

      (2) imitation by inversion. This is one of changing the direction of the original melodic intervals so that the ascending interval in the original melody becomes a descending one in the inverted version and vice versa.

      (3) imitation by retrogression. In this case the original melodic idea is repeated note for note in the

reverse order. This device is also called crab or cancrizans imitation. It can also be used in combination with imitation by inversion.

(4) imitation by augmentation. Here the original melodic idea is repeated in another voice but in notes of twice the time value of the original.

(5) imitation by diminution. The original melodic idea appears in another voice in note values one-half the time value of the original.

c. The technique of using pre-existing material even went so far as to employ complete polyphonic works in shorter forms in the larger works. (See Parody Mass under Vocal Forms in this chapter.)

d. Formal organization was episodic in the case of most of the strictly polyphonic works, both secular and religious. Compositions consisted of a number of sections, each treating its thematic material individually and exhaustively. In the highly developed polyphonic forms such as the motet and Mass there was rarely any repetition of a previously used musical section or text. Each section constituted the complete treatment of a line of text.

e. Secular poetic song forms were often characterized by a formal organization which used a principal refrain in contrast to other musical phrases.

f. With the exception of the Mass, all works were in single rather than multiple movements.

g. Dance forms were based on folk idioms and generally consisted of an application of the principle of repetition and contrast.

2. *Melody*

a. Melody is the determining factor in Renaissance music. Consequently, all musical expression is the result of melodic treatment. Harmony and rhythm cannot be analyzed apart from melodic structure.

b. Melodies are modal in structure.

c. Melody is distinctly vocal in style and limited to a range which rarely exceeds the octave. Wide skips are avoided, and most melodic movement is diatonic or restricted to the tones of the scale being used. Chromaticism, the use of other than the seven natural tones of the model scale, flattened or sharpened tones, is rare.

d. Melodic form is determined by textual rather than musical considerations.

3. *Rhythm*

a. Rhythm is free from strict metrical phrasing. However, many rhythmic clichés are used, including syncopation.

b. The restrictive isorhythmic devices of the Gothic period disappear in the fifteenth century although there are some examples of this method of rhythmic organization to be found among the early Renaissance composers.

c. Rhythmic phrases are generally long, free from metrical accent, and often overlap between the voices.

d. Rhythms are often complex as a result of the problems of polyphonic writing and the metric intricacies of the texts.

4. *Harmony*

a. Harmony is a result of simultaneous sounding of more or less independent lines of melody, and not a result of functional harmonic patterns. The composer has no preconceived notion of the chordal background which functions within a tonal system, and therefore compels him to use certain tones for each of the melodic parts at any one place. Such a predetermined function of harmony slowly makes its appearance at final cadences, however, and begins to point the way to the dominance of harmonic considerations over melodic voice leading.

b. Harmony is essentially intervallic rather than chordal. The relation between the tones of the melodic lines, particularly in reference to the cantus firmus, is of prime importance in determining the melodic progression and the treatment of dissonance. These relationships are intervallic rather than chordal.

c. Harmony is a consequence rather than a determinant in musical structure. Since rules and conventions governing voice leading are determined by treatment of intervals between voices, that which strikes the ear as harmonic progression is a result of voice relationships rather than the basis for harmonic construction.

5. *Texture*

a. The texture of Renaissance music is predominately polyphonic. Even in the late Renaissance where a tendency toward homophonic treatment is found in secular songs, the accompanying voices are treated more or less as independent melodies rather than as mere chordal accompaniments.

b. In the sixteenth century there are works in which harmonic texture is used as a contrast to the predominating polyphonic texture. These passages are designated as being in "familiar style," suggesting that this might have been a practice generally used in folk or popular music.

c. Due to the independence of voice leading, there is much overlapping of rhythmic, melodic, and harmonic cadences.

6. *Media*

a. The human voice, both in solo and ensemble, was the generally accepted media of performance for all Renaissance music.

b. Instruments of all kinds were used to reinforce the voice in both sacred and secular music.

c. Instruments began to be used independently in the sixteenth century, particularly the organ and stringed keyboard instruments, the harpsichord and clavichord.

d. Groups of string or wind instruments were often used toward the end of the Renaissance period. Consorts of viols or recorders in all their various sizes and ranges were commonly employed.

e. The lute, which held a place of importance parallel to the piano in the nineteenth century was the most popular single instrument.

IV. Practice and Performance

1. Use of specific types of voices and instruments was left to the judgment of the performers, availability, and range demands of the particular voice parts.

2. Notation indicated only relative rather than absolute or fixed pitch. Accommodation to vocal and instrumental range determined the actual pitch of any given performance.

3. Clefs to designate the pitch names and relationships of the notes on the staff were used before the Renaissance. By the sixteenth century, however, regular use was made of the C and F clefs to designate the ranges corresponding to our modern soprano, alto, tenor and bass voices. The G or treble clef began to displace the soprano C clef in the latter part of the sixteenth century.

4. No interpretive directions as to tempi, dynamics, or phrasing are to be found in the music of the period.

5. Dependence on the common practice of specific periods and schools led to lack of notational directions in many cases. The use of sharps or flats written above the notes in modern editions indicates the editor's decision that these were included in performance, but not in notation, a practice known as "musica ficta," as described in the chapter on "Gothic."

6. Another term which may have been applied to devices of performance was called "musica reservata." There is little agreement as to its meaning but several of its interpretations suggest that performance was often regulated by commonly understood practices of improvisation for which no detailed directions were necessary at that time.

7. The practice of using a succession of first inversion triads or sixth-chords was known as fauxbourdon. The composer duplicated a soprano melody at the sixth below, and a singer extemporized a fourth below the soprano. The result was a series of sixth-chords which marked the beginning of the use of the third and the full triad as a basic harmonic element.

V. Vocal Forms

1. *Motet.* Various types of motets were written in the fifteenth and sixteenth centuries. The isorhythmic motet (see chapter on Gothic) continued in use until the middle of the fifteenth century.

> Ex: Isorhythmic motet: *Veni Sancte Spiritus,* Dunstable
> TEM p. 87
> Rec. HSE-9101 Side 1

Many new methods of composition were applied to motet writing, but the cantus firmus in long held notes continued in use through the last half of the fifteenth century. However, the principal motet form of the Renaissance was that developed by Josquin Des Prez which consisted generally of a work in four to six voices with imitative treatment. The motet was usually made up of a number of sections, nonrepetitive, each of which treated a portion of the text. The texts were always in Latin and taken either from the liturgy of the Mass or from the Bible. The individual voices were most likely to overlap from one section to another, consequently well defined harmonic cadences were generally lacking except at such marked divisions as changes in meter, or at the final cadence of a section.

Ex: *Parce, Domine,* Obrecht
MM p. 55
Rec. HS-9038 MM r. 1

Ex: *Tristis est anima mea,* Lassus
MM p. 78
Rec. HS-9039 MM r. 2

Ex: *Magnificat octavi toni,* C. Morales
TEM p. 108
Rec. HSE-9101 Side 2

Ex: Polychoral motet: *Laudate Dominum,* Hassler
TEM p. 138
Rec. HSE-9101 Side 2

2. *Mass.* The Mass is the only important composite form used in the Renaissance, and as such is made up of a series of movements each of which is similar in structure and form to the motet. Each of these movements provides a musical setting for one of the five principal parts of the Ordinary of the Roman Catholic Mass, Kyrie, Gloria, Credo, Sanctus and Agnus Dei. As in the motet, the composer employed secular, sacred, and freely invented canti firmi, as well as imitative techniques for organizational purposes.

The largest proportion of Masses were those based on pre-existing material; plainsong, folk song, motets, or polyphonic secular works.

One type often called the plainsong Mass, constructed on appropriate and different canti firmi for each of the parts of the Mass (the Kyrie on a plainsong Kyrie, the Gloria on a plainsong Gloria, etc.) continued to be used as in the single Mass composed by Guillaume de Machaut. (See chapter on Gothic.)

The cantus firmus Mass using a single cantus firmus which appeared in each of the several parts of the composition was the most frequently composed style in the Renaissance. This cantus firmus might consist of an entire pre-existing melodic idea or only a portion of it. It might be quoted literally or paraphrased in all movements while reserved to the tenor voice, or it might be paraphrased throughout each movement and appear in all voices imitatively.

Ex: Cantus firmus Mass on a secular tune: *Missa, Se la face ay pale,*
Dufay
MM p. 43
Rec. HS-9038 MM r. 1
Ex: Cantus firmus Mass on a plainsong: *Missa Pange Lingua,* Des
Prez
Das Chorwerk, Vol. 1. Möseler Verlag
Rec. DGG ARC-3159

A special type of Mass developed in the sixteenth century
was called the Parody Mass. This form is an even more complex
extension of the technique of basing the parts, as well as the
whole, on a pre-existing composition. In the case of the Parody
Mass, a polyphonic motet was used as a basis for imitative development. The motet could be used in its entirety or in fragments throughout the several movements of the Mass. A motet
was usually selected from among the composer's own works as
the basis for a Parody Mass.

Ex: Parody Mass: *Missa Veni sponsa Christi,* Palestrina
MM p. 86
Rec. HS-9039 MM r. 2

Names given to the preceding types of masses were taken
from the motets or canti firmi from which they were derived,
i.e. *Missa Pange Lingua.* Relatively few masses were composed
entirely on original material freely invented.

Ex: *Missa Papae Marcelli,* Palestrina
Eulenberg Ed.
Rec. DDG ARC-3074

3. *Hymn.* These were polyphonic strophic settings of Latin
poetic religious texts in which each verse of text was repeated
to the same setting. The upper voice was generally predominately melodic.

Ex: *Veni creator spiritus,* Dufay
Das Chorwerk, Vol. 49 Möseler, Verlag
Rec. DDG ARC-3003

4. *Chorale.* The hymn tunes and their four part chordal
settings which were adopted for use in the German Protestant

church by Luther and his musical collaborators are generally called chorales, German Protestant Chorales, or Lutheran Chorales. The texts were in the vernacular language, generally German. The tunes were often taken from older Latin hymns or specifically composed to appropriate texts, but a rich source was the secular folk melody. These chorales in their simple form are usually binary with the first section repeated. The melodies which are predominantly in the upper voice are slow moving, and the cadences very marked and strong.

Ex: *Komm, Gott Schoepfer, Heiliger Geist,* Walter
    TEM   p. 120
    Rec.   HSE-9101   Side 2

5. *Psalm Settings.* These were the hymns of the French Protestant movement, the Huguenots. They were simple settings, generally in chordal style, with some free polyphonic treatment. The dominant melody, as in the German Chorale, is in the upper voice. Rhythmically, these psalm settings were somewhat more lively than the German Chorales, and the texts were, of course, in French.

Ex: *Mon Dieu me paist,* Goudimel
    TEM   p. 126
    Rec.   HSE-9101   Side 2

6. *Anthem.* Anthems were the motets of the Anglican Church. They follow the structure of the Renaissance motet in the settings of the English texts. Two types were used, the full anthem which is like the traditional four part hymn, and the verse anthem which presents an innovation in the motet style in the late sixteenth century. In the verse anthem, soloists and chorus with instrumental accompaniments were used with an alternation between solo and choral sections.

Ex: Verse Anthem; *This is the Record of John,* Gibbons
    Novello and Co., Anthems No. 831
    Rec.   DDG   ARC-3053

Ex: Anthem; *Heare the voyce and prayer of thy servaunts,* Tallis
    TEM   p. 133
    Rec.   HSE-9101   Side 2

7. *Frottola.* This is a derivation from a dance form and represents the most important of the strophic forms developed in the late fifteenth and early sixteenth centuries in northern Italy. It is a kind of sophisticated folk song, generally chordal in structure, and characterized by variously arranged patterns of two contrasting musical ideas. One pattern commonly used is abaabab. The frottola was written in three or four voices. However, the lower voices were probably played on instruments, as well as sung.

> Ex: *O mia cieca e dura sorte,* Cara
> TEM   p. 97 and 99
> Rec.   HSE-9101   Side 2

8. *Madrigal.* The madrigal is the most highly developed of all the Renaissance secular vocal forms. Originating in Italy, composers of all schools set the lyrics of Italian poets to music in this form and it flourished in the latter half of the sixteenth century. The madrigal soon arrived in England where an independent school of composers in a short time rivaled the Italians in quantity and quality of its production in the settings of English lyric poems. It was generally a through-composed (non-repetitive) type of composition in contrast to the verse-refrain madrigal of the 14th century. It varied from a chordal type similar to the frottola to imitative polyphonic examples. In some respects the madrigal was a secular counterpart of the sacred motet, as were all these highly developed secular forms. However, it was usually much more gay in melodic and rhythmic devices.

There were also madrigals of a serious nature, though most of them were settings of lyrics which spoke of love — often unrequited love. Instances of the deliberate use of musically expressive devices to fit the text are not infrequent. These so-called "madrigalisms" consisted of textual interruptions by rests, chromaticisms, naive attempts to make the music illustrate the text by means of rhythmic and melodic tone painting, etc. Frequent changes of rhythm are often used. Madrigals were written in three to five voices. Toward the end of the sixteenth century there was a distinct tendency to write madrigals in homophonic style with a predominating principal, or solo, voice. The ballet madrigal, most common in England, was of this type and was strophic in structure.

> Ex: *S' io parto, i' moro,* Marenzio
> MM   p. 100
> Rec.   HS-9039   MM   r. 2
> Ex: *Thyrsis, sleepest thou?* Bennet
> MM   p. 109
> Rec.   HS-9039   MM   r. 2

9. *Ayre.* This was a late development in England and was a purely homophonic song in strophic style. The accompanying voices were usually played on the lute, though they could be either sung or played. Its most distinguishing characteristic was its strophic form.

> Ex: *My Thoughts Are Winged with Hope,* Dowland
> TEM   p. 189
> Rec.   HSE-9102   Side 1

10. *French Chanson.* This term embraced the whole of the polyphonic secular writing to French texts of the fifteenth and sixteenth centuries. The fifteenth century chansons were generally in the repetitive fixed forms of the rondeau, virelai, etc. In the sixteenth century the fixed forms were abandoned and there is a truly polyphonic treatment in imitative style. Like the motet, the chanson is usually in sections and is constructed in a through-composed manner. The sections, however, are short and marked with simultaneous cadences in all voices. There is also a tendency to homophonic texture. Rhythms are faster and lighter than in the motet. Most of the sixteenth century chansons were in four voices and the top voice usually carried the principal melodic burden.

> Ex: *Adieu m' amour,* Binchois
> MM   p. 48
> Rec.   HS-9038   MM   r. 1
> Ex: *Pour ung plaisir,* Crequillon
> MM   p. 64
> Rec.   HS-9038   MM   r. 1

11. *Polyphonic Lied.* This is the German counterpart of the Italian and English madrigal and the French chanson. Almost without exception these were polyphonic settings of folk song melodies. In some instances these settings were almost strictly chordal. However, an imitative polyphonic treatment developed in the last half of the fifteenth and first half of the sixteenth centuries.

Ex: *Oho, so geb' der Mann ein' n Pfenning,* Senfl
  TEM p. 177
  Rec. HSE-9102 Side 1

12. *Quodlibet.* The quodlibets were a type of polyphonic composition in which several popular or folk songs of the day were combined to make a humorous poly-textual unit.

Ex: *Fricasee',* anon.
  TEM p. 170
  Rec. HSE-9102 Side 1

13. *Other Secular Forms.* A large body of traditional strophic forms such as the villancico, virelai, ballata, rondeau, etc., were employed both monodically and polyphonically in the fifteenth century. They retained their fixed forms of the earlier period (see chapter on Gothic) though they were often more simple in formal and rhythmic structure. The principal melody was placed in the uppermost part, and settings were generally chordal with little imitation. The formal musical structure of these songs was determined by their strict poetic forms.

Ex: Villancico: *Soy contento y vis serrido,* Encina
  TEM p. 94
  Rec. HSE-9101 Side 1
Ex: Meistersinger Melody: *Gesangweise,* Hans Sachs
  TEM p. 105
  Rec. HSE-9101 Side 2

VI. Instrumental Forms

While instruments were popularly used in the performance of music during the Renaissance, there was actually no real independent instrumental writing until very late in the sixteenth century. Consequently, there are very few purely instrumental forms that are unrelated to the polyphonic style of vocal music. In fact, the greatest amount of instrumental performance was either in duplication of, or substitution for, actual voice parts in polyphonic vocal works. Some works written specifically for instruments in the sixteenth century displayed a consideration for the special technical capabilities of those instruments then in use.

1. *Canzona.* The instrumental canzona which appeared in the sixteenth century was at first a mere instrumental arrangement, or transcription, of the vocal chanson. It was written for either lute or keyboard performance. Subsequently, composers wrote original instrumental works in the style of the vocal chanson. Keyboard canzonas as well as canzonas for instrumental ensembles varied from the conventional imitation of the sectional character of the vocal chansons (see Chanson under vocal forms) to the spectacular poly-choral type of the Venetian school, composition in which alternating sections in varying rhythms and textures were performed by alternating choirs of instruments.

>Ex: Canzona francese: *deta Pour ung plaisir,* Gabrieli
>MM   p. 64
>Rec.   HS-9038   MM   r. 1

2. *Ricercar.* The ricercar is the instrumental equivalent of the vocal motet. Like the motet, it was constructed in several sections. Each section had a different musical theme which was treated imitatively and contrapuntally. The ricercar written for instrumental ensemble was closely patterned after the vocal motet with numerous sections and melodic themes. The fact that many such works were published with instructions "to be sung and played" indicated their affinity to vocal forms.

The organ ricercar, on the other hand, while basically the same construction, tended to use fewer themes and sections, and therefore the treatment of the themes was much more elaborate and longer. Contrapuntal imitation was the principal element of form.

There was also a type of non-imitative ricercar for the lute, organ and instrumental ensemble. These were unlike the imitative ricercar and motet and seem to have been written more for study purposes since they tend to exploit the technical possibilities of the instruments.

> Ex: *Ricercar No. 7*, Willaert
> HMS   Vol. IV   p. 51
> Rec.   RCA   LM-6029-1   HMS   Vol. IV

> Ex: *Ricercar arioso*, Andrea Gabrieli
> HMS   Vol. IV   p. 61
> Rec.   RCA   LM-6029-1   HMS   Vol. IV

3. *Fantasia.* This was a title of rather ambiguous nature, given to instrumental compositions in the sixteenth century. It was often used to indicate compositions in various forms. The name probably referred to the improvisatory nature of such works as the ricercar in free form, but in strict contrapuntal style. The title was used to cover a wide variety of compositions published at the very end of the sixteenth century, many of which were free ricercars and chansons in tablature form.

> Ex: *Three part Fantasia, No. 3*, Gibbons
> HMS   Vol. IV   p. 53
> Rec.   RCA   LM-6029-1   HMS   Vol. IV

> Ex: *In Nomine*, Gibbons
> TEM   p. 202
> Rec.   HSE-9102   Side 2

4. *Prelude.* Another name which was applied very loosely to a variety of compositions which originally served to introduce a liturgical ceremony. In the fifteenth and sixteenth centuries it was used to designate a free type of idiomatic keyboard music, often very short and in a homophonic style. It usually exploited the technique of the keyboard. Unlike the canzona or ricercar, the prelude does not derive from any vocal form, but

represents the first type of truly instrumental music. The English virginal composers often used the term to describe a virtuoso type of keyboard composition.

> Ex: Praeambel für Laute, Neusidler
> GMB   p. 88
> Rec.   BG-548

5. *Toccata.* A form of keyboard composition deriving its name from the Italian "toccar," to touch. The toccata exploited a rather improvisatory style of writing in which florid homophonic scale and chord passages were combined with imitative sections. Most characteristic of the toccata is its adherence to keyboard idiom and its unchanging tempo.

> Ex: *Toccata Quinta, Seconda Tuona,* Merulo
> TEM   p. 152
> Rec.   HSE-9102   Side 1

6. *Variation.* The variation is a form that is basically repetitive. It uses a newly invented, or a pre-existing, melodic idea, which is presented in a succession of altered versions. The problem confronting the composer is to maintain the relationship between the successive versions and at the same time provide interest through the alterations. In the sixteenth century the beginnings of this form employed the device of altering the contrapuntal texture by the use of imitative figures, or by embellishing the melody by ornamentation and rapid scale passages, etc.

Variations for lute and keyboard in the early sixteenth century Spanish school illustrates the contrapuntal type, while the keyboard variation of the English school is representative of the figured variation.

> Ex: *Variations on the song "Cavallero,"* Cabezon
> HAM   p. 144
> Rec. EA-0026
> Ex: *Loth to depart.* Farnaby
> MM   p. 115
> Rec.   HS-9039   MM   r. 2

7. *Dance Forms.* There are only a few instrumental dances in polyphonic style to be found in the fifteenth century. Those which are known come from the *Muenchener Liederbuch* and the *Glogauer Liederbuch,* the two large collections of dances and songs dating from c. 1460. The sixteenth century, however, is a period dominated by dance forms and is often called "the century of the dance." Sixteenth century dances are characteristically paired like the pavane-galliard and the passamezzo-saltarello. In these cases the first dance of the pair is in slow duple meter, followed by the second in a fast triple meter. In many instances the second dance is merely a rhythmically changed version of the first dance. This was particularly true of the German *Tanz* and *Nachtanz,* or Tanz and Proportz. In this case the second dance assumes the characteristics of a variation on the first. The structural form of the dance is basically binary. The pairing of two dances and the actual grouping of several dances at the end of the sixteenth century indicated the desire to write instrumental works of a larger scope. These are among the first examples of the instrumental suite which was to become a standard form in the Baroque period.

Ex: *Der Prinzen-Tanz; Proportz,* anon.
MM   p. 74
Rec.   HS-9038   MM   r. 1

Ex: *Paduan and Intrada,* Puerl
HMS   Vol. IV   p. 51
Rec.   RCA   LM-6029-1   HMS   Vol. IV

Ex: *Pavana for the virginal,* John Bull
TEM   p. 161
Rec.   HSE-9102   Side 1

Ex: *Passamezzo d'Italie,* anon.
TEM   p. 194
Rec.   HSE-9102   Side 2

VII. Important Composers

Because of the large number of composers found in the Renaissance, it is necessary to explain the basis upon which the following selection has been made. These composers represent important innovations in style and technical devices of composition. Moreover, they are often the leaders of a particular school of composition or of a national group. While their works represent a high quality of Renaissance music, their inclusion does not mean that their works were always superior to some composers who have been omitted from this list.

1. Dunstable, John (c. 1370-1453) was an English composer and early master of counterpoint influential in establishing the Burgundian School. He is especially noted for his interesting contrapuntal lines composed around the plainsong melody.

> Ex: *Six Motets*
> Musica Britannica   Vol. VIII   p. 58
> Rec.   DDG   ARC-3052

2. Dufay, Guillaume (c. 1400-1474) is considered the master of the Burgundian School. His works show a strong preference for the upper voices, both melodically and rhythmically. The use of instruments is often indicated. He wrote in all the religious and secular forms of his time.

> Ex: *Ave Regina Coelorum*
> HMS   Vol. III   p. 42
> Rec.   RCA   LM-6016-2   HMS   Vol. III

3. Binchois, Gilles (c. 1400-1460) was also one of the Burgundian group, and is best known for the excellence of his secular works, especially the chanson. Like others of his time, the stylistic features were essentially the same in both sacred and secular polyphony.

> Ex: *Filles a marier*
> HMS   Vol. III   p. 45
> Rec.   RCA   LM-6016-2   HMS   Vol. III

4. Ockeghem, Johannes (1430-1495) was a pupil of Dufay and the leader of the Flemish School. His development of devices of imitation served as models for those who later perfected the

a cappella style. He was also one of the first to write in four part polyphony.

> Ex: Chanson: *Fors seulement*
> Collected Works, Breitkopf and Härtel
> Rec. DGG ARC-3052
> Ex: Mass: *Fors seulement*
> HMS Vol. III p. 47
> Rec. RCA LM-6016-2 HMS Vol. III
> Ex: Sanctus from the *Missa Prolationum*
> MM p. 51
> Rec. HS-9038 MM r. 1

5. Des Prez, Josquin (c. 1450-1521) was of the Flemish School, one of the greatest composers of all time, and the first to make music a really expressive art. He was fortunate to have the majority of his compositions published during his lifetime. Because of this fact, coupled with his genius, he was well-known and had considerable influence on other composers. In general, his sacred works are contrapuntal in style, but many of the secular works tend toward homophonic practices, perhaps due to the influence of the Italian frottola.

> Ex: *Missa Pange Lingua*
> Das Chorwerk Vol. I Möseler Verlag
> Rec. DGG ARC-3159
> Ex: Frottola: *El Grillo*
> HMS Vol. III p. 55
> Rec. RCA LM-6016-2 HMS Vol. III
> Ex: Chanson: *Je ne me puis tenir d' aimer*
> HMS Vol. III p. 55
> Rec. RCA LM-6016-2 HMS Vol. III
> Ex: Motet: *Tribulatio et angustia*
> HMS Vol. III p. 58
> Rec. RCA LM-6016-2 HMS Vol. III
> Ex: Motet: *Ave Maria*
> MM p. 58
> Rec. HS-9038 MM r. 1

6. Isaac, Heinrich (c. 1450-1517). While Isaac was a Flemish composer, he was at one time court composer to Maximilian

in Vienna, bringing the Flemish style to Austria. While he wrote many masses, motets, etc., it was his polyphonic settings of choral melodies that make his music memorable.

> Ex: *Missa Carminum*
>   Das Chorwerk, Vol. VII, Möseler Verlag
>   Rec.   West   WL-5215
>
> Ex: Polyphonic Song: *Innsbruck ich muss dich lassen*
>   HMS   Vol. III   p. 75
>   Rec.   RCA   LM-6016-1   HMS   Vol. III

7. Obrecht, Jacob (1452-1505) was born in the Nether-lands. He carried on the innovations of Okeghem, but added an expressive quality that followed the meaning of the texts. He also used four voices, the lower one becoming more a true bass line, leading to the frequent employment of the authentic cadence. He was also one of the first composers to have a large number of his works published during his lifetime.

> Ex: Motet: *Si oblitus fuero*
>   HMS   Vol. III   p. 51
>   Rec.   RCA   LM-6016-2   HMS   Vol. III

8. Senfl, Ludwig (c. 1490-1543) was a Swiss, but held musi-cal positions in Germany. He was known as a singer and a composer of church music. As a pupil of Isaac, he cultivated the Flemish style. He was also noted for the charm of his polyphonic settings of the German lied. Luther praised Senfl as the "Prince of all German music."

> Ex: *Ach, Elslein, liebes Elslein*
>   Antiqua Chorbuch, Teil II, Edition Schott   4256   p. 82
>   Rec.   SPA-58

9. Willaert, Adrian (c. 1490-1562) was a Flemish composer who became the founder of the Venetian School, numbering among his pupils such masters as Andrea Gabrieli and Zarlino. He held the post of Master of the Chapel at St. Mark's where he introduced a style of writing for two antiphonal choirs. While

his sacred music is of a high quality, he is perhaps best known for his madrigals, a form which he raised far above the level of the popular frottola.

> Ex: *Ricercar No. 7*
> HMS   Vol. IV   p. 51
> Rec.   RCA   LM-6029-2   HMS   Vol. IV

10.   Tallis, Thomas (c. 1505-1585) was an English organist and composer. He was the first to use the English language in settings of the liturgy of the Anglican Church. He also wrote a large number of motets and masses, using Latin.

> Ex: Motet: *Adesto nunc propitius*
> HMS   Vol. IV   p. 34
> Rec.   RCA   LM-6029-2   Vol. IV

11.   Cabezon, Antonio de (1510-1566), an important Spanish composer and organist, was a strong influence on many European composers for the organ and other keyboard instruments. He also made keyboard arrangements of the vocal music of Josquin Des Prez and other Flemish composers.

> Ex: Variations on the Song "Cavallero"
> HAM   p. 144
> Rec.   EA-0026

12.   Clemens, Jacobus (non Papa) (c. 1510-c. 1556), a Flemish composer, was especially noted as one of the more progressive composers of the early sixteenth century in his use of chromatic harmonization. His best works are the masses and motets.

> Ex: *Souterliedekens a 3*
> American Institute of Musicology
> Complete works of Clemens, Vol. II
> Rec.   Cantate 642220

13.   Gabrieli, Andrea (c. 1520-1586) was an Italian composer of the Venetian school, a pupil of Adrian Willaert, and

uncle and teacher of Giovanni Gabrieli. After extensive travel in Germany and Bohemia, Andrea became organist at St. Mark's in Venice where he achieved a great reputation as organist. He was a prolific composer of both choral and instrumental music, ranging from massive sacred works to the madrigal. Many larger compositions exhibit the polychoral tradition of the Venetian school established by Willaert.

> Ex: Canzona Francese: *deta Pour ung plaisir*
> MM   p. 64
> Rec.   HS-9038   MM   r. 1

14. Monte, Philippe de (1521-1603), a Belgian, was a friend of Roland de Lassus and was influenced by the Flemish style. He is best known for his expressive madrigals.

> Ex: Mass: *Benedicta es*
> HMS   Vol. IV   p. 24
> Rec.   RCA   LM-6029-1   HMS   Vol. IV

15. Palestrina, Giovanni Pierluigi (c. 1525-1594), an Italian composer, was generally considered the greatest master of Renaissance Catholic music. His most important post was that of director of the Cappella Giula at the Vatican. Palestrina is noted for the perfection of a purely vocal style, commonly known as the a cappella style. His music is characterized by a high degree of technical perfection with diatonic melody and a smooth texture that culminated in a rare beauty of sound that is almost transcendental in its implications. His *Missa Papae Marcelli* has become a model for the purest religious style of Catholic music.

> Ex: *Missa Papae Marcelli*
> Eulenberg, Ed.
> Rec.   DGG   ARC-3074
> Ex: Motet: *Stabat Mater*
> Eulenberg, Ed.
> Rec.   DGG   ARC-3074

16. Lassus, Roland de (Orlando di Lasso) (1532-1594) was also a product of the Flemish school, but was international

in his music. His fame rests mainly on his religious music, however he was equally effective in Italian and German madrigals and French chansons. He wrote over two thousand compositions. Historians rank him as the greatest of the Flemish composers, and along with Palestrina, one of the most important of the Renaissance composers.

> Ex: *Missa VIII Toni, "Puisque j' ai perdu"*
> Breitkopf and Härtel, Ed.
> Rec. DGG ARC-3077

> Ex: Chanson: *Je l' aime bien*
> Breitkopf and Härtel, Ed.
> Rec. DGG ARC-3076

> Ex: Villanella: *O la, o che bon echo*
> Breitkopf and Härtel, Ed.
> Rec. DGG ARC-3076

17. Byrd, William (1543-1623) was one of the greatest composers of English sacred music. He is best known for his superb polyphonic settings of sacred texts — music that won him the title of the "English Palestrina." He was equally skilled in keyboard music for both the organ and virginal. His *Carmen's Whistle,* a set of variations for virginal, was very popular during his lifetime.

> Ex: Motet: *Ego sum panis vivus*
> MM p. 91
> Rec. HS-9039 MM r. 2

18. Victoria, Thomas Luis de (c. 1549-1611) was a leading representative of the Roman School in Spain. He studied in Rome, probably with Palestrina. His music has a dramatic intensity and spiritual fervor that is thoroughly Spanish. He is best known for the *Requiem Mass,* but he also wrote a large number of other works, including a book of hymns for four voices.

> Ex: *Missa O Quam Gloriosum*
> Breitkopf and Härtel
> Rec. Lyr. LL-46

> Ex: Motet: *O Domine Jesu*
> MMS Vol. IV p. 23
> Rec. RCA LM-6029-1 HMS Vol. IV

19. Marenzio, Luca (1553-1599) was an important Italian madrigalist. His works show that he was a very progressive composer who made many innovations in chordal relationships and chromaticisms.

> Ex: *Scendi dal Paradiso*
> HMS Vol. IV p. 14
> Rec. RCA LM-6029-1 HMS Vol. IV

20. Gabrieli, Giovanni (c. 1554-1612) was a nephew and pupil of Andrea Gabrieli. He was the greatest composer of the Venetian School and one of the first to write for a combination of voices and instruments. One of his best known works in this medium was the *Sacrae Symphoniae*. He achieved massive sonorities with his polychoral technique. He is often regarded as the first to develop orchestration and to use a wide range of dynamics as in his *Sonate Pian'e Forte*.

> Ex: *Sacrae Symphoniae, in ecclesiis*
> HAM p. 175
> Rec. RCA LM-6029-2 HMS Vol. IV
> Ex: *Sonata pian' e Forte*
> HAM p. 198
> Rec. Bach-611

21. Morley, Thomas (1557-1602), an English composer and publisher, is best known for his madrigals and ballets. He was the publisher of the Triumphs of Oriana, a set of twenty-five madrigals by twenty-three composers — each madrigal in honor of Queen Elizabeth. He was also the author of the first English treatise on Music, "*A Plaine and Easie Introduction to Practicall Musicke.*"

> Ex: *Thyrsis and Milla*
> HMS Vol. IV p. 48
> Rec. RCA LM-6029-2 HMS Vol. IV

22. Gesualdo, Don Carlo (c. 1560-1613) was an Italian madrigalist whose works represent the extreme of chromaticism reached in the last years of the Renaissance. The harmonic results achieved by Gesualdo, while often described as mannerism, are indicative of a growing consciousness of the strength of musical expression and of the ideals of the dawning Baroque era.

> Ex: *Moro Lasso a mio duolo*
> TEM   p. 181
> Rec.   HSE-9102   Side 1

23. Hassler, Hans Leo (1564-1612) was a German who studied in Italy with Andrea Gabrieli. He adapted the Venetian style of the German lied and created a rather strong German musical style. He wrote in all the current and vocal and keyboard forms, both Renaissance and early Baroque, but was best known for his settings of German polyphonic songs and chorales.

> Ex: *Nun fanget an*
> Antiqua Chorbuch, Schott, Ed.
> Rec.   SPA-58

24. Monteverdi, Claudio (1567-1643) not only spans the final years of one period and the beginning of another by virtue of his life span, but he was one of the first composers to employ consciously two different practices; a "prima prattica," (stilo antico), and a "seconda prattica," (stilo moderno). While he wrote works in the "first practice" which were typical of the Renaissance such as his sacred choral works and madrigals, it was his use of the "second practice" which marked his contribution to the emerging Baroque and made him historically important. This will be discussed more fully in the chapter on the Baroque.

25. Weelkes, Thomas (c. 1575-1623) was one of the greatest of the English madrigalists. He was well in advance of his time in his characterization of text. He also wrote numerous anthems and services for the Anglican Church.

Ex: *O care thou wilt dispatch me*
HMS   Vol. IV   p. 17
Rec.   RCA   LM-6029-1   HMS   Vol. IV

VIII. Other Composers

Italy

Annibale (Il Padovano) (c. 1527-1575)
Merulo, Claudio (1533-1604)
Ingegneri, Marco Antonio (1545-1592)
Vecchi, Orazio (c. 1550-1605)
Gastoldi, Giovanni (........d. 1622)

Austria and Germany

Paumann, Conrad (c. 1410-1473)
Finck, Heinrich (1445-1527)
Hofhaimer, Paul (1459-1537)
Gallus, Jacobus (Handl) (1550-1591)
Eccard, Johannes (1553-1611)
Franck, Melchoir (c. 1579-1639)

England

Taverner, John (c. 1495-1545)
Farnaby, Giles (c. 1560-1640)
Bull, John (c. 1562-1628)
Wilbye, John (1574-1638)
Gibbons, Orlando (1583-1625)
Farmer, John (fl. 1591-1601)
Bennet, John (fl. 1599-1614)

Netherlands

La Rue, Pierre de (........d. 1518)
Verdelot, Philippe (........d. 1550)
Gombert, Nicholas (c. 1490-1556)
Arcadelt, Jacob (c. 1505-1560)
Rore, Cipriano de (1516-1565)

Spain

Milan, Louis (c. 1500-after 1561)
Morales, Cristobal de (c. 1500-1553)

IX. Important Writers on Music

A number of theoretical treatises on music were written during the Renaissance. These works were generally in Latin, the language of the scholar, and usually written in a learned style that often obscures rather than illuminates. However, these writings are the actual sources from which our knowledge of all musical matters not revealed by the actual music is drawn. Without these works many problems of reconstructing Renaissance music would be without authentic solutions, for they offer clues to, as well as the detailed explanations of, notation, tuning, performance, instrumental construction, rules of theory, and countless other areas puzzling to the present day scholar. Many of these works contain unique examples from the music literature of the times that would otherwise be unavailable. In several cases the authors wrote more than one work. In such cases the important one has been listed with its original title and date of writing or publication, as well as any modern edition or translation.

1. Ramos de Pareja, Bartolomé (c. 1440-1491) Spanish theorist. His *Musica Practica,* Bologna, 1482, is a landmark in the science of harmony, particularly in its instruction concerned with intonation. Ramos, through his division of the monochord, established the ratios of 4:5 and 5:6 for the major and minor thirds.

2. Tinctoris, Johannes (1436-1511) was a Belgian theorist and composer. His *Terminorum musicae diffinitorium,* Naples, 1473, is the oldest known dictionary of musical terms. An English translation appeared in London in 1849. Another work was published during his lifetime and several manuscripts were published in Coussemaker's complete edition of the writings of Tinctoris in 1875.

3. Gaforio, Franchino (1451-1522) was an Italian theorist. *Practica Musicae Franchino Gaforio Laudenis in IV libris,* Milan, 1496, is Gaforio's magnum opus. It deals with rules of counterpoint and a discussion of practices in composition, as well as the current practices of performances.

4. Aaron, Pietro (1480-1545) was an Italian theorist. *Toscanello in Musica,* Venice, 1523, is one of a number of valuable

works of Aaron who is considered among the most important theorists of the early sixteenth century. This work, his most important, contains descriptions of contrapuntal rules, chord formations, etc., as employed in his day.

5. Agricola, Martin (1486-1556) was a German theorist whose *Musica instrumentalis deudsch*, Wittenberg, 1529, is an authoritative work on the instruments of the time and a valuable source for the history of notation. Agricola wrote a number of other theoretical works as well.

6. Glareanus, Henricus (1488-1563) was a Swiss philosopher, theologian, historian, poet, and musical scholar. His *Dodecha-chordon*, Basle, 1547, advocated the completion of the modal series to twelve and greatly influenced the concept of modality and tonality. There is a German translation of this work published in 1888.

7. Zarlino, Gioseffo (1517-1590) was an Italian theorist. In the *Instituzioni armoniche*, Venice, 1558, Zarlino discusses various topics concerning music of his day in the four books that make up his major work. These include rules of counterpoint, intonation, text, treatment and the general excellence of music.

8. Morley, Thomas (1557-1602) was an English composer and theorist. His *A Plaine and Easie Introduction to Practicall Musicke*, London, 1597, (Reprint 1937) is one of the earliest treatises on music published in England. A discourse on all phases of music making, this is the most important English book on musical theory in the Renaissance. A modernized edition was published in 1952.

Excerpts in English from several of the foregoing works can be found in *Source Readings in Music History* by Strunk:

Ramos:	pp. 200-205
Tinctoris:	pp. 193-200
Glareanus:	pp. 219-228
Aaron:	pp. 205-219
Zarlino:	pp. 228-262
Morley:	pp. 274-281

X. Manuscript Sources

Until music printing became a practicality in the sixteenth century, the manuscript collections constituted the most valuable source of actual music of the Renaissance. These manuscripts were usually made by anonymous copyists and were treasured in the libraries of monasteries, churches and royal courts. Of the countless manuscripts written before the end of the fifteenth century, when the printing of music had not yet displaced the collecting of musical works in handwritten form, certain monumental collections stand out as important. In many cases these are the sole sources of folk and composed music.

1. Old Hall MS. Written about 1450 at the Catholic College of St. Edmunds in Old Hall, England, and reposing there at the present, it contains a large number of Mass compositions and hymns. There is a modern edition of this work published in 1935-38 by Ramsbotham and Collins.

2. The Trent Codices are seven volumes of fifteenth century polyphonic music both sacred and secular. They represent one of the richest collections of representative works of about seventy-five fifteenth century masters of polyphony. A large part of this collection has been printed in the *Denkmäler Der Tonkust in Oesterreich Volumes* 7, 11, 19, 27, 31 and 40 in modern notation.

3. Among the collections of purely secular songs, the chansonniers and liederbuecher of France and Germany respectively are especially noteworthy. The *Copenhagen Chansonnier* of the fifteenth century contains thirty three polyphonic chansons and is representative of a number of such collections. It is available in modern edition also. Of the German collections, the *Glogauer Liederbuch,* the *Lochaimer Liederbuch* and the *Muenchner Liederbuch* contain vocal and instrumental polyphonic and monophonic settings of German folk songs and composed works. All three of these are published in modern editions.

XI. Suggested Readings

Cannon-Johnson-Waite	pp. 142-212
Ferguson	pp. 122-239
Grout	pp. 130-225
Harmon-Mellers	pp. 185-365
Lang	pp. 168-313
Oxford, Vol. III	pp. 107-500
Reese, R.	pp. 3-883
Sachs, HER	pp. 100-171
Ulrich-Pisk	pp. 102-205
Wold-Cykler	ch. 7

XII. Further References

Andrews, H. K. *An Introduction to the Technique of Palestrina.* London: Novello, 1958.

Bukofzer, Manfred. *Studies in Medieval and Renaissance Music.* New York: W. W. Norton, 1950.

Carpenter, Nan Cooke. *Music in the Medieval and Renaissance Universities.* Norman: University of Oklahoma Press, 1958.

Einstein, Alfred. *The Italian Madrigal.* Princeton: Princeton University Press, 1949.

Fellowes, E. H. *The English Madrigal Composers.* London: Oxford, 1950.

Gray, Cecil and Haseltine, Philip. *Carlo Gesualdo, Prince of Venosa. Musician and Murderer.* London: Paul, Trench, Trubner, 1926.

Jeppeson, Knud. *The Style of Palestrina and the Dissonance.* London: Oxford, 1927.

Lowinsky, Edward E. *Secret Chromatic Art in the Netherlands Motet.* New York: Columbia University Press, 1946.

Walker, Ernest. *A History of Music in England.* London: Oxford, 1952.

The inner principal group of the high altar in the Augustin
Church of Freibourg, Switzerland, by Peter Spring. 1592-1601.
Courtesy Baerenreiter Bild-Archiv.

Chapter

5

Baroque
1575-1750

I. Sociocultural Influences on Music

The word Baroque, probably derived from the Portuguese meaning an irregularly shaped pearl, was first used as a term of scorn for those art works, particularly architecture, produced from the end of the sixteenth century to the middle of the eighteenth century. While the word still carries with it some derogatory meaning, it is widely used to designate all the arts and music of this era. Applied to such a long period and to such diverse countries as Italy, France, England and the vast territories that came under Germanic influence, it had various phases. Its division into early middle and late Baroque did not occur simultaneously in all areas. In general, Baroque art is considered excessively decorative, dramatic, flamboyant, and emotional. There is a tendency to fuse the arts wherever possible; architecture, painting and sculpture, for example, are combined in the domed ceilings of the seventeenth and eighteenth century churches; music, literature, painting, architecture and sculpture are all combined in the opera or "drama per musica." Consequently, there is often a confusion of media; painting tries to portray what sculpture can do better; music tries to be literary, etc. The intense desire to express an idea, a feeling, the artists' own deep convictions and emotions often led to excesses in all forms of art. The tendency to ascribe these violent expressive qualities to lack of taste or to the desire to cover poor workmanship placed the Baroque forms in a position of disfavor in the late eighteenth and nineteenth centuries. A reappraisal of the Baroque in the twentieth century as representative of a period of violent and revolutionary upheavals, however, gives a new insight into the deep-lying motives which find expression in what seems at first a very superficial kind of art.

.The whole Baroque movement had its inception in Italy as a part of the Counter Reformation. Its influence and spirit spread rapidly into all parts of Europe, particularly into southern Germany and Austria where the Catholic Counter Reformation was most successful in its struggle with the Protestant North. Despite its first association with the Catholic Counter Reformation, the Baroque spirit became an equally vital part of the Protestant Reformation, and in fact pervaded all forms of artistic expression both spiritual and secular. Some important movements in religion, government economics and science that were partially responsible for the activity of the Baroque are as follows:

1. The struggle between Roman Catholicism and Protestantism known as the Thirty Years' War dominated the first half of the seventeenth century, especially in northern and central Europe. This devastating struggle delayed the development of the Baroque musical life in the German lands for better than a generation. However, both the Catholic Church, which in this series of wars partially regained its political influence, and the Protestant Church which developed a clear cut form of its own, adapted the prevailing magnificence of style to their own purposes.

2. The rise of absolute monarchies and the unification of national states played an important part in the creation of national styles, since the monarchs and princes were among the most important patrons of a lavish musical life. The courts of the Louis of France and Hapsburgs of Spain and Austria were examples of centers that stimulated the production of the larger and more spectacular forms of musical expression like the opera. Smaller courts, such as those of the German princes and dukes,

were influential in cultivating an intimate kind of music for both salon and chapel. The courts of the Dukes of Weimar and the Princes of Anhalt-Cöthen are examples of these smaller but highly cultural courts.

3. Intensive colonization during the seventeenth and eighteenth centuries gave rise to a wealthy merchant class. This wealth supplied the basis for the rich independent cities that were to provide a suitable climate for the establishment of a commercial theater and its musical production, the opera. Cities like Venice and Hamburg are good examples of such a concentration of merchant wealth and their musical theaters became internationally famous during this period.

4. There was a great interest shown in all fields of scholarly inquiry in the Baroque era. Discoveries through the application of inductive reasoning were most spectacular in the field of the sciences — physiology, astronomy, mathematics, physics. The success of scientific examination in these fields influenced musicians to apply methods of science to problems of music and led to a systematic development of the techniques and materials of musical art. Such works, discoveries and devices as Bach's *Art of the Fugue*, Rameau's *Treatise on Harmony*, Morley's *A Plaine and Easy Introduction to Music*, the practice of well-tempered tuning and the perfection of the violin family are all examples of the urge to systematization and scientific inquiry.

5. Affectations in all the arts are a calculated and planned emotional expression leading to a stylization of devices. A phenomenon of the Baroque is that such arts as literature, music and painting have as their aim these affectations, mannerisms and expressive qualities. Architecture achieves these affectations by means of such devices as the arch without its keystone and the twisted stone columns as decorative elements whose function is no longer architectural, but expressive. Music discovers the way to affect these same qualities in the tension created by dissonance within the tonal system of Baroque harmony. All the arts abound in examples of affectations and expressive feeling.

II. Function of Music

1. While a great deal of religious music was written for purely liturgical purposes, especially in the Lutheran church, an increasing amount of religious music for instruments was used for nonliturgical purposes. Some of this nonliturgical music was used for preludes, postludes, and to provide a musical background for quasi-religious purposes: marriage ceremonies, the dedication of a new building, the elevation of a civil or religious official to office, etc.

2. A great amount of music in the latter part of the Baroque period was written for amateur performers in the households of the aristocracy and the wealthy class. While most of this music was instrumental, vocal music also was included. Music of this type was truly chamber music, meant more for the pleasure of the performer than for an audience.

3. Music for private entertainment was cultivated in the households of the aristocracy where small bands of musicians provided both the compositions and performances of dinner music, dances and even ensemble concerts that ranged in style from the purely utilitarian to that of real aesthetic quality.

4. In the large wealthy courts, ballet and opera were first performed as a special kind of entertainment for the princes and the courtiers. The opera soon developed into a very popular form of public entertainment, first in Italy and soon over all of Europe. Performances of purely instrumental character were rarely given for the general public.

5. The oratorio was the religious counterpart of the opera. Because of the subject matter and manner of presentation it did not assume as popular a position as opera, but it did find importance in public performance as a kind of choral concert.

6. Special festive occasions often called for vocal music as well as instrumental music. The secular cantata was often employed for such events with texts that referred directly or allegorically to the occasion.

7. There was no institutional organization for teaching the musical arts. Young boys who showed interest and talent either were taught by their own musical fathers or relatives or were attached to the household of a composer-performer. Without doubt many compositions were written for the teaching of such prospective musicians. Such works as the *Little Organ Book* of J. S. Bach was undoubtedly in part, at least, the result of providing exercise material for his four musical sons. Geminiani's *Art of Violin Playing* was a more systematic approach to instrumental pedagogy. Instruction in performance and composition was restricted to the aspiring musician and to the households of the aristocracy and wealthy burghers.

III. Characteristics of Style

For the first time in the history of western European music two styles flourished side by side: (1) the Renaissance style, the "stilo antico" which carried over into the Baroque period; (2) the new Baroque style itself, often called "stilo moderno." The following characterizations apply to the "stilo moderno" or "nuovo musiche," which is typically Baroque. It must be realized, however, that many composers, sometimes some of the most important, continued to use characteristics of Renaissance style.

The "stilo moderno" was characterized by several stylistic compositional devices peculiar to the Baroque itself. One of these devices was given the Greek name of "monody." This was a manner of writing in which the melodic line was supported by a very simple chordal accompaniment. Originally the melodic line, or monody, was something midway between speech and song. The alleviation of the monotony of this form of musical declamation by means of passages that were more melodic in character eventually gave rise to the distinction in monodic style between recitative and aria.

Another characteristic of the Baroque music was the "stilo concertato." In the concertato style the composer used various forces, instrumental and vocal, in compositions which are both the result of harmonic or contrapuntal cooperation and also the planned contrast of instruments or voices against one another either as soloists or as groups. Many of the vocal and instrumental forms of the later Baroque are derived from this style of writing.

The "stilo concitato" or excited style was another device of writing whereby the music interpreted the words or moods of the dramatic action: the use of tremolo in the strings of the orchestra or rapidly sung syllables to a repeated note by the voice are typical of this style.

1. *Formal Organization*

  a. In the newly devised recitative the text dominated over formal structure.

  b. Contrapuntal development of the thematic material continued to be used in works which were wholly or partially contrapuntal — the fugue, toccata, and the chorale prelude.

  c. Homophonic forms generally depended upon simple statement and contrast of melodic material.

  d. The variation principle was used in both homophonic and contrapuntal forms such as theme and variation, passacaglia, chorale variation, etc.

  e. Sequential patterns were a frequent device of formal organization.

  f. A great number of solo instrumental works for the keyboard instruments, both organ and harpsichord, were written in a style which suggested improvisation. Rapid scale passages, decorations, chordal figuration, etc., in a free fantasy-like vein were characteristic of such compositions. Sometimes such improvisatory passages were obviously used for a display of a brilliant technique, and were dictated by this consideration rather than purely musical ones.

  g. The establishment of the principle of tonality led to clear cut phrase and period construction in formal design.

2. *Melody*.

Melodic writing varies from the declamatory style of the recitative, which might be regarded as almost a negation of melody, to the extremely florid style of the late Baroque arias and instrumental melodies.

a. The recitative, an invention of the early Baroque composers, represented a melodic idea whose structure was determined solely by verbal considerations.

b. Melody gradually assumed vocal and instrumental idiomatic styles, but these were often interchangeable. It was not uncommon to find purely vocal design applied to instrumental writing and vice versa. Both instrumental and vocal music employed melodic line of extended range. The desire for vocal display and the use of homophonic style account for this phenomenon in vocal music, while the continued perfection of keyboard instruments and the strings made an extended instrumental range possible.

c. The bel canto (beautiful singing) style emphasized beauty of vocal sound and brilliant florid technique. Composers provided for this demand by writing melodies which were musically scintillating but not necessarily dramatically expressive. In conformity with this demand, melodies often deteriorated into spectacular vocalises with ornamentation either written in or left to the discretion of the singer.

d. Melody in homophonic music was essentially one of balanced phrase and period, usually in four or eight measures.

e. Melody was often based on chordal outline.

f. While the upper melodic line was dominant in the homophonic style, there existed a kind of polarity between the melody and the bass line which was in itself a melodically conceived part.

3. *Rhythm*

    a. Rhythm was generally simple and tempo constant.

    b. The importance of the moving basso continuo gave a certain driving, almost motoric, feeling to both instrumental and choral works written in contrapuntal style.

    c. The rapid change of harmony induced by the melodic basso continuo also made for a driving harmonic rhythm, the movement given to music by changes in harmony, which added its force to the total rhythmic motion.

4. *Harmony*

    a. There was a distinct break from the modal to the major-minor system of tonal relationship.

    b. Harmony's chordal nature was determined by a system of numbers placed under the notes of the bass line. This device was called by various names: thorough bass, figured bass, basso continuo or merely continuo.

    c. The melodic character of the bass line suggested rapid changes of harmony, especially in the works of the late Baroque.

    d. Chromaticism, or use of dissonance, was freely employed in early Baroque for expressive purposes in vocal works. In the late Baroque both instrumental and vocal composition made use of chromaticism. The system of equal tempered tuning of keyboard instruments made possible the chromatic changes that were necessary for extended modulations, which were changes from one key to another.

    e. Even in works which were essentially contrapuntal, Baroque counterpoint was based on major-minor tonality rather than the modality of the Renaissance.

5. *Texture*

    a. Homophonic texture was employed exclusively in the opera and in solo arias of all kinds. Many instrumental forms such as the sonata da camera, keyboard sonatas, and suites were also predominately homophonic.

b. A distinct harmonic counterpoint was used in religious choral works as well as in many types of instrumental compositions such as the fugue, chorale prelude, variations on a ground, etc.

c. The tendency in purely homophonic forms to include contrapuntal techniques and the harmonic richness of contrapuntal forms tended to make the texture of most Baroque music rather thick and opaque.

d. There was great emphasis on contrasting textures, especially in the concertato style. The common contrast of large massed groups with small ones was enhanced by the general use of contrapuntal treatment for the large and homophonic treatment for the smaller groups.

6. *Media*

   a. Most of the modern instruments were in use in the Baroque era.

   b. The violin family was perfected and gradually displaced the viols by the end of the period.

   c. There was a real idiomatic feeling in writing for specific instruments. Examples are especially evident in works for the harpsichord and clavichord.

   d. One of the most popular chamber music groupings of instruments is that known as the trio-sonata, a name applied both to the instrumental group and to the literature written for it. It consisted of four instruments despite its title: two treble melodic instruments (often interchangeable), a bass instrument to play the continuo part (wind or string instrument) and a keyboard instrument to realize the figured bass (usually a harpsichord).

   e. Another chamber group was the solo sonata whose name again belies the instrumentation. It consisted of three instruments — one melodic, one bass, and a keyboard instrument for the harmony.

f. There was as yet no fixed orchestral group, although orchestras were used both as accompanying groups in vocal dramatic works and as independent musical organizations. The Baroque orchestra consisted mainly of strings with a number of wood-wind instruments.

g. One of the special Baroque instrumental practices was the use of the high trumpet range called clarini. The skill developed by clarini players prompted many Baroque composers to use the trumpet as a solo instrument.

h. The Baroque organ was a small instrument with great clarity and mellowness of tone, but it lacked the ability to execute a crescendo. All contrasts in dynamics had to follow the Baroque idea of contrasting sonorities of tone, achieved on the organ by changes in registration. The limited size and pureness of tonal quality made the Baroque organ an ideal instrument on which to realize the transparent contrapuntal texture of the organ forms of the period. Practically all of the great composers of the Baroque wrote for the organ and most of them were organ performers.

i. The term clavier referred to all types of keyboard instruments, especially the harpsichord and the clavichord. The former, known variously as clavecin, cembalo, gravicembalo, spinet and virginal, was the more widely used instrument and was only displaced by the piano which was invented in 1709 by Cristofori, but not universally adopted until after the Baroque era. Much solo and ensemble music was written for the harpsichord, especially in the last half of the Baroque period.

j. For solo purposes voices came to be used in the modern classification of soprano, alto, tenor and bass.

Since vocal solos and ensemble used instrumental accompaniment, a work written for a specific voice range could not readily be performed by a different voice. As a result certain characteristic vocal parts came to be assigned to specific vocal ranges, especially in dramatic writing.

k. A vocal phenomenon unique to the Baroque was the male or artificial sopranos known as castrati. The power, range, and technical facility of the castrati voices made them a great favorite with the Baroque opera audience and accounts for many soprano arias in Baroque operas of extreme difficulty for the modern singer.

IV. Practice and Performance

1. The Baroque was the last period in which improvisation was a definite requisite of every performer. Such improvisatory techniques as the realization and actual addition of ornaments in both vocal and instrumental performance were not only tolerated but expected. In fact, in both instrumental and vocal music composers often only outlined the melodic line with the full expectation of having the performer add not only ornamentation but passing tones, scale passages and even melodic fragments to the notated melody. Vocal music was particularly given to such improvisatory additions at highly expressive points, often as dictated by the texts, and these were known as "gorgia." In the later Baroque brilliant rapid ornamentation of a virtuoso type was known as coloratura, used especially by the soprano voice.

2. In both vocal and instrumental compositions performers were expected to extend cadences, especially climactic cadences near the end of a movement or work, with elaborate improvisation. Such improvisations came to take the name of "cadenzas." In the solo arias of operas and in the solo instrumental concertos, cadenzas came to be an integral part of the work, and performers used them not only to exhibit their ability at improvisation but also their command of technical skill.

3. Closely allied to pure improvisation was the realization or completion of the harmonies indicated in the figured bass by keyboard performers. Where the figuration was present the realization consisted of improvising suitable chordal and rhythmic patterns or even contrapuntal lines. Much music, however, was not even figured so that the keyboard realization demanded the choosing of both the proper harmony and its patterns.

4. The adoption of equal tempered tuning was practically universal by the end of the Baroque period, and displaced the earlier systems of just and mean tone temperament. Tuning of some instruments varied, such as the altered tuning of the violin, known as scordatura, a device used to achieve unusual chordal effects.

5. While writing for instruments became more and more idiomatic, there was still freedom given to the choice of instruments in certain compositions. Flutes, both recorder and the new transverse or German type, as well as oboes and violins were often interchangeable in ensemble music.

6. Tremolo and pizzicato were string instrument performance techniques introduced in this period.

7. Dynamic markings such as p., f., cresc., dim., were introduced but were used very sparingly. Most dynamic variations were achieved by contrasting instrumental groups of varied size or quality.

8. Designation of ornamentation by the use of abbreviations and signs was increasingly used in the Baroque. While performers were at liberty, in fact were expected, to improvise ornamentation even though it was not marked by the composer, composers used a large variety of signs to indicate their personal wishes in the matter. While some of the ornamentation directions were in common usage, many of them took on the personal meaning of the individual composer or school to which he belonged. This has given rise to many differences of interpretation in the works of the Baroque.

9. Tempo designations such as allegro, andante, grave, etc., were also introduced but had a wide range of meaning.

V. Vocal Forms

1. *Opera.* The most significant composite vocal form originating in the Baroque period was the dramatic opera, first called drama per musica. The first impulse toward this form was given by a group of noblemen, poets, and musicians who met in Florence. This group was known as the "Camerata." They wished to create a drama in which the words should dominate the music and dictate the rhythm. The expression of this desire came to be called the monodic style. Opera generally concerned itself with secular themes shaped into dramatic form. Early opera was based on Greek myths but later works dealt with historical, legendary and fictional heroes. A distinction between opera seria (serious or grand opera) and opera buffa (comic opera) came into existence at the end of the seventeeth century.

Opera employed orchestra, chorus, and soloists. The performances were staged with appropriate scenic settings and dramatic presentation. While the first operas were performed for private showings in such surroundings as palace halls, theaters or opera houses were soon built for public presentation.

Musically the opera used a variety of formal sections such as arias, choruses, dances, duets, and other ensemble numbers. The music was exclusively homophonic in texture. Choral passages, generously used in the early operas, were finally reduced to insignificant proportions, while the solo arias received more and more attention.

The following structural styles and forms were used in the composition of the operatic form:

    a. Recitative. Short as well as long passages written in a style of highly inflected declamation are known as recitatives. This is the declamatory form of the "stilo representativo" which came to be separated from the lyrically melodic parts of the monody. By the end of the seventeenth century the clear distinction between recitative and aria had been accomplished. The recitative served to carry the narrative and acted both as a prelude to and the connecting material between the highly emotional points represented by the arias. Recitatives took on no formal structure such as the aria, but served merely as a vocal vehicle for the prose dialogue.

In more serious situations recitative might be accompanied by full orchestra. In quick moving operatic narrative it was often accompanied only by the harpsichord in realization of the figured bass. In the former case it was known as accompanied recitative, in the latter secco or dry recitative.

Ex: Recitative: *Tu se' morta* from *Orfeo*, Monteverdi
MM   p. 124
Rec.   HS-9039   MM   Rec. 2

Ex: Recitative: *Al valor del mio brando,* from *Rinaldo,* Handel
MM   p. 189
Rec.   HS-9040   MM   Rec. 3

b. Aria. The more melodic passages of the stilo representativo took on formal character and finally separated from the declamatory parts as arias. The most typical form which these arias assumed was the three part or da capo aria developed by the Neapolitan opera school. This form was almost universally adopted by the writers for all musical dramatic works, secular and religious. The aria form was often applied to ensembles such as duets, trios, etc.

Ex: Aria: *Cara sposa* from *Rinaldo,* Handel
MM   p. 189
Rec. HS-9049   MM   Rec. 3

c. Arioso. A free vocal form for solo voice that mixes the declamatory style of the recitative with the lyrical style of the aria. Like the aria, the arioso was accompanied by full orchestra. The arioso was often used to express rapid changes of mood by means of the vocal line and the orchestral accompaniment. Unlike the aria the arioso was not cast in a formal design.

Ex: Air: *O jour affreux* from *Dardanus*, Rameau
      HMS   Vol. V   p. 23
      Rec. RCA LM-6030 HMS Vol. V
Ex: Arioso: *Ach Golgotha*, from the *St. Matthew Passion*,
         J. S. Bach
      MM   p. 226
      Rec. HS-9040 MM   r. 3

d. Chorus. Choral and ensemble passages took on no specific formal character. Little or no use was made of contrapuntal texture. Homophonic texture prevailed and formal musical considerations gave way to the interpretation of the text. Because of the emphasis on solo singing choral passages were infrequent in Baroque opera and occured only because the dramatic incident required some group of persons as a necessary part of the action.

Ex: Scene from *Venus and Adonis*, Blow
      L'Oiseau Lyre Press
      Rec. RCA LM-6030-2 HMS Vol. V

Because of the great public appeal of opera by the end of the seventeenth century, certain characteristics were attached to it by virtue of its place of composition and performance. Four general schools of opera can be discerned, namely Italian, French, English, and German.

The Italian was the first and most widely disseminated. Its main centers were Florence, Venice, Rome and Naples, from which it spread to all the great political and economic centers of Europe. By the end of the seventeenth century most Italian opera had become little more than an elaborate display of solo singing. Arias in bel canto style, displaying elaborately embellished and virtuoso passages were loosely held together by inconsequential dramatic narrative sung in secco recitative. The orchestra provided an overture in Italian form and an inob-

trusive accompaniment for the vocal passages which added
nothing to the dramatic intensity of the work.

Ex: Italian Opera: *Orfeo*, Monteverdi
     Bärenreiter Edition No. 2031a
     Rec. DDG ARC-3035/6

Ex: Opera Buffa: *La Serva Padrona*, Pergolesi
     Ricordi Ed.
     Rec. DGG ARC-3039

Ex: Italian Opera: *Julius Caesar*, Handel
     Aria and Recitative: *V' adoro, pupille*
     HMS Vol. V p. 17
     Rec. RCA LM-6030-1 HMS Vol. V

French opera whose centers were the courts of the Louis of
France differed from the Italian in language and general emphasis. The French composers, influenced by the great popularity and prestige of the classic French drama, tended to emphasize dramatic sincerity and action, and wrote arias of simpler
melodic line with less demands on virtuoso technique. The inclusion of ballet episodes was an attempt to give national character to the French opera by continuing the tradition of the
ballet de cour. In the French opera the orchestra provided an
overture in the French style. It also provided the music for the
dances as well as accompaniment for the singing.

Ex: *Scene infernale* from *Alceste*, Lully
     HMS Vol. V p. 20
     Rec. RCA LM-6030-2 HMS Vol. V

Ex: Scene from *Castor et Pollux*, Rameau
     MM p. 172
     Rec. HS-9040 MM r. 3

Ex: *Chaconne* from the opera-ballet, *Les Fêtes Vénitiennes*, Campra
     TEM p. 270
     Rec. HSE-9103 Side 1

English opera is represented by very few works. The general
characteristics were adopted from French and Italian models.
The tradition of the English dramatic form of the masque to

which music was often added was influential in the few operas written.

Ex: Opera: *Dido and Aeneas,* Purcell
     Oxford University Press, Piano Score
     Rec. Elect. 90031

A truly German opera did not exist in the Baroque period though there were a number of German composers of importance. Italian opera was so well entrenched that German composers wrote in the Italian style even when using German texts. The German native form of the singspiel, in which songs of a popular nature were combined into a form of musical entertainment, was the only original form comparable to opera.

Ex: Scene: *Ach! Nero ist nicht Nero mehr,* from *Octavia,* Keiser
     HMS Vol. V p. 26
     Rec. RCA LM-6030-2 HMS Vol. V
Ex: Aria from *Croesus,* Keiser
     TEM p. 277
     Rec. HSE-9103 Side 1

2. *Oratorio.* The oratorio employed the same forces as the opera, but was distinguished from it in that it usually did not use dramatic action or stage settings for presentation. Originally performed in the oratory of the church in Italy, by the end of the Baroque era it had become a musical dramatic form based on a religious but nonliturgical theme, and presented in concert form. The oratorio, while it employed soloists, tended to emphasize the chorus and usually contained a number of large choral movements.

The forms of the solo and small ensemble movements were identical with those of opera though often of more reserved character. The choral movements, however, were almost exclusively contrapuntal in style, ranging from strict to free fugal forms.

The oratorio frequently used a dramatic character known as the narrator (storicus or testo) who introduces and often narrates the story of the work by means of recitative. In this case the other dramatic characters use recitative only in introducing their aria and ensemble numbers.

Ex: *Jepthe,* Carissimi
      GMB p. 244
      Rec. DDG ARC-3005
Ex: Chorus: *Draw the Tear,* from *Solomon,* Handel
      MM p. 200
      Rec. HS-9040 MM r. 3
Ex: Oratorio scene: *Rappresentatione di Anima e di Corpo,* Cavalieri
      TEM p. 208
      Rec. HSE-9102 Side 2

3. *Cantata.* The cantata was used in several forms and for several purposes. There were both solo and choral cantatas written for liturgical and nonliturgical religious purposes, as well as secular occasions.

The structure of the cantatas was essentially the same in all instances. Small instrumental groups were employed for accompaniment with solo instruments often used in obligato fashion with the voice. Soloists and chorus provided the vocal forces. The forms of the aria, ensembles and choruses were those used in the opera and oratorio. Cantatas might be regarded as miniature, intimate types of oratorio of a chamber music variety. The only difference between the solo cantatas and the choral cantatas was the forces employed. Solo cantatas were written for a single solo voice. Choral cantatas used a chorus and usually some soloists.

While both Roman Catholic and Protestant composers wrote cantatas, those written by the Lutheran composers in the sixteenth and seventeenth centuries comprise the greatest wealth of church music of this period. These were liturgical cantatas and might be said to represent a kind of musical sermon since most cantatas were written for specific holy days in the church calendar.

Ex: Cantata: *Laudate Dominum,* Buxtehude
      Bärenreiter Ed.
      Rec. DGG ARC-3103

Ex: Cantata: *Wachet Auf*, J. S. Bach
Eulenburg Ed.
Rec. WEST-18394

Ex: Chorale and Chorus from *Christ lag in Todesbanden*, J. S. Bach
MM pp. 208, 215
Rec. HS-9040 MM r. 3

Ex: Cantata da camera: Recitative and aria from *Stravaganze d'
Amore*, Marcello
TEM p. 304
Rec. HSE-9103 Side 2

4. *Motet.* The Baroque composers continued the tradition
of the unaccompanied choral motet of the Renaissance. The
texture, however, was the typical tonal counterpoint of the Baroque period and not the modal counterpoint of the Renaissance.
The motet was generally of liturgical nature and was used in
both the Roman Catholic and Lutheran churches.

Ex: Motet: *Ich lasse dich nicht*, J. C. Bach
Möseler Verlag
Rec. RCA LM-6030-1 HMS Vol. V

5. *Passion Music.* The settings of the passion of Christ as
narrated in the four gospels of the New Testament were frequently set for both Catholic and Lutheran church use. These
settings were actually oratorios whose texts were restricted to
the Biblical quotations concerning Christ's trial and crucifixion,
and such other commentary as the composer might select in
keeping with this subject. A narrator took the part of the Evan-
gelist and sang all the narration that was not in direct quotation
in recitative style. Other soloists took the parts of the Biblical
characters and sang those solos which were commentary on the
story. The chorus represented the people, soldiers, priests, etc.,
and also sang choruses based on the commentary. In some Passion
settings for the Lutheran church, the German Protestant Chorales were also used. Other than these deviations the work was
constructed in the same manner as the oratorios of the period.

Ex: *St. Matthew Passion*, J. S. Bach
Eulenburg Ed.
Rec. DGG ARC-3125-8

6. *Spiritual Concerto*. Works variously known as "concerti ecclesiastici" and as "Geistliche konzerte" were frequently composed in the concertato style. They were restricted to a few voices with continuo or sometimes a few concerted instruments. Many of them were for only a single voice. The German composers of the seventeenth century used this type of composition most frequently since it could be used in much the same manner as a cantata in the Lutheran service.

Ex: Sacred Cantata: *O Herr, hilf*, Schütz
   MM   p. 135
   Rec. HS-9040   MM   Rec. 2

Ex: Chorale concerto: *Erschienen ist der herrliche Tag*, Schein
   TEM   p. 217
   Rec. HSE-9102   Side 2

7. *Mass*. The Catholic Mass continued to be set by composers. In typical Baroque style it takes on a dramatic character with addition of orchestral accompaniment and the frequent division of the various sections into solo and ensemble as well as choral settings. Even the da capo aria form is employed in some instances.

Ex: *B minor Mass*, J. S. Bach
   Eulenburg Ed.
   Rec. 3 Ang. 300C

8. *Anthem*. Baroque composers continue to write anthems (see Renaissance vocal forms) for the Anglican Church. The verse anthem with introduction of dramatic style was most typical of the Baroque era.

Ex: Verse Anthem: *Hear, O Heavens*, Humfrey
   HMS   Vol. V   p. 38
   Rec. RCA   LM-6030-2   HMS   Vol. V

9. *Solo Song*. Solo songs, though not constituting a major form were frequently written, especially by the German composers. They were strophic, usually of folk-like character in binary or ternary form of arias with instrumental accompaniment.

Ex: Solo Song: *Meine Seufzer Meine Klagen,* Erlebach
      HMS   Vol. V   p. 18
      Rec.   RCA   LM-6031-1   HMS   Vol. VI

VI. Instrumental Forms

It will be noted that the instrumental forms of the Baroque fall into a number of general types from which the more specific forms associated with the period emerged. Certain continuous or single movement forms were developed from the Renaissance models, but there was also a desire to devise larger instrumental forms. This desire was realized by combining several separate movements into a composite form. While these efforts can, for convenience, be divided into the following general types, it must be understood that the characteristics of one type often were found in another, and that often some compositions and some composers represent a mixture of types.

1. Compositions which grow out of, and display, impro- visatory style:

   a. Toccata. The toccata, frequently called prelude, was a continuation for keyboard of the Renaissance toccata (see Renaissance instrumental forms). In the mature Baroque style the improvisatory toccata was coupled with sections in imitative contrapuntal style. A final crystallization of form was revealed in the toccata which framed a fugal middle section between two rhapsodic improvisatory parts. The toccata frequently was treated as a single movement independent of the fugue with which it was paired. In this case it was likely to be of purely improvisatory nature.

      Ex: *Toccata in E Minor for Organ,* Pachelbel
            MM   p. 156
            Rec.   HS-9039   MM   Rec. 3

   b. Prelude. The name is freely used to describe an introductory movement, usually one of improvisatory character. It is often applied to the toccata form itself.

In the late Baroque, preludes coupled with fugues were usually rhapsodic in character.

Ex: *Prelude and Fugue in E flat for Organ,* J. S. Bach
Eulenburg, Ed.
Rec. Col. KL-5262

2. The single movement imitative contrapuntal forms:

a. Ricercar. A composition written for harpsichord or organ, the Baroque ricercar, in contrast to that of the Renaissance, is a work without contrasting sections in which one theme is developed imitatively. The distinction between ricercar and fugue is more one of rhythmic drive than formal organization. The ricercar is inclined to be more modal in harmonic structure, exploits its thematic material with less climactic contrast, makes less use of sequential treatment, and uses thematic material that is more slow moving and potentially less rhythmically significant.

Ex: *Ricercar dopo il Credo,* Frescobaldi
MM p. 144
Rec. HS-9039 MM Rec. 2

b. Fantasia. A keyboard composition usually for organ, the fantasia was a larger and more complex kind of ricercar. It employs a single theme which is often presented in a series of sections so that the entire work takes on the form of contrapuntal variations on a theme.

The term fancy was used in England to designate works of this general nature written for an ensemble or consort of viols or wind instruments. It should be noted that the name fantasia was also given to improvisatory single movement works which were paired with the later fugues like the prelude and toccata.

Ex: *Fantasies for 3, 4, 5, 6, 7, Viole da Gamba,* Purcell
Nagels Musik-Archiv
Rec. DGG ARC-3007

Ex: *Fantasie,* Telemann
TEM p. 297
Rec. HSE-9103 Side 2

c. Fugue. The fugue is an imitative contrapuntal form
built on a single theme known as the subject imitated
in two or more individual voices. The exposition of
the subject alternately in the tonic and in the dominant
keys (the latter form of the subject is known as the
answer) emphasizes the tonic-dominant harmonic
relationship as a means of achieving formal development. Fugues, in contrast to the ricercars from which
they were developed, used subjects of more melodic
and rhythmic character. They often employ a persis-
tent counter-subject along with the principal subject
and develop the subject through various key changes,
rhythmic treatment, sequential appearances, etc. Episodes, or sections in which the subject does not appear
in its entirety, alternate with repeated appearances
of the subject in some or all of the voices. While the
fugue is generally a single movement of comparatively
brief duration, it is possible through the general acceptance of the system of equal temperament tuning
to present the fugal material in a great variety of key
relationships so that the single movement could be
drawn out to considerable length. A fugue with two
subjects is called a double fugue.

While the fugue is essentially an instrumental form,
especially well adapted to organ and other keyboard
performance, the principle of fugal development is
found in many of the other instrumental forms and
also in the large choral works of the Baroque period.
It represents the highest development of the harmonic
contrapuntal technique of the period.

Ex: *Prelude and Fugue in E flat for Organ*, J. S. Bach
Peters, Ed.
Rec. Col. KL-5262

Ex: *Contrapunctus III*, from *The Art of Fugue*, J. S. Bach
MM p. 230
Rec. HS-9040 MM r. 3

Ex: *Capriccio über dass Hennengeschrey*, Poglietti
TEM p. 232
Rec. HSE-9102 Side 2

3. Compositions with several independent sections or movements with contrapuntal texture:

a. Church Sonata (Sonata da chiesa). This composition evolved from the sectional canzona of the Renaissance (see instrumental forms-Renaissance) into a rather freely designed composite form which became one of the most important in the chamber music of the Baroque period. While there are no definite forms for each of the movements, this type of composition generally uses alternating fast and slow tempos with contrapuntal or fugal style in one or more movements. The church sonata was written for various instrumental combinations; (1) any solo melodic instrument with continuo (see solo sonata); (2) it was most frequently written for two violins or other melodic instruments and continuo (trio sonata). While dance forms were regularly found in the chamber sonata, movements of the church sonata were sometimes in dance forms though not necessarily so named. The church sonata often went by the simple name "sonata," especially in the late Baroque.

Ex: *Sonata da chiesa in E minor*, Corelli
MM p. 162
Rec. HS-9040 MM Rec. 3

b. Concerto. Two forms of the concerto, the solo concerto and the concerto grosso, were the final instrumental contributions of the Baroque period. These two forms differed only in that the solo concerto used a

single instrument as soloist, while the concerto grosso
used a group of soloists, generally three, in contrast
to the larger mass of orchestral sound.

Three movements are most frequently employed:
an allegro, a slow movement in a closely related key,
and a shorter fast movement in the original key. Each
of the movements is constructed on the plan of alternating soloist (or soloists-concertino) and full orchestra (tutti or ripieno). While soloists and orchestra may
be given different themes, usually the entire thematic
material is presented by the full group and then developed by the soloist or soloists in turn. The solo
concerto and the concerto grosso were never designed
to display the technical virtuosity of the soloists. However, they offered the Baroque composer the possibility of combining the concertato idea, the polarity
of bass and treble melody, the concept of clear major-
minor tonality and the use of a number of separate
movements, into a single idealized instrumental form.

Ex: *Solo Concerto for Flute and Orchestra,* op. No. 3
        Vivaldi
        Eulenburg Ed.
        Rec. DGG ARC-3116

Ex: *Concerto Grosso in C Major,* Handel
        MM   p. 182
        Rec. HS-9040 MM Rec. 3

Ex: *Brandenburg Concertos,* J. S. Bach
        Eulenburg Ed.
        DGG ARC-3156/7

Ex: *Concerto: La primavera,* Vivaldi
        TEM p. 286
        Rec. HSE-9103 Side 2

c. Orchestral Overture. While this term was used in
    various connotations, two forms growing out of the
    Italian and French opera are typical of the multiple
    movement work under this heading, the French Over-
    tures and the Italian Overtures. They differ mainly
    in the order of the three sections that make up the

complete work. The French Overture consists of a slow, pompous, richly harmonic section that is followed by a lively, driving fugal section, and concludes with a return to the opening slow section or at least a part of it. The Italian Overture reverses the order of movements to fast, slow, fast. Both types were used as pure orchestral forms as well as orchestral openings to operas.

Ex: *Overture to Armide,* Lully
    MM   p. 152
    Rec.   HS-9039   MM   Rec. 2

Ex: *Overture to Il trionfo dell' onore,* A Scarlatti
    Carisch Ed.
    Rec.   Cetra-1223

Ex: *Sinfonia* to the opera, *La Caduta de Decem Viri,*
      A. Scarlatti
    TEM: p. 261
    Rec.   HSE-9103   Side 1

4. Compositions based on a pre-existing or original melody or bass:

   a. Theme and Variation. An extension of the same form used in the Renaissance in which a melody either original, or pre-existing, (more often the latter) is presented in a number of variations. In the Baroque such compositions became more idiomatic for the particular instrument for which they were written, often exploiting the technical aspects of instrumental performance. Two kinds of variation were employed. One type is of a contrapuntal character in which the melody remains intact as it wanders from voice to voice while the counterpoint changes in each variation. The other type is essentially homophonic; the harmony remains the same throughout while the melody above the harmony is ornamented or changed in the subsequent variations.

Ex: *La Follia,* Corelli
Schott Ed.
Rec. DGG ARC-3008

Ex: *Goldberg Variations,* J. S. Bach
Eulenburg Ed.
Rec. DGG ARC-3138

b. Passacaglia and Chaconne. While there are those who contend these two names designate different forms, both are basically variations on a repeated bass line (ostinato bass) of four to eight measures. Sometimes this ostinato melody can be found in voices other than the bass so that the basic theme assumes the character of a harmonic pattern. Passacaglias and chaconnes were written for all types of instruments and combinations although those for keyboard are the more frequent.

Ex: *Passacaglia and Fugue in C minor,* J. S. Bach
Peters Ed.
Rec. Col. ML-4500

Ex: *Chaconne for Violin,* Vitali
Schirmer Ed.
Rec. Epic LC-3414

c. Chorale Prelude. A generic type of organ music in which a chorale tune is the basis of the composition. In some instances the chorale tune acts as a theme for a set of variations. Such works are known as chorale partitas or chorale variations. In other instances the chorale tune is used as the basis for a fantasia, and the work is then known as a chorale fantasia. By far the most popular, however, is a single setting of the chorale tune which might vary from a highly developed fugal treatment to a rather simple homophonic presentation. This form probably originated as a prelude to the actual singing of the chorale by the congregation in the Lutheran Church.

Ex: *Chorale Prelude, In dulci jubilo,* Buxtehude and
J. S. Bach
HMS Vol. VI p. 26
Rec. RCA LM-6031-2 HMS Vol. VI

Ex: *Chorale Prelude, Christ lag in Todesbanden,* J. S.
Bach
MM p. 212
Rec. HS-9040 MM r. 3

Ex: *Chorale Prelude, Nun komm, der Heiden Heiland,*
Buxtehude
TEM p. 237
Rec. HSE-9102 Side 2

5. Compositions with dance-type sections:

a. Suite. The idea of extending an instrumental piece by
joining a number of dance movements of different
rhythms and tempos was an extension of the Renaissance device of pairing dances (see dance forms in
Renaissance). The most conventionalized suite was
written for the harpsichord, (keyboard suite), in
which four dances were combined to form a complete
work. These dances are the Allemande, Courante,
Sarabande, and Gigue. Each dance is generally in a
binary form with the first part ending in the dominant
key and the second half returning to the tonic.
The dances have no thematic relationship to one
another and the only unifying factor is the constancy
of key between all the dances. While the four dances
named were considered the basic dances of the suite
(partita in German, also Ordre in French), other
dances, even those in current ballroom use, were often
added to, or substituted for, the original ones. Each
dance retains its original rhythmic character but is
cast in an idealized form with no practical use in mind.

Ex: *Suite in E minor,* Froberger
MM p. 147
Rec. HS-9039 MM Rec. 2

Ex: Lute piece: *Tombeau de Mademoiselle Gaultier,*
D. Gaultier
TEM p. 227
Rec. HSE-9102 Side 2

b. Chamber Sonata (Sonata da Camera). This is the ensemble form of the suite written as a solo sonata or trio sonata, but often using larger groups. Adherence to the basic four dances was less likely to be found in the chamber sonata. Additional and substitute dances were often used. A prelude frequently prefaced the chamber sonata, and movements other than dances, such as the aria, are often found.

Ex: Trio Sonata: *Troisieme Concert Royal,* Couperin Editions de l' Oiseau Lyre, Complete Works of Couperin, Vol. VII
Rec. DGG ARC-3148

Ex: *Violin Sonata in E Minor,* Op. 2, No. 9, Vivaldi Schirmer Ed.
Rec. BG-566A

c. Orchestral Suite. As in the chamber sonata, there was no definite adherence in the orchestral suite to the basic four dances, and additional movements both dance and otherwise were freely used. The orchestral suite was often called an overture since the first movement is frequently in the form of the French Overture.

Ex: *Suite No. 1 in C major for Orchestra,* J. S. Bach Eulenburg Ed.
Rec. Epic LC-3194

6. Keyboard Sonata. The original use of the term sonata to differentiate instrumental from vocal works was often retained in the Baroque period. A number of keyboard compositions therefore bear the names sonata, though they do not resemble either of the two typical sonata types of the Baroque, the chamber or church sonatas. Some of these sonatas were in a number of movements and some were single movement works. Generally simple binary or ternary forms were used for the individual movements which varied from dance-like character to song types, usually homophonic in texture.

Ex: *Sonata in C minor,* D. Scarlatti
MM p. 179
Rec. HS-9040 MM Rec. 2

Ex: *Biblical Sonatas,* Kuhnau
Broude Ed.
Rec. DGG ARC-3095

VII. Important Composers

1. Caccini, Giulio (c. 1546-1618) was an Italian singer and composer associated with the Florentine Camerata. His performance of the new type of monodic composition, "musica in stile rappresentativo," was looked upon as the ideal of this style. His most important work was the collection of madrigals and arias published under the title *Nuove Musiche,* the preface to which gives one of the clearest and most detailed descriptions of the manner of performance of the new monodic style.

Ex: Madrigal: *Dovró dunque morire*
MM p. 120
Rec. HS-9039 MM Rec. 2

2. Peri, Jacopo (1561-1633) was a member of the Florentine Camerata. His *Dafne* may be considered the first opera in the new monodic style. He was noted for his masterly handling of pedal-point basses, a device which suited his delight in somber subject matter.

Ex: Three pieces from the opera *"Euridice"*
GMB p. 186
Rec. (No recording available)

3. Sweelinck, Jan Pieterzoon (1562-1621) was a celebrated Dutch organist and composer. Two contributions to organ literature are outstanding; his development of the organ chorale variation which led to the organ prelude, and his use of monothematic treatment in the ricercar which resulted in the form known as the fugue. While he also wrote a great number of vocal works in the Renaissance style, his organ compositions are early

Baroque. His numerous pupils, mostly Germans, made him the founder of the famous north German organ school.

> Ex: *Chorale Variation: Ach Gott, von Himmel sieh' darein*
> HMS   Vol. IV   p. 62
> Rec.   RCA-6029-1   HMS   Vol. IV

4. Monteverdi, Claudio (1567-1643) was the greatest of the early Italian Baroque composers and the creator of the first great operatic masterpiece in modern style. In his *Orfeo* he adapts the Florentine recitative style to the use of closed forms such as the aria and dance song. He was equally at home in the Renaissance polyphonic and the Baroque monodic idioms. His madrigals are among the finest of the Italian school, but even here he shows his association with the modern school of the Baroque through his close attention to word and mood expression. Monteverdi also used an enlarged orchestra and made some specific selection of instruments in his dramatic works. His harmonic usages for expressive purposes caused much adverse criticism, particularly by one Giovanni Artusi. Among his works are eight books of madrigals, a number of operas the most important of which are *Orfeo, El Riterno Di Ulisse, L' Incoronazione De Poppea,* as well as dramatic scenes and religious music.

> Ex: *Orfeo*
> Chester Ed.
> Rec. DGG   ARC-3035-6

5. Praetorius, Michael (1571-1621), a German composer and theorist who devoted himself entirely to the writing of Lutheran choral works. His most important contribution to music history was made in his treatise, *Syntagma Musicum.*

> Ex: *Wie Schoen leuchtet der Morgenstern*
> HMS   Vol. IV   p. 39
> Rec. RCA LM-6029-2   HMS   Vol. IV

6. Frescobaldi, Girolamo (1583-1643), an Italian organist and composer was an important link in the history of fugal form.

While he wrote no works actually called fugues, his monothematic ricercars were among the most important forerunners of
this form. As a teacher of Froberger his influence in the development of composition and performance of the south German organ
schools was paralleled only by Sweelinck's influence in the north.
He was recognized as one of the greatest organists of his day,
having been appointed organist at St. Peter's in Rome. His compositions include the typical organ forms of the early Baroque
such as toccatas, capriccios, ricercars, and canzonas. A collection of such works composed for church use is his *Fiori Musicali*
(Musical Flowers).

> Ex: *Fiori Musicali*
> Bärenreiter Ed.
> Rec. DGG ARC-3054

7. Schütz, Heinrich (1585-1672) was the greatest German
composer before Bach. Evidence of his importance is the oft
repeated designation of Schütz as the father of German music.
His contacts with Italian music of the late sixteenth and early
seventeenth centuries led him to write a great number of vocal
works to German texts of a dramatic religious nature that introduced the new Baroque style into Germany. He adapted recitative, thorough-bass, concertato idiom to works for the Lutheran
service, and laid the foundation for the great art of dramatic
church music in his *Sacred Symphonies, Sacred Songs,* and *Little
Sacred Concerti* which finally blossomed into the cantatas and
passion musics of Bach and his contemporaries. A recent revival
of Schütz's work has revealed a starkness and simplicity of dramatic presentation that make such works as *The Seven Last
Words, The Christmas Story, The Resurrection of Our Lord,* and
his *Passion Music* extremely popular after three hundred years.

> Ex: *Seven Last Words*
> Eulenburg Ed.
> Rec. RCA LM-6030-1 HMS Vol. V

8. Schein, Johann Hermann (1586-1630) was another German who helped introduce Italian monody and instrumental

music into Germany. His choral adaptations for the organ were representative of the great interest in this form. A collection of twenty suites for strings called the *Banchetto Musicale* represented some of the earliest instrumental works written in Germany. He also wrote a great number of sacred and secular vocal compositions.

Ex: *Banchetto musicale, Suite No. 5*
Moeck Ed.
Rec. DGG ARC-3153

9. Scheidt, Samuel (1587-1654) is often considered the most important German organ composer of the first half of the seventeenth century, particularly in his treatment of the chorale in true organ style. His greatest published work, *Tabulatura Nova,* was a collection of figured chorales, toccatas, fantasias, hymns, and other works for the organ. Though his main contribution was in organ compositions, he wrote many choral works as well.

Ex: *Tabulatura Nova*
Ugrino Ed.
Rec. DGG ARC-3107

10. Cavalli, Pier Francesco (1602-1676) was celebrated as an opera composer in his native Italy, where he held the position as maestro di Cappella at St. Mark's in Venice. He was also well known in France and Austria. While he wrote church works his forty-one operas gained him wide recognition. His greatest operatic successes were *Jason, Cerce,* and *Hercules The Lover.* Cavalli's wide recognition attests to the rapid rise and acceptance of Italian opera in countries other than Italy.

Ex: Duet: *Musici della selva* from *Egisto*
HMS Vol. V p. 11
Rec. RCA LM-6060-1 HMS Vol. V

11. Chambonnieres, Jacques Champion (c. 1602-1672) is regarded as the founder of the French clavecin school. As the teacher of Couperin the Elder, d'Angelbert, and others, his

influence was felt not only in France but throughout Europe. He was first chamber musician to Louis XIV. His wide recognition influenced the German harpsichord composers from Froberger to J. S. Bach. His compositions were exclusively for the harpsichord.

> Ex: Keyboard Music
> HMS Vol. VI p. 20
> Rec. RCA LM-6031-2 HMS Vol. VI

12. Carissimi, Giacomo (1605-1674) was an Italian composer who applied the new devices of the monodic style to religious music, particularly the oratorio. His masterpiece, *Jeptha,* is an example of his position as the founder of the oratorio.

> Ex: *Afferte gladium,* from *Judicium Salomonis*
> MM p. 129
> Rec. HS-9039 MM Rec. 2

13. Froberger, Johann Jakob (1616-1667) was a German organist and pupil of Frescobaldi whose techniques he introduced into Vienna. He wrote many works for the organ, and is credited with having created the keyboard suite and established the order of dances within it: Allemande, Courante, Sarabande and Gigue.

> Ex: *Suite in E minor*
> MM p. 147
> Rec. HS-9039 MM Rec. 2

14. Cesti, Marc' Antonio (1623-1669) was a well-known Italian opera composer whose works gained him wide recognition. *Il Pomo D' Oro* (The Golden Apple) produced in Vienna in 1667 is regarded as his masterpiece.

> Ex: *E dove t' aggiri* from *Il Pomo d' oro*
> HMS Vol. V p. 12
> Rec. RCA LM-5030-1 HMS Vol. V

15. d'Angelbert, Jean-Henri (c. 1628-1691) was a French composer, pupil of Chambonnières. His collection, *Pièces de*

clavecin avec la maniere de les jouer — Pieces for the Harp-sichord with Instructions for their Performance, contains suites, arrangements of airs from Lully's operas and variations as well as instructions on how to play figured bass.

Ex: *Prelude, Allemande, Sarabande* from a suite for harpsichord
  HAM   Vol. II   p. 96
  Rec. (No recording available)

16. Lully, Jean-Baptiste (1632-1687) was the most dis-tinguished opera composer of the seventeenth century in France though he was actually an Italian by birth. He succeeded in establishing a true French opera which was in effect a reform of the traditional Italian opera of his time with its many musical excesses. He was able to give the French opera a greater measure of dramatic sincerity through his handling of dramatic recitative, arias and instrumental accompaniment. He established the ballet as a part of the French opera as well as the French overture. His musical production was not exclusively operatic, however, since he composed a great number of ballets for Molière's plays, and even some independent instrumental music and religious choral works. Among his operatic masterpieces are *Cadmus and Hermione, Alceste, Armide Et Renaud, Thésée,* and *Persée.*

Ex: *Scene infernale* from *Alceste*
  HMS   Vol. V   p. 20
  Rec.   RCA   LM-6030-2   HMS   Vol. V

17. Charpentier, Marc' Antoine (1634-1704) was a French composer, pupil of Carissimi, and mostly concerned with writing of religious works; masses, motet, and oratorios. He also wrote operas and smaller dramatic works for the stage, but suffered disfavor at the hands of Lully.

Ex: Oratorio scene: *Le Reneiment de St-Pierre*
  TEM   p. 242
  Rec.   HSE-9103   Side 1

Ex: Mass and Symphony: *Assumpta est Maria*
  No score available
  Rec.   Vox-8440

18. Buxtehude, Dietrich (c. 1637-1707) was a famous German organist and composer. Buxtehude influenced J. S. Bach who made a two-hundred mile journey on foot from Arnstadt to Lübeck to hear Buxtehude play in 1705. Buxtehude's works include all the current forms of organ music, much choral music and a variety of chamber and harpsichord compositions.

> Ex: Chorale Prelude: *In Dulci jubilo*
>   HMS   Vol. VI   p. 26
>   Rec. RCA LM-6031-2 HMS Vol. VI

19. Pachelbel, Johann (1653-1706) was a middle German organist and composer mainly of organ works though he also wrote for the other keyboard instruments. His fugues are of utmost importance not only because of their influence on Bach's writing in this form, but for their intrinsic artistic value.

> Ex: *Toccata in E Minor*
>   MM   p. 156
>   Rec. HS-9040 MM Rec. 3

20. Corelli, Arcangelo (1653-1713) was an Italian, one of the first great violin virtuosos, and a composer of great importance. He is looked upon as the founder of modern violin technique with its intricacies of bowing, performance of double stops and chord effects. He was not a prolific composer, his entire output consisting of six opus numbers or collections of which four are devoted to trio sonatas, one to violin and keyboard, and one to the concerto grosso. The latter represents a new form of composition of which Corelli is recognized as the creator. Handel was acquainted with Corelli and was undoubtedly influenced by his instrumental writing.

> Ex: *Concerti grossi Op. 6 No. 8 "Christmas Concerto"*
>   Eulenburg Ed.
>   Rec. Epic LC-3264
> Ex: *Sonata Op. 5 No. 12 in D. Minor "La Follia"*
>   Schott Ed.
>   Rec. DGG ARC-3008

21. Purcell, Henry (c. 1659-1695) was England's most famous Baroque composer, and his death in 1695 brought to an end any important musical contribution from a native English composer for the next two hundred years. Despite a very short life his works are numerous and representative of all areas of composition, church, dramatic, and instrumental. He was equally gifted as an instrumental and vocal composer. Among his most important works are the numerous anthems and religious choral compositions; the collection of twelve trio sonatas published during his lifetime, and his one opera, *Dido and Aeneas,* a work still frequently performed. Purcell was singularly gifted in his ability to compose on a ground bass and a number of the famous arias from his opera, notably Dido's aria, *When I am Laid in Rest,* are constructed in this form.

Ex: Opera *Dido and Aeneas*
      Oxford University Press, Ed.
      Rec.   Elect-90031

Ex.   *A New Ground*
      MM   p. 159
      Rec.   HS-9040   MM   Rec. 3

22. Scarlatti, Alessandro (1660-1725) was known mainly for his contributions to the style of the Neapolitan opera of which he wrote over one hundred. He also added a rich literature of chamber and orchestral music as well as religious cantatas and masses to Italian music of the Baroque. Scarlatti established the da capo aria in the Neapolitan opera, a form which was generally adopted for all dramatic arias.

Ex: Quartet: *Idolo mio ti chiamo Tito* from *Tito Sempronio Gracco*
      HMS   Vol. V   p. 16
      Rec.   RCA   LM-6030-1   HMS   Vol. V

23. Kuhnau, Johann (1660-1722) was a German composer whose works for the harpsichord are the most important among his other instrumental and vocal compositions. He was J. S. Bach's immediate predecessor as cantor at St. Thomas Church

in Leipzig. His most important works are his sonatas for harpsichord, especially the group of six entitled *Biblical Sonatas* which are early examples of program music in which Biblical stories are illustrated by means of musical allusion.

Ex: *Biblical Sonatas*
Broude Ed.
Rec. DGG   ARC-3095

24. Couperin, François (1668-1733) was a member of a famous French family of musicians. He was known as Couperin, le Grand, because of his enormous skill as an organist. His religious compositions, mainly for the organ, constitute a large part of his works. His most numerous and renowned compositions, however, are those instrumental works which he wrote for the harpsichord during the last part of his life. The many "Ordres" or suites for clavecin consist of dances which are often programmatic in nature. He also wrote *The Art of Playing the Clavecin* which was of wide influence. Among his best known works are the *Concerts Royaux*, the four volumes of *Pièces De Clavecin*, and *Les Gouts Réunis*, the latter consisting of a number of concerted pieces written for strings and clavecin. Couperin's works are characterized by the polarity of bass and melodic line and use of ornamentation typical of the "gallant" style of his time.

Ex: *Troisième Concert Royal in A Major*
Editions de l' Oiseau Lyre. Complete Ed. Vol. 7
Rec. DGG   ARC-3148
Ex: *La Galante*
MM   p. 169
Rec. HS-9040   MM   Rec. 3

25. Vivaldi, Antonio (c. 1669-1741) was the most celebrated of all the Baroque Italian masters and probably the most musically prolific. While he wrote a large number of operas, oratorios, secular cantatas and church music, his present fame rests in his concerti grossi and solo concertos. These number over

four hundred. Vivaldi was a priest in the Roman Catholic Church and for many years was in charge of the musical program of the Ospitale della Pieta in Venice, a home for orphaned and foundling girls. It was in discharge of this duty that he wrote most of his instrumental and smaller choral works which were performed by the girls in the institution. Among the most famous of the concerti grossi are the works known as *L'Estro Harmonico* (Harmonical Whim), *Gimento dell' armonia e dell' invenzione* (The Struggle between Harmony and Invention) and *Le Stagioni* (The Four Seasons). J. S. Bach was especially influenced by Vivaldi's concertos and transcribed several for clavier.

Ex: *Concerto for Flute and String Orchestra, Op. 10 No. 3 "Il Gardellino"*
 Schott Ed.
 Rec. DGG ARC-3116
Ex: *Concerto Grosso Op. 3 No. 11 in D minor*
 Eulenburg Ed.
 Rec. DGG ARC-3116

26. Telemann, Georg Philipp (1681-1767) was perhaps the most prolific of German composers of the late Baroque. His compositions covered every conceivable field of musical performance. Some concept of his enormous output can be gained from the fact that he wrote some forty operas, about three thousand cantatas and motets with orchestra or organ, six hundred overtures, forty-four passion settings, and equally numerous works for special occasions such as funerals, weddings, coronations, consecrations, etc. His fame was considerably greater during his lifetime than that of J. S. Bach whose life-span was contained within that of Telemann. The last forty-six years of his life were spent in Hamburg where he was city director of music. He took this position in preference to that of cantor of St. Thomas Church in Leipzig. The latter position was then assumed by Bach who was second choice to Telemann in the eyes of the church council. Telemann remained relatively unknown during the nineteenth and early part of the twentieth centuries. However, the revival of interest in Baroque music during the past

twenty years has brought his music to the fore again, particularly the orchestral and chamber music.

Ex: *Concerto in D major for Trumpet, 2 Oboes and Continuo*
Sikorski Ed.
Rec. DGG ARC-3119

Ex: *Partita in G major for Recorder and Continuo*
Bärenreiter Ed.
Rec. DGG ARC-3043

27. Rameau, Jean Philippe (1683-1764) was well known in his day as a musical theorist, organist and composer. His early career was that of organist in several of the great cathedrals of France. While serving in this capacity at Clermont-Ferand he wrote his famous *Treatise of Harmony* in 1722. In this work he stated his system of chord building on super-imposed thirds; the conception of a chord in all its inversions as one and the same entity; and the idea of a fundamental bass by which chord progressions are determined. His lasting fame, however, is based mainly on his dramatic compositions, of which the works *Les Indes Galantes* (The Gallant Indians) and *Castor and Pollux* are his masterpieces. Besides a long list of dramatic works — ballets, operas, and incidental music for drama — Rameau wrote a considerable amount of works for clavecin and chamber groups typical of the Baroque period. Rameau's dramatic works were exceptional for their expressive melodic line, originality of instrumentation, and richness of harmonic idiom. Rameau's ideas aroused violent interest both antagonistic and favorable, first between those who favored him and those who favored Lully, and later between his adherents and the "Encyclopedists." The latter exchange was known as the "War of the Buffoons." The perennial charges against the operatic innovator that were leveled against Monteverdi before him and Gluck and Wagner after him were leveled at Rameau. His critics found his works lacked melody, were filled with illogical harmony, and used orchestral instruments in a noisy fashion.

Ex: Opera: *Castor et Pollux*
      Durand et Fils Ed.
      Rec. Decca, D-9683

28. Bach, Johann Sebastian (1685-1750) is recognized as one of the greatest composers of all times. He was a member of what is, perhaps, the most interesting musical family in history. Well over one hundred members of the Bach family in Thuringia were occupied in whole or in part in musical activities. Of this number some twenty were performers and composers of special significance, including both ancestors and offspring of Johann Sebastian.

At fifteen years of age Bach spent a short time of study with his brother Johann Christoph in Lüneburg. A year as violinist in the orchestra of the Duke of Saxe-Weimar was followed by his first real post as organist in Arnstadt in 1704. He left Arnstadt in 1707 to take the post of organist in Mülhausen. In 1708 he moved again, this time to Weimar where he was made court organist and chamber musician to the Duke of Weimar. In 1714 he was raised to the rank of chamber musician and remained in this post until 1717. During this time he made a reputation for himself as one of the great organists of his day as well as a composer of a wide variety of works in both secular and religious fields. In 1717 he accepted the post of chapelmaster and director of chamber music to the Prince of Anhalt at Cöthen. Here Bach composed most of his orchestral and chamber music. His wife Barbara died in 1720 and in 1721 Bach married Anna Magdalena Wülken a gifted musician whose handwriting is often found in early manuscripts of Bach's works.

In 1723 Bach succeeded Kuhnau as cantor of the Thomas School in Leipzig, a post he held until his death in 1750. As organist and director of music at the two principal churches in Leipzig, Bach composed most of his great church music during the next twenty-seven years.

Among the many visits he paid to other cities in the capacity of organist, organ installer, and composer, none was more famous than the one to the court of Frederick the Great in Potsdam where his second son, Karl Philipp Emanuel, was chamber musician. It was during this visit that Bach improvised upon a theme given him by Frederick, a theme which he later used as the basis for his work known as *The Musical Offering*. An unsuccessful eye operation in 1749 caused Bach to become totally blind, and in 1750 he died from a stroke of apoplexy.

Bach represents the culmination of an era, particularly through his great emphasis on the vocal contrapuntal style. He was a master of the art of tonal counterpoint and his *Art of the Fugue* is a veritable exhaustive treatise dealing with all manners of contrapuntal devices illustrated in the canons and fugues which comprise the work. His skill in handling fugal treatment is evident in all types of compositions, instrumental, vocal, secular and religious. In his use of instruments he foreshadowed the future in music. He composed in every conceivable form except that of the opera. While the great preponderance of his works were written for the church, there is much of his instrumental output that is strictly secular in nature. Even the smallest works, however, demonstrate his care and attention to compositional excellence. His mastery of counterpoint within the tonal system is comparable to that of Palestrina within the modal idea.

It was more than half a century after his death before any measurable appreciation of his great contribution to the history of music was realized. Mendelssohn brought Bach to the attention of the musical world of the nineteenth century with a performance of the *Saint Matthew Passion* in Leipzig in 1829.

A great number of Bach's works were lost in manuscript. A comparatively small amount was published during his lifetime. Despite the great loss the complete edition begun in 1850 by the Bach Gesellschaft contained forty seven volumes. A second complete edition is now in process of publication.

Among the great masterpieces remaining today are the following works listed under vocal and instrumental headings:

Vocal works: *Mass in b minor, The Saint Matthew Passion, The Saint John Passion, The Christmas Oratorio,* two *Magnificats,* approximately one hundred and ninety church cantatas, over twenty-five secular cantatas, and many other short works.

Instrumental Works: *The Art of the Fugue, The Musical Offering, The Italian Concerto for Harpsichord, The Goldberg Variations for Harpsichord, The Well Tempered Clavier,* suites, partitas, and inventions for harpsichord, *Four Overtures (Suites) for Orchestra, The Brandenburg Concertos, Six Solo Suites for Violoncello, Three Sonatas and Three Partitas for Solo Violin,* numerous works for organ, including chorale preludes, toccatas, preludes, fantasias and fugues, and concertos for harpsichord and violin as well as numerous sonatas for instrumental combinations.

> Ex: *Goldberg Variations for Harpsichord*
> G. Schirmer Ed.
> Rec. DGG ARC-3138

> Ex: *The Art of the Fugue*
> Peters Ed.
> Rec. DGG ARC-3082/83

> Ex: *The Brandenburg Concertos*
> Eulenburg Ed.
> Rec. DGG ARC-3105/6

> Ex: Cantata: *Ich hatte viel Bekümmernis*
> Eulenburg Ed.
> Rec. DGG ARC-3064

> Ex: *Saint Matthew Passion*
> Eulenburg Ed.
> Rec. DGG ARC-3125/8

29. Scarlatti, Domenico (1685-1757), the greatest of the Italian composers for the keyboard, was one of the most original composers in the history of music. While he wrote works for the church and for the operatic stage, his greatest contribution was his more than five hundred compositions for the harpsichord. He was the son and pupil of Alessandro Scarlatti. After a very productive youth in Italy he took a post with the Portuguese court in Lisbon where he became music master to the Princess

Maria Barbara. It was for her that he composed the works that were to make him famous, the *Esercizi per gravicembalo*, (*Exercises for the Harpsichord*), which usually go by the name Sonatas today. When the princess married the heir to the Spanish throne, Scarlatti moved to Madrid where he spent the remainder of his life from 1729 to 1757 as master of the salon. His sonatas are the finest example of late Baroque writing for the harpsichord. Scarlatti manages to exploit the instrument to the utmost in these works and in so doing lays the foundation for future keyboard technique. Many of the works call for such innovations in performance as the crossing of the hands, etc. The sonatas of Scarlatti reflect the whole gamut of moods from the gay and dance-like, which often include Spanish rhythms, to the song-like and romantic.

> Ex: *Sonatas*
> G. Schirmer Ed.
> Rec. Col. SL-221

30. Handel, Georg Friedrich (1685-1759) was a compatriot of Johann Sebastian Bach, and one who shares with him the distinction of bringing an era to a close. In contrast to Bach, Handel was a cosmopolitan composer who added to his German heritage a wide study and firsthand knowledge of the Italian musical style, and practiced these accomplishments during most of the last fifty years of his life in England. Handel was something of a musical prodigy, for after instruction on organ, oboe, and harpsichord as well as in counterpoint and fugue he assumed the position as assistant organist in Halle, his native city, at the age of twelve. During this year he also composed a number of choral and instrumental works. In 1702 Handel went to Hamburg where he was associated with the opera until 1706. In the same year he went to Italy where he became successful as a composer of Italian opera and dramatic oratorios. In 1710 he returned to Germany as chapel master to the Elector of Hanover, a relationship that resulted in his going to England when this prince took over the throne of England.

From this time on Handel was occupied with a variety of activities: teacher, director of the Royal Academy of Music (an institution whose prime purpose was the production of Italian opera in London) composer, opera impressario, and traveler. His main compositional area was that of opera until 1741, when he turned to the composition and production of oratorios. It is in the latter field that he achieved a lasting fame.

In general it might be said that Handel reflects the past in his emphasis on the vocal media, but foreshadows the future in his predominantly homophonic style. His compositions, both secular and religious drama, reveal a spirit of grandeur, for there is always something of the pomp of the court about all his works. He wrote twenty-seven oratorios and over forty operas as well as a great quantity of other vocal forms such as anthems, masques, cantatas, and vocal solos and ensembles. Handel was also a prolific composer of instrumental compositions which include all the Baroque forms: concerti grossi, harpsichord suites, organ concerti, chamber music for strings, winds, and keyboard, and large orchestral works. Among his vast number of works a few stand out as masterpieces: the oratorios, *The Messiah, Samson, Judas Maccabaeus, Solomon, Israel in Egypt, Saul;* the operas, *Alcina, Julius Caesar, Rinaldo, Xerxes;* for orchestra, *The Water Music, The Fire-works Music* and *Twelve Concerti Grossi for Strings.*

Several incomplete and often inaccurate editions of the works of Handel have been issued from time to time. In 1955 work was begun on a new complete edition issued by the Georg Friedrich Handel Gesellschaft of Halle.

> Ex: *Concerti Grossi,* op. 3
>   Bärenreiter Ed.
>   Rec. DGG ZRC-3139/40
>
> Ex: *The Messiah*
>   G. Schirmer Ed.
>   Rec. West-3306
>
> Ex: *Acis and Galatea*
>   Chrysander Ed.
>   Rec. Osieau 50179/80

31. Pergolesi, Giovanni Battista (1710-1736) whose short life fell entirely within the eighteenth century was, however, still representative of the Baroque style of composition. He wrote both instrumental and vocal music, but it was his opera buffa compositions which were to bring him fame. Pergolesi wrote three of these works which were performed between the acts of his serious operas. The most famous of these is *La Serva Padrona* which still is found in the opera repertoire. While a large number of trio sonatas, solo sonatas and concertos in the Baroque style are ascribed to Pergolesi, it is doubtful that many of them are his work. A number of religious works were published, the best known today being the *Stabat Mater*.

Ex: Opera Buffa: *La Serva Padrona*
      Ricordi Ed.
      Rec.   DGG   ARC-3035/6
Ex: *Recitative and Aria* from the opera Buffa; *Liviettae Tracollo*
      TEM   p. 314
      Rec.   HSE-9103   Side 2

VIII.   Other Composers

Italy

    Cavalieri, Emilio del (c. 1550-1602)
    Banchieri, Adriano (1568-1634)
    Rossi, Salomone (1587-1630)
    Landi, Stefano (1590-1655)
    Mazzochi, Domenica (1592-1665)
    Marini, Biago (1595-1665)
    Legrenzi, Giovanni (1626-1690)
    Stradella, Alessandro (1642-1682)
    Vitali, Giovanni Battista (1644-1692)
    Steffani, Agostino (1654-1728)
    Torelli, Giuseppe (1658-1709)
    Lotti, Antonio (1667-1740)
    Bononcini, Giovanni (1670-1747)
    Albinoni, Tomaso (1671-1750)
    Abaco, Evaristo Felice dall' (1675-1742)
    Durante, Francisco (1684-1755)

Porpora, Nicola (1686-1768)
Marcello, Benedetto (1686-1739)
Geminiani, Francesco (1687-1762)
Veracini, Francesco Maria (1690-1750)

France
Cambert, Robert (1628-1677)
Lalande, Michel-Richard de (1657-1726)
Leclair, Jean Marie (1697-1764)

England
Lawes, Henry (1596-1662)
Locke, Mathew (c. 1630-1677)
Humfrey, Pelham (1647-1674)
Blow, John (1648-1708)

Germany
Franck, Melchior (c. 1579-1639)
Tunder, Franz (1614-1667)
Kerll, Johann Caspar (1627-1693)
Strungk, Nikolaus Adam (1640-1700)
Bach, Johann Christoph (1642-1703)
Biber, Heinrich Ignaz Franz von (1644-1704)
Krieger, Johann (1651-1735)
Muffat, Georg (1653-1704)
Erlebach, Philipp Heinrich (1657-1714)
Fux, Johann Joseph (1660-1741)
Boehm, Georg (1661-1733)
Keiser, Reinhard (1674-1739)
Graupner, Christof (1683-1760)
Walther, Johann Gottfried (1684-1748)
Fasch, Johann Friedrich (1688-1758)
Hasse, Johann Adolph (1699-1783)

IX. and X.[1] Important Writers on Music

1. Bardi, Giovanni de' (1534-c. 1612) was an Italian aristocrat who through his philosophical and literary interest founded the

[1]From this point on IX and X will be combined because original manuscripts lose their general importance due to the vast amount of music published.

Florentine Camerata, the group whose investigation led to the first operatic composition. His writings, all in Italian, are concerned with speculations concerning the "new music." An English translation of the major portion of a *Discourse on Ancient Music and Good Singing* addressed to Giulio Caccini is published in Strunk's *Source Readings in Music History*.

2. Artusi, Giovanni Maria (c. 1540-1613) was an Italian writer on music. *L'Artusi ovvero dello imperfezioni della moderna musica, Venice 1600* (Artusi, concerning the imperfections of modern music) is a representative critical essay. Artusi was very conservative in his musical philosophy and is remembered mainly for his criticism against the "new style" as represented by Monteverdi at the opening of the seventeenth century. The foregoing essay cited is partially translated in Strunk's *Source Readings in Music History*.

3. Praetorius, Michael (1571-1621) was a German musician composer and theorist. His *Syntagma Musicum,* Wittebergae, (1615-1618) (Musical encyclopedia), appeared in three volumes. The first, written in Latin, deals with ancient church music and secular instruments. The second volume, in German, is an exhaustive treatise on the instruments of the Baroque period and represents the most important source of information in this area. Forty-two woodcuts depicting the principal instruments add to its importance. The third volume contains accounts of secular music. This total work is, perhaps, the most valuable treatise written during the Baroque period. Reprints of the second and third volumes were made in 1929 and 1916 respectively.

4. Mersenne, Marin (1588-1648) was a French theorist. His *Traite de l' Harmonie Universelle,* Paris 1627, (Treatise Concerning Universal Harmony), was published in an expanded form in 1636-7 as *Harmonie Universelle*. It includes a discourse on harmonic theory and an especially valuable description, both verbal and pictorial, of all the instruments of the seventeenth century. An English version of this work was published under the title *Harmonie Universelle: The Books on Instruments,* 1957.

5. Simpson, Christopher (c. 1610-1669) was an English violist and composer. *The Division Violist or an Introduction to the Playing Upon a Ground,* London, 1659, is a book of instruction in the playing of the viol and improvisation. A modern edition was published in 1958.

6. Fux, Johann Joseph (1660-1741) was a German composer and theorist whose most important work was *Gradus ad Parnassum,* Vienna 1725 (Steps to Parnassus). An English translation was published in 1943. This work became a standard text in contrapuntal instruction and was studied by such masters as Mozart and Haydn, and used by such distinguished teachers as Cherubini and Albrechtsberger. It was of great influence in the teaching of counterpoint for well over a century.

7. Couperin, François (1668-1733) was a French composer, organist and clavecinist. *L'Art de toucher le clavecin,* Paris 1716, (The art of playing the harpsichord) described Couperin's manner of performance of his clavecin pieces and is of greatest importance in its description of the manner and style of playing the keyboard literature of the seventeenth and eighteenth centuries.

8. Mattheson, Johann (1681-1764) was a German composer and writer. His *Grundlage einer Ehren-Pforte, woran der tüchtichsten Capelmeister, Componisten, Musikgelehrten, Tokünstler,* etc., *Leben, Werke, Verdienste,* etc., *erschienen sollen,* Hamburg 1740, (Foundation for a triumphal arch on which the lives, works and successes of the greatest directors, composers, learned musicians, and artists shall be inscribed) was a biographical dictionary which is a source of historical information of the period.

9. Rameau, Jean-Philippe (1683-1764) was a French composer and theorist. His *Traite de l' Harmonie,* Paris 1722 (Treatise on Harmony) presented the revolutionary idea of a harmonic system in which the chords were built on thirds and were classfied in all their inversions as the same chord. Excerpts from the *Traite de l' Harmonie* are translated in Strunk's *Source Readings in Music History.*

10. Geminiani, Francesco (1687-1762) was an Italian violinist, composer and writer. *The Art of Playing the Violin,* London 1730, was first published anonymously and was the first method for violin instruction to be written. In 1751 it was published under Geminiani's name as *The Compleat Tutor for the Violin.* A facsimile edition was published in 1952. This work is of utmost importance in the study of principles of violin playing of the Baroque era.

11. Tartini, Giuseppe (1692-1770) Italian violinist, composer and theorist, wrote a number of theoretical works dealing with his discovery of combination tones and other theories concerning harmonic structure.

12. Hotteterre, Jacques (d. c. 1760) was a French flutist. His *Principles de la flute traversiere ou flute d'Allemagne, de la flute a bec ou flute douce et du hautbois,* Paris 1707, (Principles of playing the tranverse or German flute, the recorder or sweet flute and oboe) is the earliest work on the performance of the three wood wind instruments.

XI. Suggested Readings

Cannon-Johnson-Waite	pp. 247-286
Bukofzer, *Music in the Baroque Era*	
Ferguson,	pp. 183-225, 235-320
Grout	pp. 266-410
Harmon-Mellers,	pp. 366-569
Lang	pp. 314-550
Sachs HER	pp. 172-236
Ulrich-Pisk	pp. 206-311
Wold-Cykler	ch. 8

XII. Further References

David, Hans T. and Mendel, Arthur. *The Bach Reader.* New York: Norton, 1945.

Flower, Newman. *Handel.* London: Cassell and Co., 1959.

Geiringer, Karl. *The Bach Family.* New York: Oxford, 1954.

Grout, Donald J. *A Short History of Opera.* New York: Columbia University Press, 1947.

Kirkpatrick, Ralph. *Domenico Scarlatti*. Princeton: Princeton University Press, 1953.

Newman, William S. *The Sonata in the Baroque Era*. Chapel Hill, University of North Carolina Press, 1959.

Schrade, Leo. *Monteverdi*. New York: Norton, 1946.

Spitta, Philipp. *Johann Sebastian Bach*. New York: Dover Publication, 1951.

Terry, Charles Sanford. *Bach*. London: Oxford, 1928.

Concert at the court of Frederick the Great. After an engraving of Peter Haas. Courtesy of Baeren-reiter-Bild-Archiv.

Chapter

6

꒰ꇇꭍ

Classicism
1725-1800

I. Sociocultural Influences on Music

The term Classic is used here to designate the music of the eighteenth century. This term has also been used by historians to describe all the arts that are concerned mainly with problems of form, logic, balance and restrained expression, and that were also based on models of Greek and Roman art. Unfortunately, there are no such models for Classic music to emulate. Consequently the term, as applied to music, refers to the works of those eighteenth century composers whose music gives the impression of clarity, repose, balance, lyricism and restraint of emotional expression. The Classic period is one of the high points of music history and was nourished by a number of important developments in the patronage and function of music during this time.

1. Austria and Germany became the center of a very vital musical activity. It must be noted that in these countries there were a large number of courts that were able to maintain their independence. This was in contrast to France and England, where almost all aristrocratic life had come under the influence of a central power. In Austria and Germany, however, these small courts gave up much of their political and economic independence, but maintained their artistic and social status. There was even great rivalry among them in artistic and social matters.

Moreover, a long tradition of instrumental music, an abundance of talent, a natural love of music among all classes, great artistic ambition combined with great wealth — together these made the perfect conditions for an enthusiastic patronage.

2. Composers depended upon the patronage of a court or aristrocratic society that was very discriminating in its tastes. This society was not only sophisticated and elegant, but disclaimed any affinity for being profound, or showing its emotion. The Age of Reason had placed a premium on intellectual pursuits and looked with a good deal of suspicion on any reliance upon feelings.

3. The concert hall and opera house became established institutions. This made it possible for all classes to enjoy the fruits of creative activity, whether aristocratic or not.

4. Publishing houses became well established and exerted a strong influence on both composers and the public. They not only made performances of musical works more widespread, but publishers were in a position to champion certain composers — often at the expense of others.

5. There was a general decline in the patronage of the church toward serious music. While there were certain reform movements in both Protestantism and Catholicism during the eighteenth century, none of them provided a suitable climate for a continuous growth of religious music. Certainly the rather shallow attitude of aristocratic society did little to maintain the religious music at the level of the Baroque.

II. Function of Music

1. Music in the Classic era served a highly sophisticated and aristocratic society. Its most common function was to provide delightful entertainment for guests in exclusive salons.

2. A larger but still discriminating audience patronized public concerts of orchestral music and the elegant spectacle of opera.

3. Music also served an important function in the home, for this was an era of amateur musical performances, both vocal and instrumental. Many serious composers were called upon to write chamber music as well as vocal solos and ensembles for amateur consumption.

4. Naturally, music for dancing was in popular demand for a society that loved gaiety and entertainment.

5. While the church was not a major consumer of serious music, it still demanded that composers write sacred music for its services in the spirit of secularism that prevailed.

III. Characteristics of Style

All the characteristics of style applied to all forms in the Classic. All of the following stylistic qualities were present to some extent in all of the classic forms, vocal or instrumental.

1. *Formal Organization.*

   a. Musical form was predicated on the idea of one melody being contrasted homophonically with a second melody, leading to the A-B-A formula. This was partly in protest against the complications of polyphony and partly an effort to create a form that could be grasped and enjoyed by all — aristocrat with discriminating taste and middle-class bourgeois.

   b. Forms are precise and clear, with sections being clearly marked off by cadences.

   c. All Classic music is characterized by a symmetry of form. Musical periods are perfectly balanced, usually in units of four measure phrases.

   d. Folk music in all its forms and idioms was gradually introduced into serious music. This was especially true of Haydn, who used some Croatian melodies and rhythms in his music. No doubt this reaching into folk music was due to the rather wide range of the

Classic audience. Folk elements also appeared in opera and song.

2. *Melody.*

　　a. There was an emphasis on lyricism with smooth melodic contours. Ornaments were often written out and became a lyric part of the melody.

　　b. Melodic configuration was frequently based on chordal structure.

　　e. Melodies were extended to the double phrase and more. This was in contrast to the generally short, cryptic melodic devices of earlier music.

　　d. Melodic devices such as ornaments, sequential patterns, etc., became formalized to a point of being cliché́s.

3. *Rhythm.*

　　a. Classic composers usually used very simple and constant rhythmic patterns that were clearly punctuated by rhythmic cadences.

　　b. All parts have the same rhythmic patterns. Polyrhythms were no longer used as in earlier music.

　　c. An important formal device of rhythm was the Alberti bass which is the breaking up of the triad into broken chord figures with a repeated rhythmic pattern (Fig. 7).

Figure 7

　　d. Silence became a part of the element of rhythm. Strong cadences are sometimes followed by a measure of silence in order to heighten the effect of the cadence.

e. The tempo of a movement, or section, is always constant from beginning to end.

4. *Harmony.*

a. Harmony is tonal with a harmonic rhythm that moves slowly and subordinate to the melody. This results in a predominately homophonic style.

b. Because the bass no longer served a melodic function, the Baroque polarity between soprano and bass disappeared. Consequently, the device of the basso continuo was discontinued.

c. Harmony is generally simple, rarely using anything more complicated than primary chords and sevenths.

d. There is a formal key relationship between themes and between movements of forms. This key relationship serves to provide contrast and interest without introducing new material. In the exposition of the sonata-allegro the first theme is in the tonic. The second theme is in the dominant of the original, or the relative major if the first is in a minor key. The development usually contains a number of modulations away from either the tonic or dominant with a return to the tonic. In the recapitulation the second theme is in the tonic, thus reconciling the key relationships and enabling the movement to end in a tonic cadence. The key relations between movements are less varied. In general all movements are in the same key with the exception of the second movement, which is in the sub-dominant, dominant, or relative minor. If the first movement is in minor, the last movement is sometimes in the parallel major.

e. The most commonly used cadence was the IV V I with the final tonic on a strong beat (Fig. 8).

Figure 8

The feminine cadence was also frequently employed. This is the usual authentic cadence, but with the final tonic on a weak beat (Fig. 9).

Figure 9

5. *Texture.*
   a. The texture of Classic music is essentially homophonic, with lyric melody predominating.
   b. Even when polyphonic texture is present, there is a clarity and transparency of line that gives the music an almost filigree effect. In orchestral music this clarity of texture is emphasized by means of contrasting tonal coloring.

6. *Media.*
   a. The most popular means of musical expression was instrumental — the orchestra, chamber music (both strings and winds) and solo instruments.

b. The Classic period saw the division of the instruments of the orchestra into four major groups; strings, wood-winds, brass and percussion. With the exception of the percussion, each group became a complete choir in itself. Moreover, the harpsichord was no longer used for the bass line and to fill in the harmonic texture.

c. While the harpsichord had been the household in-strument during the Renaissance and the Baroque, it was superceded by the piano during the late eigh-teenth century.

d. Instrumental chamber music became very popular. The large number of amateur performers and the in-timacy of aristocratic society supplied a suitable cli-mate for its development. Some of the finest of all Classic music can be found in the literature of the string quartet, piano quintets, trios, sonatas, etc.

e. Another media very much in demand was opera. Tes-timony of this can be seen in the large number of operas composed by both major and minor composers.

f. Aside from opera, vocal music was of minor impor-tance, but remained in the form of religious music, folk songs and the lied.

IV. Practice and Performance

1. Dynamics became commonplace. This was another means of achieving contrast, but instead of changing the texture as in the Baroque tutti and concertino, the Classic composer employed crescendo and diminuendo as well as sudden changes from FF to PP.

2. Composers gave explicit directions in dynamics, tempi, phrasing, and all other interpretive matters, leaving little for the performer's imagination.

3. While ornaments were not always written out, there was a precise formula for the designation of each figure. It is in this

area that the Classic composer depended upon tradition and consequently the correct interpretation of ornaments is a serious problem for today's performer.

V. Instrumental Forms

1. *Sonata.* The most important form of the Classic era is the sonata, an abstract instrumental form of large dimensions in three or four separate movements. It was developed from the seventeenth century dance suite and trio-sonata. It was also undoubtedly influenced by the Italian operatic overture. A normal organization of a Classic sonata consists of (1) a sonata-allegro movement; (2) a slow two- or three-part song form, or a variation form; (3) a minuet; (4) a rondo, or sonata-allegro. On occasion this last movement is a variation-form, but in any event it is always in a fast tempo. If there are only three movements, the minuet is omitted. A sonata is the name used for this form when written for one or two instruments. When written for more than two instruments, it takes the name of the particular ensemble, such as a symphony, trio, etc. There is a potential universatility about the sonata. It is the only form that is divorced from religion, drama, and the dance. It also has more universal appeal than the polyphonic forms such as the fugue because it is less complicated intellectually. K. P. E. Bach is the composer who was mainly responsible for the sonata, although he cannot be credited with its invention.

> Ex:[1] *Sonata No. 10, K. 330, C major,* Mozart
> *Symphony No. 40, K. 550, G minor,* Mozart
> *Piano trio No. 3, C major,* Haydn

2. *Sonata-Allegro.* The sonata-allegro is by far the most representative single form. Its organization is based on the structural idea of the presentation of two contrasting themes, or musical ideas, their development and their final reconciliation

---

[1]Because there are a large number of scores and recordings by numerous publishers and recording companies for almost all music from the classic era to present day, specific editions and recordings will be omitted.

in a restatement. The following is the plan of the Classic sonata-allegro:

Exposition ‖: Th. I. (maj.) trans. Th. II. Dom. trans. Cl. Th. :‖
Th. I. (min.) trans. Th. II. Rel. trans. Cl. Th. :‖

Development ———— Varied treatment of material of the exposition in distant keys followed by a cadence.

Recapitulation ———— Th. I. tonic maj. trans. Th. II. tonic trans. Cl. Th. tonic‖
Th. II. tonic min, trans. Th. I. tonic maj. trans. Cl.‖ Th. tonic

(Th. I is first theme; trans. is transition; Th. II is second theme; Cl. Th. is closing theme. The outline below the line is the pattern when the movement is cast in a minor key.)

Composers sometimes prefaced the sonata-allegro with a slow introduction to serve as a musical device to quiet the audience and gain its attention. There was usually no connection between the musical material of the introduction and the thematic material of the sonata-allegro. This introductory section was most often used in the symphony.

Ex: *Symphony No. 101, D major (Clock), first movement,* Haydn
   Sonata No. 14, C minor, K. 547, first movement, Mozart
   Quartet No. 1, F major, Op. 18, Beethoven

3. *Symphony.* The symphony is a sonata for orchestra and is normally in four movements. The use of a larger group of instruments called for a much more extended composition. The varied tonal possibilities of the orchestra made it possible to have a greater variety of style, more extended climaxes, and a more complex development section. The first movement of the symphony was often preceded by a slow introduction.

There were two important "schools" of classic symphony composers: The Mannheim School with Stamitz as its most important composer and the Viennese School of Haydn, Mozart, and Beethoven.

Ex: *Symphony No. 1, Op. 21, in C major,* Beethoven
      Symphony No. 92, (Oxford), Haydn
      Sinfonia a 8 in D, Johann Stamitz

4. *Solo Concerto.* This is in the pattern of the sonata, but generally omitting the minuet, thus making it a three-movement form. The first movement is a sonata-allegro in which the orchestra presents the whole exposition and then the solo instrument enters either with a direct statement of the theme, or an introduction, and then the theme. The development follows with the solo instrument pitted against the orchestra. In place of the subordinate theme in the recapitulation, there is usually a brilliant cadenza — a free improvisation on the themes by the performer, although this was sometimes written out by the composer. The second and third movements follow that of the sonata with optional cadenzas.

Ex: *Concerto for Cello and Orchestra in B flat,* Boccherini
      Concerto for Piano and Orchestra, No. 20, D. minor, K. 466, Mozart

5. *Chamber Music.* All kinds of small instrumental ensembles, using the forms of the sonata come under this heading. These forms were called Trios, Quartets, Quintets, and Sextets and were for various combinations of string and wind instruments. However, the String Quartet was the most common. When the piano was used in combination with string instruments, the form was designated as a Piano Trio, Piano Quartet, Piano Quintet, etc.

Ex: *Piano Trio, No. 1 in G,* Haydn
      Piano Quartet, No. 2 in E flat, K. 493, Mozart
      Quartet, No. 19 in C, K. 465, Mozart

6. *Rondo.* The rondo is also predicated on the idea of repetition of a theme after a contrasting melodic idea. It differs from the sonata-allegro form in that it has no development section and that the principal theme is always repeated in the tonic. The typical form is as follows: A-B-A-C-A-B-A. In a major key

B is usually in the key of the dominant. If A is in a minor key, B is in the relative major. C which is in the tonic is usually a melodic idea of minor significance or merely an episode between the repetitions of A.

Ex: *String Quintet in G Minor, K. 516, last movement,* Mozart
Sonata No. 2, A major, Op. 2, last movement, Beethoven

7. *Variation-form.* The variation was still popular in the Classic period. It was used extensively as the second movement of keyboard sonatas and also in some quartets and symphonies. In the Classic period, the variation-form was primarily homophonic. Variations were both harmonic and melodic, using contrasting tempi and rhythmic patterns as well as changes in tonal coloring.

Ex: *Clarinet Quintet, A major, K. 581, last movement,* Mozart
Quartet in C Major, Op. 76, second movement, Haydn
Variation for piano in F minor, Haydn

8. *Minuet and Trio.* This is the only dance form to survive in the Classic sonata. While it was a two-part form in the Baroque, it became a three-part from in the Classic. Its plan is as follows (note that each of the sections is a three-part song form):

A	Minuet	A	B	A
B	Trio	C	D	C
A	Minuet	A	B	A

Ex: *Eine Kleine Nachtmusik, Serenade for String Orchestra, K. 525, Menuetto,* Mozart
Symphony No. 101, D major (Clock) third movement, Haydn

9. *Three-part Song Form.* The three-part song form is more instrumental than its name indicates. It is based on lyric melody in a simple A-B-A, and was often used as the second movement of a sonata.

Ex: *Sonata No. 1 in F minor, second movement,* K. P. E. Bach
Symphony No. 101, D major (Clock), second movement, Haydn

10. *Polyphonic Instrumental Forms.* The polyphonic forms of the Baroque were not completely discarded during the Classic.

However, they were most often used as musical devices rather than complete forms. For example, the first theme of a sonata-allegro was sometimes cast as a fugato (fugal passage). Fugal passages were also often used in the development sections. Both Haydn and Mozart made extensive use of the fugue in this manner and used polyphonic forms as complete movements in some of their later works. In contrast to the Baroque fugue, however, the subjects were usually longer and of a more lyric character.

Ex: *Quartet, B major, K. 387, last movement,* Mozart
 Symphony No. 41, C major, K. 550, last movement, Mozart

11. *Overture.* The eighteenth century overture was a sonata-allegro type structure. It was associated almost exclusively with the opera and was used as an expression of mood preparatory to the first scene. In the late eighteenth century composers began to incorporate material from the main body of the opera into the overture.

Ex: *Overture to Orfeo ed Euridice,* Gluck
 Overture to Marriage of Figaro, Mozart

12. While the sonata was the dominant form of the Classic era, there were also serenades, divertimenti, cassations and notturni. These were a continuation of the earlier suite and symphonies of the Baroque, but were now based on the Classic characteristics of style. They could be written for any group, from small chamber groups to a full orchestra.

Ex: *Divertimenti, Op. 31,* Haydn
 Serenata Notturna, D major, K. 239, Mozart

VI. Vocal Forms

1. *Opera.* Opera in the eighteenth century underwent considerable reform from the stereotyped practices of the Neapolitan school. These reforms were realized in the works of Gluck, who thought of himself as a reformer of opera, and by Mozart. In general, it can be said that the structure of opera became much more fluent and subtle than that of the Baroque. The relation between music and drama was somewhat restored. No

longer were singers left to their own devices in improvising dazzling vocal effects that had little to do with the story. No longer was the stage mechanic more important than the composer. There was a strong emphasis upon skillful characterization of the protagonists, together with a greater dramatic force. The principle of the sonata-form structure was applied with great success to operatic scenes and arias. Each became a closed form, complete in itself. The following are the important closed forms that are found in all Classic opera:

- a. Recitative. The recitative was both secco and orchestrally accompanied and had considerable musical interest, apart from carrying the narrative portions of the drama. The accompaniment itself was often highly suggestive of the atmosphere of the text.

- b. Aria. The aria in the Classic opera of Gluck and Mozart avoided the spectacular virtuosity of the Baroque opera. While the principle of the da capo aria still prevailed, it was a much more expressive musical realization of the text. As in the recitative, the orchestra created the proper mood by means of lyric melody and tonal coloring.

- c. Choruses and Ensembles. The operas of Gluck and Mozart use the chorus as an effective part of the drama. Ensembles, especially in Mozart, are marvelous examples of subtle musical dramatization. In contrast to the homophonic texture of the aria, these choruses and ensembles are usually polyphonic. Each member of the ensemble is often declaiming elements of counterplots and intrigue along with the main story. In essence this is both musical and dramatic counterpoint.

> Ex: *Orfeo ed Euridice,* Gluck
> *Marriage of Figaro,* Mozart
> *Don Giovanni,* Mozart

2. *Oratorio.* The oratorio was continued in the tradition of the Baroque, but with emphasis on classic characteristics of

style. The best-known Classic oratorios are by Haydn. The *Creation* was based on a text from the Book of Genesis and the *Seasons,* a secular work on poetry by the Scottish poet, James Thomson, and translated into German. Both of these works have become successful concert pieces.

Ex: *The Creation,* Haydn
     The Seasons, Haydn

3. *Mass.* There was a general decline in the quality of religious music composed during the Classic era. Much of what was composed was written for liturgical use, but was also appropriate for the concert hall. The Mass was the favorite of these forms and consisted of the setting of the Ordinary of the Mass with soloists, chorus and orchestra, and was symphonic in nature.

Ex: *Missa Solemnis in D minor, (Nelson Mass,)* Haydn
     Mass in C. (Coronation), K. 317, Mozart

4. *Lied.* The Classic lied replaced the ornamented pathos of seventeenth century arias and songs. The lied was characterized by simple folk-like melodies and was usually strophic (the same melody and harmonic substance for each stanza of the poem). Some of the finest strophic songs were written in the late eighteenth century by Mozart and Haydn to the poems of Goethe.

Ex: *An Chloe K. 524,* Mozart
     My Mother Bids Me Bind My Hair, Haydn

5. *Vocal Polyphony.* While homophony was the basic texture of Classic vocal as well as instrumental music, polyphony still prevailed in some forms. This was especially true in operatic ensembles and in the chorus sections of the Mass and Oratorios. Examples can be found in the ensembles of the *Marriage of Figaro* and *Don Giovanni* by Mozart. Haydn's *Creation* and Mozart's *Requiem Mass* show examples of polyphonic texture in religious vocal music. In addition, most classic composers wrote short vocal canons and polyphonic choruses, often on light,

comic texts for social singing. Both Haydn and Mozart wrote many of these delightful works.

Ex: *Der Greis,* Haydn
    Piu non si trovano, K. 549. Canzonetta for two sopranos and bass, Mozart

VII. Important Composers

1. Sammartini, Giovanni (1701-1775) was an Italian composer who was also a pioneer in the development of the Classic sonata. He is also known for his chamber music in the Classic style. He was Gluck's teacher. The principal works that survive today are a number of sonatas for chamber ensemble, especially the string quartet.

2. Gluck, Christoph Willibald (1714-1787) was an opera composer who initiated many reforms that eventually laid the foundations for the later opera composers. However, his reforms had little immediate effect on the composers of his own time. Gluck, after writing in the traditional Italian style, finally came to the conclusion that the dramatic force of the libretto must be the most important aspect of opera. To achieve this he made the following innovations: (1) He eliminated virtuosity, substituting lyric simplicity; (2) He strove to create musical portraits of his characters and their feelings; (3) He returned to the use of plots taken from mythology — plots that avoid the complex counterplots and minor intrigues of Neapolitan opera; (4) He made the recitative more musically expressive; (5) He used the instruments of the orchestra as a tonal palette, creating the proper mood and atmosphere by tonal coloring; (6) He used the chorus as a dramatic device to intensify the dramatic force; (7) He made the overture an introduction to the mood and spirit of the opera. His most important works were *Orfeo ed Eurydice,* 1762; *Alceste,* 1767; *Armide,* 1777; *Iphigenie en Tauride,* 1779.

3. Bach, Karl Phillip Emanuel (1714-1788) was the son of J. S. Bach and sometimes was known as the "Berlin" Bach. He was

well-known as a performer on keyboard instruments as well as a composer. He was very influential in establishing the form and style of Classic composing, and is often credited with being the first to write in the sonata-allegro form. There is no doubt but that both Haydn and Mozart were influenced by his style. He wrote more than 200 sonatas and solo works for the piano, in addition to numerous concerti and chamber music works. His sonatas show the basic form of the sonata, but there was little, if any, development of the themes in the sonata-allegro movement.

4. Stamitz, Johann Wenzel Anton (1717-1757) was the founder of the Mannheim school and made a number of important contributions to both orchestral playing and writing for orchestra. The most important of these were: (1) The first use of extensive dynamic shading in orchestral performance; (2) The introduction of the clarinet into the orchestra; (3) The introduction of the minuet into the symphony as the third movement; (4) The creation of what was known as the finest orchestra in all of Europe. He wrote about 74 symphonies, but because the symphony was perfected by Haydn and Mozart, these works are seldom performed today.

5. Haydn, Franz Joseph (1732-1809) was one of the most prolific composers of the eighteenth century. Haydn's career is a fine example of the patronage system functioning at its best. Born in Lower Austria, he received his early training as a choirboy at St. Stephens in Vienna. Aside from this schooling he was largely self-taught in music, drawing heavily upon the style of such Classic composers as K. P. E. Bach. Haydn was finally given a post as assistant Kappelmeister at the Court of Prince Esterhazy in 1761 and was to enjoy an ideal patronage for a period of over thirty years. His duties were to provide music requested by the Prince for any and all occasions. Consequently, he was called upon for every conceivable form of music from sonatas through opera and including all forms of Catholic religious music. A most important factor in the development of his orchestral music was the fact that he had an orchestra at his disposal at all times. This enabled him to experiment with various

orchestral instruments and orchestral timbres. It was Haydn who brought unity to late eighteenth century music and "perfected" the Classic style. Haydn wrote an enormous amount of music; much of it has been lost and the remainder is only now being published in a complete edition. His more important works are the symphonies (well over 100 of which 104 are published) and the 82 string quartets. His main contributions to the Classic style consist of (1) the use of a slow introduction to the first movement of the symphony; (2) enlarging the development section of the sonata-allegro and developing fragments of themes; (3) using the variation-form for the slow movement of symphonies and quartets; (4) using a more flexible orchestration that permitted melodies to be imitated in contrasting tonal coloring. Of his total creative output, the following works are his most representative: (1) the *London Symphonies* (nos. 93-104); (2) the later quartets, especially the *Emperor, Op. 76, No. 3;* and the *Lark, Op. 65, No. 5;* (3) two oratorios, the *Creation* and the *Seasons;* (4) the piano sonatas.

6. Bach, Johann Christian (London Bach), (1735-1782) was also a son of J. S. Bach. Johann Christian Bach lived and studied in Italy for a time after studying in Berlin with his brother, K. P. E. Bach. He later went to England where he became music master to the Queen of England. He was an important composer of the light homophonic genre and his music was an important source of the Classic style. He wrote numerous operas in addition to piano sonatas, symphonies and various kinds of chamber music.

7. Dittersdorf, Karl von (1739-1799) was a successful composer of Classical symphonies, church music and opera, although he was eclipsed by both Haydn and Mozart. One opera, the *Doctor and Apothecary,* still survives, as well as numerous string quartets and a few symphonies.

8. Boccherini, Luigi (1743-1805) was an Italian composer and cellist who was a great admirer of Haydn's music and who copied his style. He wrote a great quantity of chamber music, including 102 quartets and 125 quintets. His six cello sonatas

and four cello concertos are still prominent in the present day repertory of music for cello.

9. Mozart, Wolfgang Amadeus (1756-1791) was a composer whose creative inventiveness and lyric genius place him among the three or four "giants" of music. Born in Salzburg, Mozart showed evidence of a great creativity from infancy. His youth was spent in the atmosphere of the Salzburg Court where his father was a violinist. His genius was recognized early and his talents as a performer and as a composer were displayed to almost all of Europe through tours to the important courts and musical centers. In spite of almost ideal conditions for a successful career and despite his superior talents, Mozart's life was one of struggle and disappointment. In contrast to Haydn, Mozart never really had a patron. He was one of the first independent composers who had to struggle for recognition and commissions without the security of a permanent post. Without patronage, Mozart was forced to write in every popular form of his day in order to interest people in his music. His death and burial in a pauper's grave came just as he was gaining some public acclaim for his opera, *The Magic Flute,* a recognition that might have brought him the security of a permanent position.

In style, Mozart was a conformist. He refined and polished the Classic forms, but made no major innovations over those made by Haydn. It should be noted that Mozart knew Haydn and their friendship probably influenced Mozart's mature works. While there are many similarities between their styles, Mozart is distinctive in the following ways: (1) in general, his melodies are more lyric, more extended, and more subtle in their lyric expressiveness; (2) He seldom repeats phrases note for note, but makes some minute change in ornaments, rhythm, harmonic structure, or dynamics; (3) He seldom uses the slow introduction to his symphonies; (4) He indulges in more chromaticism in both melody and harmony, thus foreshadowing the romantic style; (5) In his chamber music especially, all parts become equal in importance.

While he did not follow the devices of Gluck's reforms, his refined classic taste, his innate feeling for, and love of the theater led him to write what was perhaps the happiest solution to the problems of combining pure music and extra-musical ideas. Mozart's operas can be placed in three general classifications: (1) opera buffa, the most important of which are *Marriage of Figaro, Cosi fan Tutti,* and *Don Giovanni;* (2) The German operas — *The Magic Flute* and *The Abduction from the Seraglio;* (3) The Italian style operas — *La Clemenza di Tito* and *Idomeneo.*

It is difficult to pick out the major works from Mozart's total output of over 600 compositions. However, there are a few that can stand out from the rest as monuments to his creative genius. Mozart did not number his works chronologically by the usual opus numbers, but Ludwig von Köchel compiled a chronological catalog in the middle of the nineteenth century. This catalog was recently brought up to date by the late Alfred Einstein and this numbering system is used today. Mozart's works are designated by the letter K and the appropriate number.

Of his total number of works, attention is called to the following: (1) the last three symphonies, *E flat major, No. 39* (*K. 543*), *G. minor, No. 40,* (*K. 550*); *C major, No. 41* (*K. 551*) (2) Among the string quartets there is a group known as the "Ten Celebrated Quartets" Köchel numbers (387), (421), (428), (458), (464), (465), (499), (575), (589), (590). The *Clarinet Quintet in A major* (*K. 581*) must also be included in the great works of chamber music. (3) Mozart also wrote chamber music for winds and strings. Among these are: *Serenade in D major for winds and strings,* (*K. 320*), *Divertimento in D major for String quartet and 2 horns,* (*K. 334*), *Sextet for String Quartet and 2 Horns* (*K. 552*). (4) *Violin Concertos in G. major,* (*K. 216*), *D. major,* (*K. 218*), *A major,* (*K. 219*). (5) Of the 25 piano concertos, the following are performed most often: *C major,* (*K. 415*), *B flat major,* (*K. 450*), *G major,* (*K. 453*), *and D minor,* (*K. 466*). (6) His most representative piano sonatas are those in *C minor* (*K. 467*), *C major* (*K. 545*), *B flat major* (*K. 570*), *and D major* (*K. 576*). (7) While he wrote a number of religious works, his *Requiem Mass* is his crowning achievement in this medium.

10. Cherubini, (Maria) Luigi (1760-1842) was the last important composer to show the classical restraint that identifies him as a Classic composer even though he lived well into the nineteenth century. He was born in Italy where he became a successful Italian opera composer. He soon made Paris his permanent home and his creative life was mainly French influenced from then on. His French operas were influenced by Gluck's reforms, but never achieved a great success. Perhaps his best opera is *Médée* which has been revived in recent years. Other French operas are *Lodaiska* and *Les Deux journées*. Two *Requiem Masses* show a high quality of church music that is noted for its superb counterpoint.

11. Beethoven, Ludwig van (1770-1827) must be considered as both a Classicist and a Romanticist and will be discussed more fully in the chapter on Romanticism. While the greater portion of his compositions reveal the characteristics found in the Romantic style, his earlier works conform to the pattern of the Classic. It is generally accepted that those works written before 1802 are patterned after the traditions of Haydn and despite an occasional outburst of impatience with the harmonic and dynamic simplicity of Classicism, his acceptance of the tradition is fairly complete. The important earlier works included the piano sonatas up to Opus 53; the first three piano concerti; String Quartets, Opus 18; and the First and Second symphonies.

VIII. Other Composers

Germany

> Quantz, Johann Joachim (1697-1773)
> Richter, F. X. (1709-1789)
> Bach, Wilhelm Friedemann (1710-1784)
> Wagenseil, Christoph (1715-1777)
> Monn, George Matthias (1717-1750)
> Cannabich, Christian (1731-1798)
> Haydn, Michael (1737-1806)

Italy

Jommeli, Niccolo (1714-1774)
Piccini, Niccolo (1728-1800)
Cimarosa, Domenico (1749-1801)

France

Rousseau, Jean Jacques (1712-1778)
Gossec, François (1734-1829)
Grétry, André (1741-1813)

England

Arne, Thomas (1710-1778)
Boyce, William (1710-1779)

IX. and X. Important Writers on Music

Because Classicism was concerned mainly with form there was little philosophizing about music. Most of the writers were seeking to formalize musical performance and consequently gave detailed instructions as to how to play instruments and also how to interpret the various devices of musical practice. A few of the more important writers and their works are listed following. Note that in most cases the writers were also creative artists, or at least performers.

1. Quantz, Johann Joachim (1697-1773) was a composer and flutist as well as the author of *Versuch einer Anweisung, die Flöte Traversiere zu spielen,* Berlin, 1752; (Essay on Instruction for playing the Transverse Flute). While the title suggests a method for flute, Quantz deals with problems and questions of the general musical practice of his time. This work has not been translated into English, but excerpts can be found in *Source Readings in Music History* by Oliver Strunk.

2. Rousseau, Jean Jacques (1712-1778) was a French writer, philosopher, and sometimes music scholar and composer. His *Dictionaire de musique* was published in 1767. This work contains many of Rousseau's articles written originally for the *Encyclopedie* to which he was a major contributor.

3. Gluck, Christoph Willibald (1714-1787) wrote an important treatise on opera, the *Preface to Alceste*, Vienna, 1769. *Alceste* was composed in 1767 but the printed score appeared in 1769. It is in this preface that Gluck seeks to establish the aesthetics of his musical theories concerning opera. He also gives an account of what he believed to be serious abuses of the true purpose of opera in the Italian school. This preface appears in Strunk's *Source Readings in Music History*.

4. Bach, Karl Phillip Emanuel (1714-1788) wrote *Versuch über die wahre Art, das Clavier zu spielen*, Berlin, 1753-1762, (Essay on the True Art of playing Keyboard Instruments) (New York, 1949). This work is still an authoritative source of information on the traditions of performance of Classic music for the keyboard. It is also very valuable in the realization of classic ornaments and embellishments. There are excerpts in *Source Readings in Music History* by Oliver Strunk.

5. Mozart, Leopold (1719-1787) was the author of *Versuch einer gründlichen Violinschule*, Augsburg, 1756, (Treatise on the Fundamental Principles of Violin Playing) (London 1951). Leopold Mozart was the father of Wolfgang Amadeus and an eminent violinist and teacher. This work is one of the first successful methods of violin playing. Along with K. P. E. Bach and Quantz, he gives us an account of the musical practice of the Classic era. Excerpts of this work can also be found in Strunk's *Source Readings in Music History*.

6. Hawkins, Sir John (1719-1789) was an English music historian who wrote *A General History of the Science and Practice of Music*, London, 1776, republished in 1875. Hawkins' history, published about the same time as Burney's history, is filled with reliable information, especially about the musical scene in eighteenth century London.

7. Burney, Charles (1726-1814) was the most important English music historian of the eighteenth century. *A General History of Music*, London, 1776, reprinted New York, 1957, is the first important history of music in English. It contains many interesting comments on the contemporary musical trends that

reveal the general attitude of both the creative musician and the public during Burney's time. Burney made extensive trips to the musical capitals of Europe and wrote two volumes concerning the musical scene on the Continent.

XI. Suggested Readings

Cannon-Johnson-Waite	pp. 287-340
Ferguson	pp. 321-362
Grout	pp. 411-469
Harman and Mellers	pp. 581-630
Lang	pp. 530-733
Sachs-HER	pp. 237-254
Ulrich-Pisk	pp. 312-424
Wold-Cykler	ch. 9

XII. Further References

Burney, Dr. Charles. *An Eighteenth Century Musical Tour in Central Europe and the Netherlands.* New York: Oxford, 1959.

Burney, Dr. Charles. *An Eighteenth Century Music Journey in France and Italy.* New York: Oxford, 1959.

Carse, Adam. *The Orchestra in the Eighteenth Century.* Cambridge, England: W. Heffer, 1940.

Dent, E. J. *Mozart's Operas,* rev. ed. New York: Oxford, 1947.

Einstein, Alfred. *Mozart: His Character and Work.* New York: Oxford, 1945.

Geiringer, Karl. *Haydn, A Creative Life in Music.* New York: W .W. Norton, 1946.

Geiringer, Karl. *The Bach Family.* New York: Oxford, 1954.

Grout, Donald J. *A Short History of Opera.* New York: Columbia University Press, 1947.

Helm, Ernest E. *Music at the Court of Frederick the Great.* Norman: University of Oklahoma Press, 1960.

The third act of Richard Wagner's *Die Meistersinger von Nürnberg* presented by the Vienna State Opera. Courtesy of the Photographic Archiv of the Austrian National Library.

7

꘏

Romanticism
1800-1910

I. Sociocultural Influences on Music

The early nineteenth century saw the rise of a style of music, literature and art that we refer to as Romantic. The nineteenth century was a time of dramatic thought and action. It was also a time of strong contradictions between capitalism and socialism, freedom and oppression, logic and emotion, science and faith. The consequence of these contradictions was a change in the thinking of people, especially creative artists. An intellectual change took place in the minds of composers that was many sided, complex and often incompatible. Consequently it is impossible to say there is a definite Romantic style. Other periods of the past had a core of accepted beliefs and practices that drew composers together with a similarity between their music. Romanticism, on the other hand, had the tendency to isolate creative personalities — for their practices and beliefs were often in opposition and, like Romanticism itself, complex. However, the following are a few of the important sociocultural events and ideas which influenced composers to display Romantic qualities.

1. The revolutionary spirit that finally exploded in the French Revolution infused artists with the ideals of liberty and individualism. In terms of music, there were several Romantic results. There was a general impatience with the rules and restraints of Classicism. Just as the Revolution opposed the eighteenth century status quo, so music revolted against the prac-

tices of Mozart and Haydn. To be different was the goal and the Romantic period was to witness a great variety of musical experiments to achieve individualism. Moreover, to implement the ideals of liberty, composers sought to express their own personal convictions and to portray events and ideas as they understood them. The expression of emotion and the evocation of imagination became the primary goal of most Romantic music. In an effort to stimulate the imagination there arose a predilection for the strange and the remote, a fascination for the mysteries of the universe.

2. The Industrial Revolution caused a major change in the economic and social life of the common man and also gave rise to a wealthy capitalistic middle class. There was a general leveling of society and, while the composer did not write for the lower classes, his music was addressed to the masses to a far greater degree than before in the history of music. The wealthy middle class was the potential patron for the composer who had all but lost aristocratic patronage because of the increasing decline in the power and influence of the court. Literature and the visual arts were quick to use the injustices of the Industrial Revolution, the exploitation of the workers, the low standards of living and the social abuses of the lower classes as subjects for their works. Music, however, seems to have denied the existence of these pressing problems. While Wagner wrote a few scenes which may have revealed the bitterness of industrial exploitation, the avoidance of this theme is worthy of note. Music became more and more disassociated from real life. Composers expressed the splendor and pride of the human spirit in what seems to be an escape from reality for those who could afford the luxury of music.

3. The development of the "business" of music was also an important influence on the direction composers took in their writing. In order to cultivate the patronage of a wider and unorganized public, the composer, together with his publisher and concert manager, had to "sell" music to the public. Pub-

lication was on a different basis than it had been. In the effort
to capture audiences a dynamic and colorful personality came to
be an important asset, as can be noted in such individuals as
Liszt, Berlioz and Wagner. The concert manager, or impresario
as he was often called, was also an important figure in the business of music. His opinion as to what the public would accept
and be enthusiastic about was a strong motivation for many a
composer and performer. Another important person behind the
scenes of music was the music critic. He was a sort of liaison
between the public and the composer. His writing served not
only to interpret the composer to the public, but to set standards
of musical taste. Needless to say the composer was usually in
conflict with most of the critics, but the critic was still often
responsible for the acceptance or rejection of a composer's works.

4. While the revolutionary spirit had its origin in France,
it was in Germany and Austria that Romanticism had its strong-
est foothold and where it flourished. The French almost abandoned the Romantic ideal because of their affinity for the
Classic. Germany and Austria, however, were younger; they had
never known the oppression of a strong central absolutism and
they were also more concerned with the things of the spirit.
Because of their youthfulness there seemed to be a conscious
emphasis on folklore and historical epics in their desire to achieve
a cultural heritage equal to the older and longer established
countries. Whatever the reasons, the seeds of musical romanticism were to fall upon very fertile ground, particularly in
Vienna ·

II. Function of Music

1. Romantic music still served a sophisticated and aristocratic society as had been the case with the Classic. Aristocratic
patronage was considerably smaller than it had been in the
eighteenth century and there were practically no opportunities
for the kind of patronage enjoyed by Haydn. The intimacy of
the exclusive salon was still the ideal setting for chamber music

and solo forms. Performance, however, was no longer by amateurs, for Romantic music was usually too technically demanding for unskilled performers.

2. Outside the patronage of the exclusive salon was a large, but unorganized and unsophisticated, concert-going public which loved music. Romantic composers were constantly striving to gain the recognition of this vast audience and, in an effort to win acceptance, they were very sensitive to the likes and dislikes of these music-lovers. This middle-class listener searched for new excitement or relaxation from everyday life in music. To stir up or calm down his feelings was the function of the composer. There were two general types of music that appealed to these patrons — symphonic music and the extravagant spectacle of opera and ballet.

3. Performers, as well as composers, had the urge to be acceptable and to dazzle audiences. Composers, who were often also fine performers themselves, like Liszt and Paganini, wrote a large number of virtuoso pieces to thrill the public with technical display.

4. Because the Romantic composer expressed his own feelings and convictions, some music was written without patronage in mind. He wrote to express himself in personal documents of art. These were often experimental in nature and uncompromising so far as public taste was concerned. The last piano sonatas and string quartets of Beethoven and many songs by Schumann and Hugo Wolf are examples of this kind of expression.

5. Social dancing by all segments of society gave the composer a large market for dance music. The great popularity of the waltz made fame and fortune for composers like Johann Strauss and his son and, in addition, aroused the envy of many who may have been artistic successes, but never gained public favor.

6. The Church can no longer be considered a patron of music. There was very little music written for liturgical purposes.

The small amount of sacred music written during this time contained the personal religious feelings and convictions of the composer, expressed in music for the concert hall.

7. The teaching of music became an established profession. Many fine conservatories and schools were founded. A number of prominent performers and composers such as Liszt and Mendelssohn achieved wide recognition as teachers. To meet a pressing need for pedagogical material, composers wrote etudes and other short pieces. Fortunately, many of these works, like the *Etudes* by Chopin, are of a very high level of artistry and form an important segment of the repertory for the piano.

III. Characteristics of Style

Because Romanticism is so personal and so filled with contrasting concepts of music, not all characteristics of style are present in all forms. There are contradictions in style between groups of composers and even within the works of individual composers. There were Romantic idealists and Romantic realists. The idealists were absolutists, who insisted music must exist for its own sake without extramusical devices. The realists were the champions of program music, who believed music could and should tell a story, imitate sounds of nature, or express a visual scene. Preoccupation with literary forms is seen in the importance of the text in solo-song.

There was a contradiction between virtuosity and intimacy. Some Romantic composers excelled in spectacular virtuosity, which was expressed by brilliant technical performances and often by the resources of a vast number of performers. On the other hand, there were those who emphasized the intimacy of miniature forms and delicate textures to express their personal feelings in solo songs, chamber music and lyric piano works. There was also a contrast between nationalism and internationalism. There were composers whose aim was to extol national characteristics and feelings by using folklore, folk songs and dances. There were also Romanticists who avoided nationalistic devices in the search for a universal musical language. Nationalism became very strong in such countries as Russia, Poland, and Bohemia. In Russia a group was organized called the "Russian Five" whose aim was to develop a national music consciousness that would not be dependent upon the Italian or German tradition.

There was one concept that all Romanticists had in common which gave their music a sense of unity: their music was aimed at the evocation of emotion as its primary function. The concept is based on the premise that a feeling of musical tension is necessary to achieve a corresponding intensification of emotional response. All Romantic music, therefore, concerns itself with the problem of achieving this tension. Most Romanticists revolted against the restraints and formalism of the Classic. However, some Romantics, such as Schubert, Mendelssohn and Brahms, cast their Romantic expressions in molds of Classic forms.

1. *Formal Organization*
    a. Musical form was still predicated on the idea of contrasting melodies in the homophonic style, making the sonata still the most important type of formal organization. Rather than two contrasting melodies, there were often contrasting theme groups and sometimes only motives pitted against each other.
    b. In addition to the Classic forms that were still in use, there were free forms, such as the ballad, nocturne, fantasy, etc. These were most common in piano music. The free forms, however, were still based on contrasting themes, but usually without development sections. Sometimes, in the very short preludes or etudes, only one theme or melody might be used with changes in harmony or rhythm for the contrast.
    c. Forms are not precise and clear as in the Classic, but are often overlapping, vague and without strong cadences. Sections and even movements of the longer works often melt one into the other by means of subtle and mild cadential effects, both harmonically and rhythmically.

d. It was a common practice, in the larger forms especially, to use the same thematic material in each movement as a means of maintaining a constant expressive character. This is sometimes called cyclic, or psychological form.

e. Forms are not symmetrical or balanced. Musical phrases and periods often use uneven numbers of measures and different numbers of beats in each measure. Development sections of the sonata form have a tendency to be lengthy. It was here that the composer could use his imagination and ingenuity to best advantage.

f. Folk melodies, or at least folk-style melodies, were used extensively in Romantic music. This was especially true in nationalistic music, but was also a common practice in the music of the Romantic idealists. Folklore was especially popular in Romantic opera, where it was no doubt aimed at arousing enthusiasm among the general public.

2. *Melody*
   a. Romantic melody has a tendency to grow out of harmonic progressions and is less independent than previously. Chromaticism is frequent and helps to create harmonic tension.

   b. Melodies are not stylized as to length or form. They are frequently fragmentary with rhythmic interruptions and irregular phrases. They can also be extremely long, with many deceptive cadences.

   c. Melody is characterized by an intensity of personal feelings. Dynamic climaxes and frequent changes in dynamics serve to build the tension necessary for its expression.

3. *Rhythm*
   a. In the early Romantic, the element of rhythm remained much as it had in the Classic. From about the

middle of the century, however, rhythm comes to be more irregular and more interesting. There are often changes in the number of beats in a measure, cross-rhythms and syncopations.

b. Rhythm is often complex and rhapsodic. It sometimes avoids strong stresses in order to increase the sense of tension, especially in slower movements.

c. Tempo in Romantic music is not always constant. There are frequent indications of changes of speed and the use of tempo rubato and accelerando.

4. *Harmony*

a. Romantic harmony is still tonal, but a much weaker sense of key center was to develop all through the nineteenth century. Almost all the characteristics of harmony during this period show this gradual disintegration of the major-minor system.

b. Tonality was weakened by the fusion of the major and minor modes, using chords typical of one mode in the other.

c. Harmony makes a greater use of chromaticism, non-harmonic tones, altered chords and extensive use of ninth and thirteenth chords. All these devices serve to build harmonic tension, but also weaken the sense of key-center.

d. Strong formal cadences were usually avoided with numerous deceptive cadences to give a harmonic sense of motion and tension.

e. Key-relationships are less formalized than in the Baroque and Classic. Modulation to distant keys and sudden moving in and out of keys for short periods of time also add to tension and to the weakening of a strong feeling for a particular key.

f. Modal harmonization of folk melodies, especially in nationalism, served to open new avenues of harmonic expressiveness.

5. *Texture and Tone Color*

   a. The texture of Romantic music was generally a mixture of the vertical and horizontal elements. Polyphonic texture occurred more as a device than a style, with the lyric quality of the lied as a more dominant stylistic character. Tone-color became an integral part of the melodic and harmonic texture. Melodies were created in terms of tonal coloring with their musical expressiveness identified with specific instruments. Harmonic texture was also influenced by the new orchestration that created new colorings by unusual combinations of instruments and the subdivision of the usual choirs of instruments. A new kind of sonority is possible by such combinations as the subdivision of the higher strings or an expanded brass section.

   b. The texture also can be described as "heavy" with an opaqueness of sound as opposed to the "lighter" and transparent quality of the Classic. Even in works for solo voice, the accompaniment provides a sonority of tonal fabric that serves to blend the voice with the instrument.

   c. In orchestral works the greater number of instrumental parts gives a sense of a richer texture. In addition the texture is made even more sonorous by more subdivisions of instruments than before. For example, Wagner sometimes divides the first violin section into as many as four different parts, etc.

6. *Media*

   a. The piano became the most popular single instrument of the Romantic period because it could run the gamut of all ranges of sound and because it could be played by an individual. It became almost a musical symbol of Romanticism. Moreover, the piano was enlarged to give it a wider range and more tonal power. The instrument reached such heights of popularity that it became the favorite household instrument with every family that could afford it.

b. The orchestra grew to be the favorite large instrument of the century. It had the qualities of bigness, colorfulness and sonority which could create Romantic expression. It had been expanded from the Classic orchestra by the addition of instruments such as the English horn and clarinet, and also by the addition of more brass and percussion. Moreover the virtuosity of the orchestra was increased by technical development of already existing instruments, especially brass and wood winds. Because of its popularity, the orchestra was established as a public institution, supported by its box-office appeal and government subsidies.

c. The solo song with piano accompaniment was also a favorite medium of romantic expression. The voice is also a personalized instrument, for it combines with the literary elements of Romanticism to give an added intensity to the poetic text. Aside from the solo song and opera, vocal music was of minor importance in the period.

d. Opera is a major medium of expression in the Romantic. Combining, as it does, drama, poetry and the visual experience of action, along with music, it is able to make a powerful impression on the emotions of an audience that was truly Romantic. Its popularity can be realized by noting the large number of Romantic operas that are still in the repertory of opera today.

IV. Practice and Performance

1. Dynamics became more explicit than those of the Classic. Subtle shadings of coloring and minute gradations of loudness were indicated by a more definite terminology. Tempi were more accurately designated by the use of the metronome markings.

2. Due to the size and complexity of the orchestra, for the first time the orchestral conductor became a virtuoso. He became a performer whose instrument was gigantic and capable of every Romantic expression. The use of the baton by the conductor took him from the keyboard to the podium.

3. This was the era of massive festival performances. Because of the fondness for sonority and power, an enormous number of participants were often used. Sometimes, as in the case of Berlioz, the large orchestra and chorus were called for by the composer. At other times the usual number of performers were greatly augmented to suit the taste for massed effects. The large festival orchestra and chorus appeared in all countries and is still very popular. There have been many instances in which over a thousand performers have taken part in the performance of a single work.

4. The middle-class love for music-making led to the establishment of the choral society. Folk music, political songs and popular melodies provided the musical fare, but the artistic level was rather shallow. A few such societies made presentations of Handel and Haydn oratorios, but they had little effect on the Romantic quality of their own composers.

5. The art of improvisation was generally discarded in the practice of Romantic music, due to the complexity of its composition and the complete directions for performance. A few individuals, like Chopin and Liszt, continued to make brilliant use of it, but most of the cadenzas were written in a manner to give the effect of improvisation.

V. Instrumental Forms

As has been noted earlier, Romantic music was so individual, so personal that it is impossible to define forms in a manner that will apply to all composers. Any explanation of the stylistic character of specific forms can only be a generalization, for each Romanticist used it as his own creative imagination dictated.

1. *Sonata and Symphony.* The Romantic sonata form is still based on the organization of the Classic sonata. Some composers,

such as Beethoven and Schubert, adhered rather closely to the Classic form, but others, as Mahler and Tchaikovsky, made notable departure from it. During the early years of the Romantic era, the piano sonata retained its popularity. As the century progressed, however, the symphony became the most important sonata form. To it composers could bring more and more sonority, as well as combine music with literary ideas because of its possibilities for realism. In general, themes of a Romantic symphony are more lyric and more contrasted than in the Classic. Modulations are more varied and often without the usual preparation. Because there is less emphasis on balance and logic, there is a more sectional scheme of organization. Unity between movements is often achieved by the cyclic principle of using the same themes, or portions of them, in each movement. While emphasis in the Classic sonata is on the first movement, the Romantic often places its emphasis on the last movement. This is due to the cyclic form in which the climax, or culmination of the thematic material, takes place during the last movement. The minuet is usually replaced by the scherzo movement, a movement that is quicker in tempo and provides more contrast to the second and last movements. The variation-form is frequently used as either the second or the last movement.

> Ex: *Sonata No. 23, Op. 57 (Appassionata)* Beethoven
> *Sonata No. 2, Op. 35,* Chopin
> *Symphony No. 3, Op. 55 (Eroica)* Beethoven
> *Symphony No. 5, Op. 64,* Tchaikovsky

2. *Chamber Music.* The forms of music for chamber ensembles generally followed the forms of the Romantic symphony and sonata. The instrumentation, however, remained much the same as in the Classic period. There was an increased emphasis on virtuosity which demanded a higher degree of professional skill for performance than in the chamber music of Haydn and Mozart.

Ex: *Quartet, No. 16 in F, Op. 135,* Beethoven
      Piano Quintet in E flat, Op. 44, Schumann
      Clarinet Quintet in b, Op. 115, Brahms

3. *Concerto.* The Romantic concerto became more symphonic than its eighteenth century counterpart; technical demands made the solo parts more spectacular. In addition the
solo is much more dependent upon the orchestra for the musical
development. The double exposition of the Classic concerto is
usually abandoned. The Romantic predilection for continuous
movement and cyclic form is also apparent in the solo concerto.

Ex: *Concerto in A minor for Piàno, Op. 54,* Schumann
      Concerto in D for Violin, Op. 77, Brahms

4. *Symphonic Poem.* One of the typical forms of orchestral
program music is the symphonic poem. It was the invention of
Franz Liszt and was sometimes called a tone-poem, especially
when it was based on a poetic idea. The form is in a continuous
movement and is based on the principle of variations on a theme,
or contrasting themes, that are inspired by a program or a literary
idea. It is a metamorphosis, or transformation of themes through
various stages and forms in which the themes retain their
identity.

Ex: *Les Preludes,* Liszt
      Vltava (Moldau), Smetana
      Till Eulenspiegel, Richard Strauss

5. *Concert Overture.* The concert overture is a symphonic
work in the manner of an overture that is not associated with
an opera. In general, the concert overture does not attempt to
tell a story, but creates a mood that can be associated with a
literary theme, a place, or an event. Most works of this nature
adhere closely to the principle of the sonata-allegro.

Ex: *Hebrides Overture,* Mendelssohn
      Academic Festival Overture, Op. 80, Brahms

6. *Ballet.* While the ballet had been a part of opera in the seventeenth and eighteenth centuries, it was not until the Romantic era that it achieved consideration by composers as a unified dramatic form independent of opera. Dramatic expression is achieved by the music and a corresponding dance pantomime, both solo and ensemble, that serves the same purpose as the vocal solo and chorus in opera.

> Ex: *Creatures of Prometheus,* Beethoven
> *Swan Lake,* Tchaikovsky

7. *Symphonic Suite.* The Baroque idea of the suite was revived about the middle of the nineteenth century. However, instead of the traditional scheme of dances, it presents a free succession of contrasting movements, usually national dances or ballet movements. It is sometimes a series of extracts from a ballet, or incidental music to a play and often suggests a series of scenes, or even a story, as in a suite of symphonic poems. It was usually written for orchestra, but also appeared in the literature for piano.

> Ex: *Nutcracker Suite, Op. 71A,* Tchaikovsky
> *Peer Gynt Suite No. 1, Op. 46,* Grieg

8. *Dance Movements.* The nineteenth century saw the rise in importance of stylized dance movements for both the orchestra and solo instruments, especially the piano. Dances of a national character such as the Polonaise, Mazurka, Jota, etc., were used by many composers. Moreover a more general type, Hungarian, Spanish, and Slavonic, was also the basis of many works. These were usually idealized concert versions which are expanded and are not functional for social dancing. Sometimes dance movements which symbolized ideas or events such as the *Danse Macabre* and the *March to the Gallows* gave Romantic composers the opportunity to use realistic devices to intensify the mood or atmosphere.

> Ex: *Polonaise Fantasie, Op. 61,* Chopin
> *Mephisto Waltz,* Liszt
> *Danse Macabre,* Saint-Saens

9. *Rhapsody.* Rhapsody was a term often used in Romantic music to designate a free fantasy on themes of a national or epic character. It is a single movement form with the usual contrasts and Romantic tensions. It appears in the literature for both orchestra and piano, sometimes for a combination of a solo instrument with the orchestra.

> Ex: *Hungarian Rhapsody No. 2,* Liszt
> *Rhapsody in E flat for Piano, Op. 119, No. 4,* Brahms

10. *Variations.* While the variation-form was sometimes used as a movement of a sonata or symphony, it also held a high place as an independent form for both orchestra and piano solo. Variations were created on a pre-existing theme, or on a specially composed melody. Occasionally each variation was made to suggest a particular mood or character of an idea suggested by the theme.

> Ex: *Enigma Variations, Op. 36,* Elgar
> *Variations on a Theme by Handel, Op. 24,* Brahms

11. *Etudes.* A particular form for solo instruments was the etude. Originally it was a study piece designed for the perfection of technique, but was expanded as a concert work with emphasis on a display of virtuosity. Even when it became a concert piece, however, it never lost its function as a study piece. Each etude usually emphasized some particular technical problem. It is in a binary, or a three-part form with the usual tension of contrast and repetition.

> Ex: *Etudes, Op. 25,* Chopin
> *Transcendental Etudes after Paganini for Piano,* Liszt

12. *Occasional Pieces.* There was a wide assortment of descriptive titles attached to short forms that suggested moods or revealed the personal feelings of the composer. They are usually in two- or three-part forms, but sometimes are short enough to have but one section. Some of these forms were called nocturnes, preludes, caprices, serenades, etc. A ballad is usually a longer work that suggests the possible moods of a story without

actually defining a particular sequence of events. In addition, titles suggestive of personalities, scenes, or ideas were often applied to these shorter pieces. There is nothing except the mood and atmosphere to differentiate one from another in a formal manner.

Ex: *Nocturnes,* Chopin
Caprices for Violin, Paganini
Ballad No. 4, Chopin

VI. Vocal Forms

1. *Opera.* Opera provided the best opportunities for all aspects of the Romantic to be combined into a single form. All Romantic opera can be described as an extravagant spectacle with a tendency toward heroic and epic subjects, supernaturalism, mystery and passion. Eighteenth century opera was dominated by the Italian style with its multiplicity of closed forms, but in the nineteenth century, Italy, France and Germany each maintained its own style with special qualities that were indigenous to each. Therefore, it becomes necessary to describe briefly the form of opera in each of these countries.

a. Italian Opera. Early Romantic opera in Italy retained the Neapolitan style with a series of recitatives, arias, duets and choruses without much continuity of dramatic action. Later in the century, mainly under the influence of Verdi, it showed a greater dramatic unity and characterization of personages and events. Plots are often quasi-dramatic, but there is a general improvement in quality. The recitative and aria are still the principal closed forms with melody in the popular bel-canto style and an emphasis on virtuosity. There is also more balance between voice and instruments, but the orchestra still serves as an accompaniment, not as an equal partner.

Another facet of Italian Romantic opera is the movement known as "verismo," or realism. Realism was not limited to music, but was also shown in the choice of libretti that presented subjects from everyday life and depicted people in familiar situations.

Ex: *Lucia di Lammermoor*, Donizetti
La Traviata, Verdi
Tosca, Puccini

b. French Opera. Opera in nineteenth century France
showed some characteristics that were different from
the Italian. During the early part of the century there
was a marked distinction between Grand Opera and
Opéra Comique, but as Romanticism matured the two
styles merged into one. Opéra Comique is generally
distinguished from Grand Opera by use of some
spoken dialogue instead of a continuous musical texture. In addition, it generally was simpler in musical
expressiveness and used fewer characters with very
little chorus. These two styles were compromised in
the French Lyric opera. The theatrical aspect and the
simpler forms of Opéra Comique were combined with
the virtuosity and drama of the Grand Opera. A particular trait in all French opera was the ballet and it
became even more important during the Romantic
era. There is a unity of dramatic action with the music
that is seldom found in the Italian style. There is also
less virtuosity with more emphasis on the lyric quality
of melody. Moreover, French Romantic opera rarely
displays the intensity and passion of either the Italian
or the German but is more moderate in its music and
in its dramatic qualities.

Ex: *The Hugenots*, Meyerbeer
Carmen, Bizet
Pelléas et Mélisande, Debussy

c. German Opera. Opera in Germany presents two significant styles: (1) German Romantic opera and (2)
Music-Drama, the latter conceived and developed by
Richard Wagner. In the Romantic opera the stories
were often based on German legends and folklore with
the mystery of nature and supernatural forces serving
to intensify dramatic expression. Recitatives and arias
are still closed forms and are often based on folk-song

or folk-style melodies. Melodrama, orchestrally accompanied speech, is sometimes used for special effects. The orchestra becomes a powerful instrument in creating atmosphere, moods and even bits of realism. There is also a type of leitmotif in which particular instruments and melodies are used to identify and characterize individuals.

Ex: *Der Freischütz*, Weber

The ideal of music-drama, or the art of the future as it was called by Wagner, was that of an art form in which all the arts would be woven into one cohesive and continuous line of dramatic expression. Wagner continued the German tradition but wrote his own stories, drawing heavily upon German myths and folklore. His libretti are filled with Romantic mysticism and supernaturalism, and almost all are concerned with the concept of redemption through love. There are no closed forms, such as recitative and aria. The vocal line is a continuous melody arising out of an orchestral fabric that is also continuous, without usual cadences. The leitmotif became a unifying device in the sonorous and tension-filled musical texture. The Wagnerian leitmotif is a musical figure that is associated with a particular idea, person, object, mood or situation. Because Wagner uses the orchestra as the main source of dramatic expression, his operas are symphonic in nature. Consequently, it has been possible to have successful concert performances of much of his music without staging and even without the vocal part.

Ex: *Tristan and Isolde*, Wagner
     Parsifal, Wagner

d. Nationalistic Opera. In addition to the Italian, French and German, there were operatic developments in those countries where nationalism was strong, especially in Russia and Bohemia. These operas were also based on folklore or upon events of national significance with nationally important personages. Composers such as Mussorgsky in Russia created works that are highly original with great dramatic power without using the closed forms of the Italian and without imitating Wagner. However, it must be said they are closer to Wagner than to Verdi.

> Ex: *Boris Godunov,* Mussorgsky
> *Bartered Bride,* Smetana

2. *Oratorio.* The Romantic oratorio followed the choral tradition of Handel in the works of Mendelssohn, who added the melodic, harmonic and tonal qualities of the Romantic style. While there were very few who wrote in the Protestant tradition, there were many composers who set quasi-religious stories that were full of mysticism and Catholic symbolism to music in the manner of the oratorio. These were sometimes referred to as hybrid forms, for they are not opera, oratorios or cantatas. The orchestra generally plays a more important role, with the chorus and soloists becoming only a musical device in a symphonically conceived work. Both Liszt and Berlioz wrote a number of compositions in this fashion for performance in the concert hall.

> Ex: *Elijah,* Mendelssohn
> *L'Enfance du Christ,* Berlioz
> *La Damoiselle élue,* Debussy

3. *Sacred Choral Music.* There was very little music, written for liturgical purposes in the Romantic period. However, composers wrote Te Deums, Requiems, Beatitudes, etc., for voices and instruments. Again the emphasis was usually on the symphonic ideal rather than on the vocal qualities. These are heard most often in the concert hall, but could be used in the Church for special occasions.

> Ex: *Te Deum,* Verdi
> *German Requiem,* Brahms
> *Mass in F,* Bruckner

4. *Secular Choral Music*. While there was a great wealth of secular choral music written in the nineteenth century, only a few important works have survived and most of these are for voices and orchestra. Some composers, like Beethoven, Liszt and Mahler, used the chorus as a part of the symphonic form.

Ex: *Symphony No. 9, Op. 125*, (*choral*) Beethoven
     Song of Destiny, Brahms

5. *Lied*. The solo song occupied an important place in Romantic music. Romantic poetry was combined with the voice and piano in a highly personal and subjective musical expression. There were two basic types of formal organization used in these works namely (1) strophic plan and (2) composed-throughout. The latter has more possibilities for Romantic expression because every poetic idea can have its own music counterpart. The piano created and sustained the mood of each poem and is more of an equal partner than merely an accompaniment to supply rhythm and harmony for the vocal line. German composers set poems by such writers as Heine, Schiller and Goethe, poets who epitomized the Romantic spirit. The song cycle is a series of songs to poems by a single poet which are related by a central idea, or theme. Schubert, Schumann, Brahms and Hugo Wolf were the most important composers of the German lied. While the German lied holds the prominent place in song literature, both the French and the Russians also fostered a song literature of high quality. The French especially were helped by the French Romantic poets to create songs of exceptional lyric beauty.

Ex: *Dichterliebe*, Schumann
     Winterreise, Schubert
     Without Sun, Songs and Dances of Earth, Mussorgsky
     Five Poems of Charles Baudelaire, Debussy

VII. Important Composers

1. Beethoven, Ludwig van (1770-1827) has been listed among the composers of the Classic style, but it is as a Ro-

manticist that his greatest compositions were conceived. Born in Bonn, Germany, Beethoven displayed strong musical gifts as a child. He suffered at the hands of his father who hoped he could mold the young talent into a prodigy like Mozart. The incompetence of his father as a manager and as the head of the family finally caused Beethoven to become the sole support of his family. His gifts as a pianist, organist, violinist and composer won him an official position at the Bonn Court where he remained until 1792 when he left for Vienna, where he was to live the rest of his life. While he was first known in Vienna as a brilliant pianist a slowly developing deafness caused him to abandon performance for composition. He was the first composer in music history to live independent of the exclusive patronage of the aristocracy and to make a comfortable living from the sale of his compositions.

His life is generally divided into three periods. The first, as a pianist composer ends about 1802. Compositions from this period hold the seeds of Romanticism, but are still cast in the molds of the Classic tradition of Mozart and Haydn. The second period of maturity ends about 1814 and reveals his development as a complete Romanticist. The third and last period is somewhat of an enigma. Here Beethoven seemed to be breaking the bounds, even of Romanticism, by becoming more introspective, more profoundly spiritual, more improvisational and even recalling the contrapuntal style of the Baroque.

Beethoven was largely responsible for freeing music from the restraints of Classicism and for leading the way to individualism and subjective feeling in music. He made important contributions to the literature of every media of musical expression, especially the symphony and the string quartet. His works became models for his contemporaries as well as the later composers. Almost all of the Romanticists found justification in Beethoven for their own individualism of style. His main contributions can be summed up as follows: (1) He showed a remarkable economy of material in the sonata form that led the way to the cyclic type of multiple forms; (2) His themes were often constructed from short motives that were gradually built up and expanded into full length lyric melodies; (3) He raised the piano to a high level of use and Romantic expression; (4) He showed a polyphonic grasp of thematic development; (5) Dissonance became a functional part of his harmonic structure; (6) He achieved a new fluency in modulation that opened new possibilities of harmonic contrast and interest; (7) He changed and expanded the traditional forms of the sonata and symphony to accommodate his thematic material and expressive purpose, rather than making his material fit the forms.

Beethoven's works include nine symphonies, numerous overtures, five piano concertos, one violin concerto, thirty-two piano sonatas, twenty-one sets of variations for piano, ten violin sonatas, sixteen string quartets, nine piano trios, an opera, *Fidelio,* an oratorio, *Christ on the Mount of Olives* and the great *Missa Solemnis.* In addition to the foregoing major works there are a number of songs, miscellaneous chamber music and a number of compositions for various solo instruments. If one were to select a few works that stand out more firmly as monuments to his creative genius, the following would certainly be included: *Symphonies No. 3, Op. 55 in E flat (Eroica); No. 5, Op. 67 in C minor, No. 9, Op. 125 in D minor (Choral); String Quartets. Op. 95 in F minor and Op. 127 in E Flat; The Emperor Concerto* for Piano and Orchestra, *Op. 73 in E flat; Piano Sonatas Op. 13 in C minor (Pathetique)* and *Op. 57 in F minor (Appassionata); The Missa Solemnis, Op. 123 in D minor;* the opera *Fidelio.*

2. Paganini, Niccolò (1782-1840) was the first of the great instrumental virtuosi of the nineteenth century. An Italian violinist, he developed a spectacular technique that enabled him to dazzle his audiences. In addition, his innate showmanship gave him an almost hypnotic power over his listeners. His compositions consist mainly of virtuoso etudes for violin and a brilliant violin concerto. He had a profound effect on many Romantic composers, especially Schumann, and Liszt who tried to adapt Paganini's concepts of virtuosity to the piano.

3. Weber, Carl Maria (von) (1786-1826) was the founder of the German Romantic school of opera. His father was an amateur musician and also the director of a traveling theatrical

group. No doubt this environment helped to stimulate young Weber's imagination as a dramatic composer. He was something of a child prodigy, learning the piano and violin at an early age and also having his first piano works published at the age of 12. His important posts as a mature musician were as Capellmeister at Prague and as Director of the Opera at Dresden. In addition to his fame as a composer, he was well-known as a brilliant pianist and conductor, the first to use a baton and become a performer on the orchestra. While he composed in almost every media, his best works are for piano and the stage. The piano works are brilliant concert pieces with emphasis on virtuosity and, with the exception of the *Invitation to the Dance*, are seldom performed today. His opera *Der Freischütz* is based on a German folk tale that dwells on supernatural phenomenon, and reveals the sentimentality of middle class personages. While Weber broke with the Italian operatic tradition, he still used arias in the Italian manner. It was the chorus effects, the orchestral tonal coloring, and the stories that made the operas typically German. He suggests the later leitmotif of Wagner in identifying moods and ideas in a musical manner. The overture became a collection of the important melodies of the opera, serving as a sort of preview of what was to come. His most important operas are *Der Freischütz, Euryanthe,* and *Oberon.* The latter was first produced in England a few months before his death in 1826.

4. Rossini, Gioacchino (1792-1868) was one of the most brilliant of the early Italian Romantic opera composers. He exhibited a remarkable flow of melody in the bel canto tradition. This combined with brilliant orchestration, dynamic rhythms and clear-cut phrases made his operas popular all through Europe. One of his notable devices of orchestration was the use of crescendo by means of numerous repetitions of a phrase, adding instruments and increasing the degree of loudness with each repetition. Rossini was at his best in opera buffa and his principal works in this form are *La Gazza Ladra, L' Italiana in Algeri* and *Il Barbiere di Siviglia.* The latter became his most popular opera and was produced in almost every opera house of Europe.

5. Schubert, Franz (1797-1828) is the only Viennese composer to claim that city as his birthplace. His early musical train-

ing was as a member of the Vienna Court singers and as a student in the "Convict," a training school for the singers. Here he learned to play the violin and studied theory, as well as singing. When his voice "broke" he had to leave the school. For a time he held a post as an elementary school teacher, but gave it up after three years. After this brief period of teaching, Schubert's life was illustrative of a kind of Bohemianism often associated with the Romantic spirit. He was one of the few composers to live in poverty. He never held a position as a musician in either an institution or in an aristocratic household. Moreover, he did not even have the security of a benevolent patronage nor a steady income from the sale of his works. He eked out a precarious existence as a private tutor, sold a few compositions to publishers and had a few commissions for works. The greatest portion of his works can be ascribed to art for art's sake. His early death at the age of 31 was unquestionably hastened by actual poverty. While Schubert's piano, chamber and orchestral works are significant contributions to the literature of music, it is in the art songs that his expression of Romanticism reaches its height. The outstanding qualities of his music are his lyric melodies and harmonic coloring. Moreover, in his lieder there is a musical sensitivity to the poetic expression that makes Schubert's songs among the finest in all vocal literature. His piano works, chamber music and orchestral works are generally classic in their formal organization. The Romantic element lies in the substance of melody and harmony.

Schubert composed over 600 songs, nine symphonies, twenty-two piano sonatas, seventeen operas, six masses, about thirty-five chamber music works and numerous occasional pieces for orchestra and also for solo instruments. It is only Schubert's operas that have failed to gain recognition. Some of his best songs can be found in the two song cycles, *Die Schöne Müllerin* and *Die Winterreise*. Of his symphonies the *Unfinished, No. 8 in B minor* and the *C major, No. 9* are the best-known. The *Quartet in D minor (Death and the Maiden)*, the *Quintet in A major, Op. 144* and the *Piano Trio in B flat, Op. 99* hold a high place in the literature for chamber music. The *Piano Sonatas in C minor and B flat* are his finest works for this instrument.

6. Donizetti, Gaetano (1797-1848) was one of the most prolific of the Italian opera composers. Donizetti's music is notable for its remarkable melodies, by means of which he could express the whole gamut of emotions. Actually his harmony, rhythm and orchestration are at times tedious, but it is his talent for melody and stagecraft that caught the public's favor and served to keep many of his works popular to this day. While he wrote a vast amount of instrumental music, cantatas and church music, his operas are all that have survived. The best of these are *Lucia di Lammermoor* and the comic operas *La Fille du régiment* (The Daughter of the Regiment) and *Don Pasquale*.

7. Bellini, Vincenzo (1801-1835) is remembered for his gift of melody like all Italian opera composers. More reserved in range of expression than Donizetti, Bellini was exceedingly adept in psychological characterization. The Romantic element lies mainly in his sentimental melodies rather than in the tension of harmony and sonority of sound. All of his operas were of a serious nature and the more important works are *Norma, La Sonnambula* (The Sleepwalker), and *I Puritana* (The Puritan).

8. Berlioz, Hector (1803-1869) was one of the first of the recognized composers who did not come from a musical family, or at least a strong musical background. His father was a doctor and young Berlioz was also destined for a medical career. However, his interest in music gained the upper hand and he deserted medical studies in Paris in favor of composition. Berlioz never became a proficient performer on any instrument, nor was he a practicing musician in professional sense. His only musical post was a music librarian at the Paris Conservatory. In effect he was a free-lance composer-conductor, writing music and then arranging concerts for its performance. He wrote only in the larger forms of the overture, symphony and opera, composing virtually nothing for solo instruments or chamber music.

Berlioz was a pioneer in the area of symphonic program music. He developed the idée fixe, a recurring melody or theme that identifies programmatic ideas, persons, etc., in a purely musical manner. His most famous programmatic symphony is the *Symphonie Fantastique*. Berlioz was a master of orchestration, bringing new orchestral colors and even new sounds into the orchestral fabric. He also enlarged his orchestra to almost gigantic proportions, even planning a work for an orchestra of 465 performers. His technic of orchestration and instrumentation was set forth in his *Treatise of Instrumentation and Orchestration* published in 1844, a book which served as a dictionary of orchestration until well into the twentieth century. Berlioz was also a musical journalist, a career that enabled him to actively campaign in behalf of the Romantic ideals in opposition to the conservatism of Classicism.

His important works, in addition to the *Symphonie Fantastique* are: *Harold in Italy*, for solo viola and orchestra; *Romeo and Juliet*, for solo voices, chorus and orchestra; *The Dammnation of Faust*, a concert opera; *A Requiem Mass* and the *Childhood of Christ* for solo voice, chorus and orchestra. In addition he wrote a number of concert overtures, of which the *Roman Carnival* and *Benvenuto Cellini* are still frequently performed.

9. Mendelssohn-Bartholdy, Felix (1809-1847) was the son of a wealthy banker and the grandson of a famous philosopher. He was also fortunate in being surrounded with the finest opportunities for becoming a musician, for he had the wealth for unlimited study and a highly cultivated cultural and social background. He became a proficient concert pianist as well as a competent composer. His most important position was as Director of the Royal Conservatory in Leipzig, which he founded, and as Conductor of the Gewandhaus Orchestra, also in Leipzig. He was widely traveled and his music became very popular in many countries, especially in England. Among his other accomplishments, Mendelssohn was largely responsible for the Romantic revival of interest in the works of J. S. Bach. Mendelssohn's music is closely allied to the Classic traditions in form, the Romantic element showing in his melodies and imagination of orchestral coloring. His music has little of the passion and vio-

lence of Romanticism, but almost always expresses a serenity and a sentimentality that had a wide audience appeal.

Mendelssohn wrote a great deal of music in his short life, but his fame rests largely on his works for piano, orchestra, and two oratorios, *Elijah* and *St. Paul.* Among the orchestral works the music to *Midsummer Night's Dream, The Hebrides Overture, The Scottish* and *Italian Symphonies* are the most often performed. His *Violin Concerto in E minor* has remained a classic in violin literature. His finest large work for piano is the *Variations Serieuses in D, op. 54.* Other popular Romantic piano pieces are the *48 Songs Without Words.* The oratorio *Elijah* is perhaps the finest Romantic oratorio and was written especially for performance in England.

10. Chopin, Frederic (1810-1849) was born in Warsaw, Poland, but left his native land at the age of twenty and spent the rest of his short but creative life in Paris. He composed almost exclusively for the piano and was most successful in the shorter forms of occasional pieces such as the etude, nocturne, impromptu, mazurka and polonaise. He exploited the melodic and harmonic possibilities of the piano to a greater degree than any other composer. He concentrated on melody which he decorated with delicate and graceful passages of coloratura. He also made daring harmonic innovations with enharmonic modulations and new dissonances which often prolonged harmonic tension far beyond that of his contemporaries. Moreover, Chopin enhanced the harmonic texture of piano music by a skillful use of the pedal to increase the number of tones in a chord. He was also responsible for the development of the left-hand figuration based upon tenths rather than the fifth and octave of the Alberti bass.

Chopin's music is often associated with Polish nationalism. The *Polonaise* and *Mazurka* represent this facet of his creative output. Setting aside the larger forms as being of lesser importance, it is the *24 Preludes,* the *Impromptus,* the *Waltzes* and the *Ballads* that hold the interest of present-day pianists and their audiences.

11. Schumann, Robert (1810-1856) was the son of a book-seller, a circumstance that brought him into close contact with the writings of the new Romantic movement during his forma-tive years. After a period of law study and an unsuccessful attempt to become a concert pianist he turned his efforts toward composition and musical journalism. He founded and became editor of the *Neue Zeitschrift für Musik,* a journal devoted to musical criticism. He also taught for a time at the Leipzig Con-servatory and was Musical Director at Düsseldorf. However, organized musical activity was not congenial to his nature and he devoted most of his time to writing, composing and to con-cert tours with his wife, Clara Wieck, who was the first prom-inent woman concert pianist. Schumann suffered from a mental disorder and, after attempting suicide, was confined to an asylum where he died in 1856.

Schumann, more than other composer, became the spokes-man for the revolt against Classicism and the champion for revolutionary tendencies in music. In addition, he became the ardent supporter of such men as Chopin and Brahms and it was through his writing that much of their music became known to the concert world. His compositional efforts cover the range of music from opera through piano works and solo song. It is in the smaller forms that he is most successful. While the sym-phonies, piano concerto and some chamber works are still re-tained in the repertory, it is generally recognized that Schumann did not have the craftsmanship to mold the larger forms success-fully. Schumann's music can be characterized by its lyric melody, its vague and imaginative formal structure and its remarkable range of expression from the most tender to the heights of pas-sion. He showed his interest in Bach by using contrapuntal de-vices within the framework of Romantic harmony. His piano music is very idiomatic, making full use of the harmonic and tonal possibilities of the instrument. He had a Romantic pre-dilection for suggesting poetic titles for many of his piano and orchestral works, but admitted that the music was always com-posed before the title was attached. In the lieder he is second only to Schubert. The piano plays an almost equal role with the voice in the songs, since he often used the piano as a commentary on the vocal melody to suggest and sustain the mood of the poem in a kind of musical prologue and epilogue. His major works include a large number of songs of which the love songs are perhaps the best. The cycle *Dichterliebe* on poems by Heine represents the finest of these. The piano music includes the *Concerto in A minor, Carnival, Kreisleriana, Papillons,* the *Symphonic Etudes* and many other short forms. Also important are the four symphonies and numerous chamber music works.

12. Liszt, Franz (1811-1886) was one of the most fascinating of the Romantic personalities. As a virtuoso pianist-composer he left the imprint of his virtuosity and sentimental Romanticism on almost all subsequent pianists. Born in Hungary, he studied in Vienna and then in Paris where he became known as a concert pianist. He later settled in Weimar, Germany, where he devoted the major portion of his energies to composing and teaching with only an occasional concert tour. Liszt was deeply impressed by the virtuosity of the great Italian violinist Paganini and tried to do for piano technic what Paganini had done for the violin. In addition, he inaugurated the recital as a popular form of musical presentation. Liszt was also a popularizer of music and made innumerable transcriptions for the piano of all sorts of music from Beethoven symphonies to Schubert lieder. As a Romantic realist, Liszt was a champion of program music and was responsible for the invention of the symphonic poem. His orchestral music gives the effect of an extravagant theatrical style with a wide range of emotion from tender sentimentality to intense passion. To gain these effects he used a large orchestra and followed the lead of Berlioz in colorful orchestration.

Liszt's piano music contains brilliant technical passages, chromaticisms, sentimental melodies, and a vague sense of organization. The outstanding piano works by Liszt are *The Concerto in E flat major, The Sonata in B Minor, The Hungarian Rhapsodies, Mephisto Waltz, The Transcendental Etudes,* and numerous short virtuoso pieces. While Liszt's orchestral music has less appeal today than in the nineteenth century, the Symphonic Poems, *Les Preludes* and *Mazeppa* are the most often programmed by present-day orchestras.

13. Wagner, Richard (1813-1883), one of the most controversial figures in music history, was the arch-Romanticist of the nineteenth century. Raised in a theatrical atmosphere by his stepfather who was an actor and playwright, young Wagner's musical training was rather desultory. However, his ambition to be a conductor and a theatrical composer finally brought him conducting posts with provincial orchestras. Filled with ambition, he went to Paris where he hoped to rival the success of Meyerbeer. After a disastrous three years in Paris he finally returned to Germany. The Paris years, however, saw the completion of the operas *Rienzi* and the *Flying Dutchman,* both of which were finally produced in Dresden, but Wagner became embroiled in the revolutionary movements of the time and was forced to flee Germany.

He was to spend the next twelve years in exile, living most of the time in Switzerland. It was during these years that he formulated his theories about the opera, writing a number of essays on aesthetics, the most important of which was *Oper und Drama.* It was in this essay that he set forth the idea that the ideal art-form would be equal portions of music, drama, poetry and stagecraft. He called this art form the music-drama (the art of the future). One of the important results of his new theories was the beginning of the *Ring of the Nibelungen,* a gigantic saga of four operas to be given on successive nights: *Das Rheingold, Die Valküre, Siegfried,* and *Gotterdämmerung.* Drawing heavily on German and Norse mythology and based on the idea of redemption through love, the *Ring* is the longest and most complicated dramatic work ever to be successfully staged. The whole cycle was to take more than twenty years to complete.

In 1864 Wagner was invited to Munich by the young King Ludwig of Bavaria and it was here that *Tristan and Isolde* was first produced. Because of Wagner's expensive tastes, the drain on the Bavarian treasury was too great and he was forced to leave the country. He then moved to Lucerne, Switzerland, where he wrote *Die Meistersinger*. The *Ring* was finished in 1874. Wagner had long dreamed of a theater especially constructed for his own works and finally in Bayreuth, in Northern Bavaria, such a theater was built with revolving stage, sunken orchestra pit and every device of stage mechanics possible at that time. In 1876 the first performance of the *Ring* took place in this theater, which has since become a mecca for lovers of Wagnerian opera. His last opera was *Parsifal*, a quasi-religious drama based on the story of the Holy Grail. He died in Venice in 1883.

Critics of Wagner were usually either violently opposed to his theories and music or were ardent partisans in his struggle for recognition. As a man, he was a supreme egotist. As one writer has put it: "Wagner thought of himself as the world's greatest composer, poet, dramatist, philosopher and politician, and remarkably, he was very nearly all of these."

Wagner's musical style reveals the Romantic ideal at its greatest intensity. A few of the most important devices he used to achieve his Romantic expressiveness follow. (1) He used the leitmotif to identify people, objects, ideas, and emotions in his music-dramas. In addition to serving as a unifying device, it also convinces the listener of the reality of his Romantic illusions. (2) Wagner's music-dramas were through-composed, rather than being made up of closed forms of recitatives and arias. (3) He carried the dissolution of tonality to the very edge of atonality by the use of chromatic harmonies and vague cadences. This tendency is especially prevalent in *Tristan and Isolde*, in which he achieved climaxes of great power and tension. (4) The orchestra carries the burden of dramatic expression, thus making his operas predominately symphonic in nature. (5) Consequently, he enlarged the orchestra by adding instruments and subdividing the normal sections. This gave him a new range of tonal coloring that made it possible to reach new heights of orchestral tensions.

14. Verdi, Giuseppe (1813-1901) is the greatest figure in the history of Italian opera. He was no revolutionist like Wagner, for he never departed completely from the traditions of the closed forms of recitative and aria. He enriched the long established forms with superb melodies, dramatic scenes, and an instinctive sensitivity for the theater. Some of his earlier works were tinged with nationalism and succeeded in stirring up the patriotism of Italians for their own freedom and unity as a nation. Verdi's position as a nationalist was further enhanced by a brief period as an elected member of the Italian Parliament. His operas cover a wide range of subjects from the Egyptian story of *Aida* through the dramas of Shakespeare. With the exception of the *Requiem*, his nontheatrical works are of lesser importance. Verdi's more important operas are *Macbeth*, *Rigoletto*, *Il Trovatore*, *La Traviata*, *Un Ballo in Maschera* (A Masked Ball), *La Forza del Destino* (Force of Destiny), *Don Carlos*, *Aida*, *Otello* and *Falstaff*. All of these works are still prominent in the repertory of opera companies.

15. Gounod, Charles (1818-1893) was a French composer who is best known for his operas and for his Romantic sacred music in the Catholic tradition. His most famous works are the operas *Faust* and *Romeo and Juliette*. Both of these remain in the opera repertory of today. *Faust* was first composed as a lyric opera with spoken dialogue and was later reworked in its present form with recitatives and arias. Gounod's music is filled with sentimental lyricism and a type of mild Romanticism that was imitated by many lesser talents of his time.

16. Franck, César (1822-1880) was a Belgian organist and composer whose musical style is that of French Romanticism. He lived in Paris where he was an organist, choirmaster, and teacher of such composers as D'Indy and Chausson. His music reveals a polyphonic treatment of Romantic melody and a harmonic substance comparable to that of Wagner. There is an air of Romantic mysticism in almost all of his works. He was one of the few Romantics to write extensively for the organ, but his religious music is climaxed by the oratorio, *Les Beatitudes*. He

is best known for the *Symphony in D minor,* a *String Quartet,* and a *Violin Sonata in A major.* He also wrote a number of works for piano, including the *Symphonic Variations for Piano and Orchestra.*

17. Smetana, Bedřich (Friedrich) (1824-1884) is considered the father of Czech music. An ardent nationalist, he wrote a long orchestral work called *My Fatherland,* consisting of six symphonic poems depicting scenes from the life and history of Bohemia. The *Vltava* is the most successful of this cycle. Smetana was a disciple of Liszt and his symphonic poems are modeled after those of Liszt. A *Quartet in E minor* (From my Life) and an opera, the *Bartered Bride,* are his best known works in each of these media.

18. Bruckner, Anton (1824-1896) was an Austrian composer whose symphonic style, serious and profound, permeates everything he wrote. An organist and a deeply religious man, Bruckner wrote a number of religious works for the Catholic church, including a *Te Deum* and three *Masses.* His nine symphonies make up his major works and are marked by their great length and a rather massive tonal structure. There is also a kind of religious mysticism about all of his works, especially in the slow movements. He used song-like themes as a basis for the symphonic forms and achieved great climaxes by using them in a choral-like manner with instrumentations that suggest a full organ sound. Bruckner is looked upon as a nationalist in his native Austria.

19. Brahms, Johannes (1833-1897) was born in Hamburg, Germany, and began the study of the piano at the age of eight. By the time he was thirteen he was playing the piano in taverns to help supplement the meager income of his family. After a period of teaching and concertizing he moved to Vienna in 1863, where he was to remain until his death in 1897. While he held minor positions as director of various choral societies, he was never interested in a permanent position, but preferred to remain as an independent free-lance composer.

It was Schumann who called attention to Brahms' genius as a composer in an essay in the *Neue Zeitschrift für Musik*. Stylistically, Brahms is Romantic in his emotional expressiveness, but more Classic in his formal organization. He is sometimes referred to as a Neo-Classicist because of his devotion to the principles of the Classic sonata and the polyphonic treatment of his musical materials. He was an absolutist, writing no program music in the Romantic sense of the term. Brahms often used a motif as a basis for an entire movement, or even a complete symphony. His orchestration is always full, giving a massive kind of musical sound. Rhythmically, Brahms is exceedingly complex, using cross-rhythms with numerous shifting of accents and metric patterns. He is best known for his four symphonies: *No. 1 in C minor* (*op. 68*), *No. 2 in D major* (*op. 73*), *No. 3 in F major* (*op. 90*) and *No. 4 in E minor* (*op. 98*). Other important works are the *Violin Concerto in D major* (*op. 77*), the *Piano Concerto in B flat major* (*op. 83*), a substantial amount of chamber music, and the *German Requiem,* (*op. 45*), In addition he wrote a number of songs, *The Song of Destiny* (*op. 54*), the *Alto Rhapsody,* (*op. 53*) for chorus and orchestra.

20. Bizet, Georges (1838-1875) was one of the first French composers to be influenced by Wagner. Perhaps this influence was responsible for the failure of his earlier works, for the French generally were not sympathetic towards the Wagnerian style. Bizet's fame rests almost solely on *Carmen* which was a failure when it was first performed in 1875. In *Carmen* Bizet introduced realism into French opera. Wagnerian influences are apparent in such devices as the "death motive," but Bizet was also original in the vivacity of the music and the psychological characterizations. *Carmen* has become the most popular opera of all times. Bizet also achieved some success with incidental music to *L'Arlésienne,* a play by Daudet, but most of his music gained popularity only after his death.

21. Mussorgsky, Modest (1839-1881) was an ardent Russian nationalist and a member of the "five," a group which was dedicated to the development of a Russian style, independent of

German and Italian influences. Other members of the "five" included Balakirev, Cui, Borodin, and Rimsky-Korsakov. Mussorgsky was untutored in the basic theory of music, but possessed a great genius for creative expression. He never held a musical post, but spent most of his life as a government clerk and his early death was probably hastened by malnutrition and excessive use of alcohol. His greatest works are in the medium of song and opera, although his *Pictures at an Exhibition* for piano, and *A Night on the Bald Mountain*, a programmatic work for orchestra, have retained their popularity. His greatest gift was his ability to translate the inflection of speech into dramatic, passionate, and poetic melody. His most famous opera is *Boris Godunov* in which he created a nationalistic music-drama. Divorced from the Italian operatic tradition and yet not imitative of Wagner, *Boris Godunov* is truly an original work that had great influence on many non-Russian composers. Because Mussorgsky was unskilled as an orchestrator, his operas and orchestral music were revised and orchestrated by Rimsky-Korsakov and it was in this version that they were first introduced to the European audiences.

22. Tchaikovsky, Piotor (Peter) Ilyitch (1840-1893) embarked on a course of law study and entered government service, but gave it up at the age of twenty-three and turned to music. After only two years of intensive study he was appointed professor of composition at the Moscow Conservatory. While Tchaikovsky is associated with the Russian spirit in music, and emotionally was a nationalist, he was not a member of the "five" because he also wrote in the style of Schumann and Berlioz. His melodies are lyric with a tinge of the Slavic modal harmonies that identify them with Russian folk song. His music is sentimental and sometimes even trivial. Nevertheless, it has a directness and a range of emotional expression that has a wide appeal to all audiences. He is best known for the *Fourth, Fifth* and *Sixth* (*Pathétique*) *Symphonies*, the *Overture, Romeo and Juliet,* the *Nutcracker Suite,* the *First Piano Concerto in B flat minor,* and the ballet, *Swan Lake. Eugene Onegin,* one of two operas, is still in the operatic repertory.

23. Dvořák, Antonin (1841-1904) was another Czech nationalist. He first gained recognition through his Slavonic orchestral dances and later turned to symphonies and chamber music. His style is closer to that of Brahms, although there are suggestions of Wagnerian harmonies in his music. His best known work is the *Symphony No. 5 in E minor*, better known as the *New World Symphony*, written during a sojourn in the United States where he had come to be the Artistic Director of the National Conservatory in New York. The *New World* is based on themes that suggest Negro folk tunes, although Dvořák denied any conscious use of such material. Other works that remain alive in music literature are an overture,*Carneval, Concerto for Cello, American String Quartet, Stabat Mater,* and a number of songs.

24. Grieg, Edvard (1843-1907) was a Norwegian nationalist who wrote in the traditional style of the German Romantics inasmuch as he was trained under the influence of Mendelssohn and Schumann. However, he was successful in adapting the German style to the modal melodies and harmonies of Norwegian folk song and dances. The result was a literature of lyricism with freshness and charm. Grieg's important large works include the incidental music to *Peer Gynt* and the famous *Piano Concerto in A minor*. The special charm of his music, however, is found in the shorter works; songs, dances, and the many *Lyric Pieces* for the piano.

25. Rimsky-Korsakov, Nikolay (1844-1908) was a member of the "Russian Five" and has been credited with writing the first Russian Symphony. He was a naval officer and a self-taught musician. In spite of his lack of formal training he was appointed Professor of Instrumentation and Composition at the St. Petersburg Conservatory, a position which he held until his death. His music utilizes the true Russian folk-idiom and oriental melodic patterns. His musical output is not large, mainly because he gave a great deal of his time to revising and orchestrating the works of his friends, especially Mussorgsky. Rimsky-Korsakov's best operas are *Pskovityanka* (The Maid of Pskov), *Sniegurotchka* (Snow Maiden), and *Le Coq d'or* (The Golden

Cockerel). His orchestral works include *Scheherazade* and *Sadko*. The latter is the first Russian tone poem. Rimsky-Korsakov is also author of a textbook on orchestration, *Foundations of Orchestration,* and an autobiography, *The Chronicle of My Musical Life.*

26. *Puccini, Giacomo* (1858-1924) was the most famous and successful Italian opera composer after Verdi. He was a notable representative of the so-called "verismo style," a style which dealt with realistic subjects from everyday life and used a kind of melodramatic recitative with less emphasis on traditional subjects and forms. He was skillful in the technique of the theater and his operas contain a kind of Romantic sentimentality that caused them to rival Verdi's in popularity. Puccini's most successful operas are *Manon Lescaut, La Bohème, Tosca, Madame Butterfly,* and *Turandot.*

27. Wolf, Hugo (1860-1903) was an Austrian composer who represents the Wagnerian influence on the lied. His complex contrapuntal texture and chromatic harmony give his songs a tension and expressiveness not unlike the music of *Tristan and Isolde.* Moreover, Wolf had the capacity for a deep insight into the poetic spirit of the text. On hearing his lieder, one feels the text to be the dominant element, with melody and harmony subordinate. He uses the piano to intensify the dramatic element and not as a mere accompaniment. While he also wrote an opera and some instrumental works, it is for his more than 300 lieder that he is remembered. Many of his lieder were published posthumously and some still are unpublished.

28. Mahler, Gustav (1860-1911) was an Austrian and the last great composer of the Viennese Romantic style. He held various positions as a conductor, including the directorship of the Vienna Court Opera, the Metropolitan Opera and the New York Philharmonic Society. Mahler's symphonies (he completed nine) are dramatically conceived, colossal tone-paintings. His scores call for enormous orchestral resources comparable to those used by Berlioz. Mahler was also a skillful and imaginative orchestrator, devising new sounds and even special tunings for

strings to achieve dramatic effects. Using song as melodic material with solo voice and choral groups, his symphonies were sometimes expanded into choral works symphonically conceived. He frequently attached programmatic notes, or poetic quotations to his scores to suggest a feeling or a mood. Mahler's most important works are *Symphony No. 1 in D major; Symphony No. 2 in C minor; Symphony No. 8 in E flat major,* called the *Symphony of a Thousand* because of its great number of participants; *Lied von der Erde* (Song of the Earth) for tenor, contralto and orchestra, and *Des Knaben Wunderhorn* (The Youth's Magic Horn) a cycle of ten songs with orchestra.

29. Debussy, Claude (1862-1918) a French composer, was the leading figure of the Impressionistic movement in music, the most influential development of nineteenth century French music. Impressionism was an antirealistic movement that originated first in the fields of painting and poetry. In addition to being antirealistic, it was anticlassical; even its Romantic qualities were milder, and avoided the violence and passion of the earlier Romanticists. It was concerned with vague and transitory suggestions to evoke moods and "atmosphere." Debussy was one whose music was directly influenced by painting and literature, for he was greatly stimulated by the paintings of Monet and the poetry of Verlaine and Mallarmé. He tried to suggest the same kind of feeling as his colleagues in painting and poetry. He sought to express the shimmering effects of light and shade in painting by tone-color and chordal structure in music, sacrificing lyric melody, traditional forms and polyphonic complexities for suggestive harmonic progressions. In order to achieve a more luminous tonal coloring he destroyed the traditional function of the successive scale steps by the use of the whole-tone scale where each note has a subtle persuasion all its own. Debussy also added to musical vagueness by weakening his cadences with parallel chordal progressions.

Debussy's first important impressionistic work for orchestra is the *Prélude à l' après-midi d' un faune* (An Afternoon of a Faun), followed by *Nocturnes,* and *La Mer* (The Sea). An opera

Pelléas et Mélisande is almost a music drama with a restrained music expression to create the emotional atmosphere of Maeterlinck's drama. In addition he wrote a *String Quartet* and a number of interesting pieces for piano including *24 Preludes* including the famous *Cathédrale engloutie* (The Sunken Cathedral).

30. Strauss, Richard (1864-1949) was one of the last of the Romantic realists. Like a number of the late nineteenth century composers he was also distinguished as a conductor, both in opera and in the concert hall. It is as a composer, however, that he made his greatest musical impact for he was one of the virtuosi of orchestral writing. Strauss was a disciple of Liszt, Berlioz and Wagner, adapting their realistic methods and devices to his own uses. After a few early works in the forms of the sonata, quartet and symphony, he turned to program music for his expression. His realism is sometimes subjective in that he attached ideas and states of feeling to melodic and harmonic ideas as in the symphonic poem, *Tod und Verklärung* (Death and Transfiguration) for which he had the poet Ritter compose a poem to illustrate the music. On the other hand he used realism in a descriptive manner by suggesting scenes, movements and actual sounds of life and nature, as in the *Alpine Symphony* where he employs a wind machine and a thunder machine to portray a storm scene. Strauss' realism covers a wide range of subjects from the humorous to the hysteric.

His music is brilliantly orchestrated with dramatic and sweeping sonorities that are marked by strong harmonic dissonances and sharp contrasts in tonal coloring. He makes use of parallel chord progressions and arbitrary dissonances that obscure tonality but do not deny it. Moreover, he uses a contrapuntal fabric that ignored the traditional intervallic relationships between the moving parts that are pushed relentlessly to their climactic conclusions.

While Strauss' earlier works were mainly symphonic poems, he also made an imposing contribution to opera. His first opera of note was *Salome,* based on the text of Oscar Wilde, an opera that shocked the public of the 1900's more by its subject than its music. *Electra,* on the other hand, used sharp dissonances and strong tonal color to characterize the decadent story of hate and sordid revenge. *Der Rosenkavalier,* a comic opera written in 1911, is more Classic in its form, but still infused with the lyric sentimentality of Romanticism. While he lived almost to the middle of the twentieth century, his period of creative greatness seemed to end with *Der Rosenkavalier.* The best of his symphonic poems are *Don Juan; Till Eulenspiegel's lustige Streiche; Tod und Verklärung; Ein Heldenleben,* (A Hero's Life); *Also Sprach Zarathustra,* and *Don Quixote* (a variation for cello and orchestra). In spite of Strauss' seeming preoccupation with the larger forms of program music, a number of fine songs comprise a distinct contribution to song literature.

31. Sibelius, Jean (1865-1957) was the most important Finnish composer of the late nineteenth and early twentieth century. His style remained deeply rooted in the nineteenth century Romantic tradition. He consciously carried out a program of nationalistic musical expression, basing much of his thematic material on Finnish folk song idiom though never employing the folk melodies literally. The great preponderance of his works are for orchestra. Besides seven symphonies in the classic-romantic tradition, his most typical nationalistic orchestral compositions are the tone-poems based on Finnish legend, history and landscape. Among his best know works in this genre are *Finlandia, En Saga,* and *Pohjala's Daughter.*

VIII. Other Composers

Germany and Austria

    Hoffman, E. T. A. (1776-1822)
    Hummel, Johann (1778-1837)
    Spohr, Ludwig (1784-1859)
    Czerny, Carl (1791-1857)
    Meyerbeer, Giacomo (1791-1864)
    Marschner, Heinrich (1795-1861)
    Loewe, Karl (1796-1869)
    Lortzing, Albert (1801-1851)

Strauss, Johann (Sr.) (1804-1849)
Nicolai, Otto (1810-1849)
Franz, Robert (1815-1892)
Strauss, Johann (Jr.) (1825-1899)
Humperdinck, Engelbert (1854-1921)
Reger, Max (1873-1916)

Italy

Clementi, Muzio (1752-1832)
Spontini, Gasparo (1774-1851)
Boito, Arrigo (1842-1918)
Leoncavallo, Ruggiero (1858-1919)
Mascagni, Pietro (1863-1945)
Busoni, Ferrucio (1866-1924)
Wolf-Ferrari, Ermanno (1876-1948)

France

Boieldieu, François-Adrien (1775-1834)
Auber, Daniel-François-Esprit (1782-1871)
Offenbach, Jacques (1819-1880)
Vieuxtemps, Henri (1820-1881)
Lalo, Edouard (1823-1892)
Saint-Saëns, Camille (1835-1921)
Delibes, Leo (1836-1891)
Chabrier, Emmanuel (1841-1894)
Massenet, Jules (1842-1912)
Fauré, Gabriel (1845-1924)
D'Indy, Vincent (1851-1931)
Chausson, Ernest (1855-1899)
Charpentier, Gustave (1860-1956)
Dukas, Paul (1865-1935)

Russia

Glinka, Mikhail (1804-1857)
Rubenstein, Anton (1829-1894)
Borodin, Alexander (1833-1887)
Cui, Cesar (1835-1918)
Balakirev, Mily (1837-1910)
Scriabin, Alexander (1872-1915)
Rachmaninoff, Sergey (1873-1943)

England
  Field, John (1782-1837)
  Sullivan, Sir Arthur (1842-1900)
  Elgar, Sir Edward (1857-1934)
  Scott, Cyril (1879-

United States
  Foote, Arthur (1853-1937)
  Chadwick, George (1854-1931)
  Kelley, Edgar Stillman (1857-1944)
  MacDowell, Edward (1861-1908)
  Hadley, Henry (1871-1937)

Spain
  Albeniz, Isaac (1860-1909)

Poland
  Wieniawski, Henri (1835-1880)
  Paderewski, Ignace (1860-1941)

IX. and X.　Important Writers on Music

There was a wide variety of writings on musical subjects in the nineteenth century that can be placed in the following catagories: 1. music theory, 2. criticism, 3. history and biography, 4. aesthetics.

The teaching of music outgrew the old apprenticeship method, partly because of the large number of nonprofessionals who became interested in the processes and techniques of musical composition. Moreover, it was in conservatory and university classes that much of the music theory was taught. To meet the growing demand for a systematic approach to theory, manuals of harmony, counterpoint, form, composition and orchestration were written.

The art of musical criticism won the attention of many writers including the composers themselves. With a less sophisticated audience than in the eighteenth century there was an interest in, and a need for, interpretations and evaluations of musical works and their performances. Evaluations of music were made not only of the contemporary but also of the older composers. In addition the rise of the virtuoso performer made his performance noteworthy and reviews of his performance had a profound effect on his box-office appeal.

The most famous journals that served as sounding boards for critical writings were the *Allgemeine Musikalische Zeitung* published in Leipzig, the *Neue Zeitschrift für Musik* founded by Schumann in 1834 in Leipzig, and the *Gazette Musicale* published in Paris.

With history becoming a science and with the romantic cult of personality, both history and biography became important areas of literary efforts. The science of musicology was systematized in the late nineteenth century, a science that led to authoritative editions of older composers and definitive biographies of composers and performers.

The Romantic period, as we have seen, was a time of conflicting theories and ideas about what music could and should express. Writers on aesthetics argued the pros and cons of the various opinions regarding music. This was especially true of the conflict between program and absolute music and the new theories of opera.

1. Hoffman, Ernst Theodore Amadeus (1776-1822) was a German writer and composer. He espoused the romantic ideal of the union of the arts and wrote poetic and romantic appraisals of such composers as Mozart and Beethoven. He used the pen name of Johannes Kreisler (made famous by Schumann's Kreisleriana). His critical writings were published in the *Allgemeine Musikalische Zeitung*.

2. Fetis, François (1784-1871) was a Belgian music theorist and historian. While he wrote a number of theoretical treatises, his most famous work is the monumental *Biographie universelle des musiciens et bibliographie generale de la musique* in eight volumes, Paris, 1833-1844. This was the first fairly complete dictionary of musicians and still serves as a prime source for some composers.

3. Berlioz, Hector (1803-1869) wrote the first important treatise on orchestration, *Traite d' instrumentation et orchestration modernes,* Paris, 1844 (Treatise on instrumentation and orchestration, New York, 1948). This work remained a standard textbook on the subject until fairly recent times. In addition Berlioz made frequent contributions of critical essays to the *Gazette Musicale* and published a book of essays on orchestral music, *Les Soirees de l' orchestre,* Paris, 1853 (Evenings in the orchestra, New York: 1956).

4. Coussemaker, Walter (1805-1876) was a French music historian who wrote a number of important works on early music. His interest in ancient documents led to a number of valuable collections of early music. His major work is *Scriptorum de musica medii,* Paris, 1864-1876 (Writings of Medieval Music).

5. Schumann, Robert (1810-1856) was the founder and editor of the *Neue Zeitschrift für Musik,* published in Leipzig. His writings were militant essays propagandizing the new Romantic ideals. In the imaginary *Davidsbündler* (Society of David) the different facets of his own romantic personality were represented by the characters of Florestan and Eusebius, names he often used in signing his essays. Schumann was also the first composer to recognize the genius of Chopin and Brahms, writing enthusiastic criticisms of their music.

6. Liszt, Franz (1811-1866) also made numerous contributions to the literature about music as a critic, as a commentator on the current musical scene, and as a champion of the "modern" style of his day. He wrote a series of articles "On the Position of Artists" in which he discussed the social consciousness of composers and performers. He also wrote on church music, calling for a return to the function of music as a spiritual force.

7. Wagner, Richard (1813-1883) was the most prolific writer on music of all the Romantic composers, both in the area of aesthetics and criticism. In addition to being the author of libretti for his own operas, Wagner wrote essays and pamphlets on a variety of musical subjects. Of special significance were his writings on the problems of opera. *Oper und Drama,* Leip-

zig, 1851, outlined his theories of the "artwork-of-the-future."
His autobiography also set forth his ideas on the union of the
arts and his own thoughts on almost everything from music to
politics. He also wrote an important essay, *Religion and Art*,
that was a counterpart of his opera *Parsifal*.

8. Ambros, August Wilhelm (1816-1876) was an eminent
German historian and musicologist. His *Geschichte der Musik*,
Leipzig, 1862, was one of the first music histories that tried to
draw a parallel between developments in music and the developments in the visual arts.

9. Grove, Sir George (1820-1900) was an English historian
and musicologist. His chief claim to fame as a writer on music
is the *Dictionary of Music* and *Musicians* in four volumes, London, 1879-1889, a work that has gone through many editions and
revisions, the latest in 1954 expanded to nine volumes.

10. Helmholz, Herman von (1821-1894) was a German
scientist and an expert on acoustics. His *Lehre von den Tonemp-
findungen als physiologische Grundlage für die Theorie der
Musik*, Brunswick, 1863 (On the Sensations of Tone as a Physiological Basis for the Theory of Music, New York, 1948), laid the
foundation for modern research in the physical and physiological
aspects of musical sound and hearing. He based his work on experimentation, but drew heavily upon the researches of Rameau
and Tartini.

11. Hanslick, Eduard (1825-1904) was the most famous of
the romantic critics and aestheticians in the field of music.
While he was born in Prague, he lived most of his life in Vienna.
Hanslick was a champion of absolutism in music and his book
*Vom Musikalischen Schönen: ein Beitrage zur Revision der
Aesthetik der Tonkunst*, Leipzig, 1854 (On the Beautiful in
Music; a Contribution to the Revision of Musical Aesthetics, New
York, 1957) is his most notable work. It has been translated into
many languages, including English. In this work Hanslick argued
that the beauty of a musical composition lay wholly in
the music itself, without extramusical ideas. His opposition
to the new school of Romantic realism led to his criticism of

Wagner, Liszt, Berlioz and the other programmatic composers. In retaliation Wagner caricatured Hanslick in the character of Beckmesser in *Die Meistersinger*, a distinction that led to an undeserved lack of appreciation of Hanslick's writings. While he opposed the Wagnerian group, he wrote glowing accounts of Schumann and Brahms who represented the more classic facets of Romanticism.

12. Chrysander, Karl Franz (1826-1901) was a German music historian and critic. He shared in the editing of the monumental collection of music, *Denkmäler der Tonkunst*, five volumes, Leipzig, 1869-1871. Chrysander is best known, however, for his writings on the life and works of Handel. He started the Deutsche Handelgesellschaft (German Handel Society) and wrote a definitive biography of Handel published in Leipzig in 1858-1867.

13. Prout, Ebenezer (1835-1909) was an English theorist and teacher. He was the author of numerous textbooks on theory including harmony, counterpoint, fugue, and musical form. His text on orchestration went through many editions and has been used as a handbook of instrumentation until well into the twentieth century.

14. Riemann, Hugo (1849-1919) was a German musicologist who is generally credited with systematizing the science of musicology. He led the way in a stylistic study of types and periods of music, a specialization that has resulted in a wealth of authoritative studies by present day musicology. The list of Riemann's writings is long, but most significant is the *Musiklexikon*, Leipzig, 1882, a work that is recognized as a standard reference in music. It has gone through many editions, the latest in 1959.

15. d'Indy, Vincent (1851-1931) was one of the few successful composers to write a text on the art of musical composition, *Cours de Composition Musicales*, Paris, 1903-33 (Course of Musical Composition). A student of César Franck, d'Indy also wrote an authoritative biography of the Belgian master.

XI. Suggested Readings

XII. Further References

Abraham, Gerald. *A Hundred Years of Music*. New York: Knopf, 1938.

Barzun, Jacques. *Berlioz and the Romantic Century*. New York: Little, Brown, 1950. (2 vols.).

Chase, Gilbert. *America's Music*. New York: McGraw-Hill, 1955.

Courcy, G. I. C. de *Paganini*. Norman: University of Oklahoma Press, 1957.

Grout, D. J. *A Short History of Opera*. New York: Columbia University Press, 1947.

Locke, Arthur, W. *Music and the Romantic Movement in France*. New York: E. P. Dutton, 1920.

Newman, Ernest. *The Wagner Operas*. New York: Knopf, 1949.

Praz, Mario. *The Romantic Agony*. New York: Oxford, 1951.

Rolland, Romain. *Jean Christophe*. New York: Modern Library Ed. 1938.

Thayer, A. W. *Life of Ludwig van Beethoven*. Princeton: Princeton University Press, 1964.

Wagner, Richard. *Prose Works*. tr. W. A. Ellis, London: 1892-1899. (8 vols.)

Zetlin, Mikhail O. *The Five, the Revolution of the Russian School of Music*. New York: International Universities Press, 1959.

The New York Philharmonic and Music Director Leonard Bernstein, performing for a national audience over the CBS Television Network. Photo by Roy Stevens.

Chapter

8

༄༅

Twentieth
Century

I. Sociocultural Influences on Music

The transition from nineteenth century Romanticism to twentieth century "modernism" is, perhaps, as violent an upheaval in musical thought as was the transition from the ars antiqua to the ars nova, or from the Renaissance to the Baroque. As in the earlier revolutions, the seeds of the new are already to be found in the dissolution of the old. The audible results of this musical revolution show as wide a difference with nineteenth century and earlier musical ideas as the technological phenomena of the nuclear age differ from those of the nineteenth century. The attainment of these results has been an orderly and evolutionary one.

Because the speed of twentieth century attainments in all areas has been so accelerated, music subjected to this same acceleration has moved from one new idea to another with such rapidity that no previous era can be compared with the diversity and extremes of its expressions. The search for originality on the part of every composer has led to extremes of expression, reversion to past historical styles, neoclassicism, neoromanticism, serial composition, electronic music, microtonal music, music concrete, even "post" serial and aleatory music. The insistence on originality is so compelling that its end results often appear questionable.

The sociocultural influences which affect music are many and varied, but the annihilation of space through the application of the technological results of scientific discovery is probably the basic influence on musical creativity and production.

1. The basic scientific research already begun in the nineteenth century and continued into the twentieth led to a number of discoveries and inventions which influenced man's relationships beyond all previous imagination. The invention of methods of rapid sound communication such as the telephone and telegraph in the nineteenth century led to the further development of sound transmission and resulted in the perfection of radio, phonograph, tape recording and television, all of which have had and are having a vital effect on music. By the middle of the twentieth century, music has not only become available to almost every human being in civilized society but in many instances has become a constant accompaniment at all waking and even sleeping hours. It is now possible to have musical performance at every social activity. Music from the banal to the most esoteric, from all periods of history, music performed by all types of performers, is at the command of almost any individual through one of the modern means of transmission. Such a plethora of musical experience was never at the disposal of the wealthiest patron, secular or religious, in the past. The standard of living of western Europe and America makes it possible for almost everyone to have at his disposal one or more of the machines which perform recorded music.

2. Commercial exploitation of music through recorded media and through management of performers has had a marked influence on the course of musical composition. Because of the natural lag between the composer and the general public as the patron, the overwhelming mass of music published and distributed via the concert stage tends to emphasize the compositions of the past three hundred years. As a consequence there is a very limited audience for the contemporary composer who deviates from the tradition of the last three centuries and whose music is not likely to be "immediately acceptable." In fact, such

a limited audience is probably made up primarily of other musicians or those who through special training are capable of some understanding of the new music. As a result modern composers are often accused of writing only for the musical elite.

3. Availability of musical performance through recorded media has also been of great influence on the performance of music. Phonograph, tape, and film recordings in the possession of the individual and in use by radio, motion picture and television have been vital factors in the technological displacement of thousands of musicians. Except for a relatively few persons the pursuit of a musical career in performance must be combined with other occupations. The general employment of orchestral, chamber music, and solo performers of the nineteenth century is no longer in evidence. Even though "live" performances are still given, rapid transportation reduces the number of performers used since a few virtuosi performers are readily available. Consequently a relatively few performers can supply the needs of many concert stages, opera houses and orchestras as soloists and conductors. The emphasis on economic and artistic success tends to make these performers devote their attention to those works which are acceptable to a wide general public. Few performing artists and conductors are interested in promoting the works of living composers, and those who are must restrict their interests in the face of managerial and public pressure. There are exceptions among performers and managers, but these remain in the minority. Whereas the aristocratic patron of the eighteenth century expected his chapelmaster to compose and perform new works continuously, the twentieth century patron, the general public, expects the performer to perform little or nothing of the works of the contemporary composer who remains a "silent partner" in the musical act. It is possible that artists and managers underestimate the ability of the general public to consume modern works. A more venturesome policy might open up the concert field to the contemporary composer.

4. The invention of electric instruments for musical reproduction has also led to the invention of electronic sound producing instruments. Such instruments since 1950 have engaged

a number of composers in experimentation with not only an entirely new field of sound complexes but also entirely new possibilities in "composing" these sounds. Rhythmic complexities completely beyond the possibility of human realization are comparatively easy to achieve on electronic instruments. In addition to these instruments directly manipulated by composers are the electronic computers which invite the possibility of automatic musical composition. Programmed computers have already been used to "compose" music.

5. Two great political revolutions, that of communism and that of fascism, have made deep impressions on musical composition in the twentieth century. Fascism in Italy and its nazi counterpart in Germany were comparatively short lived. In their most virulent forms nazism and fascism, as well as communism, damned all nontraditional creativity as decadent and typical of the inherent weakness of western democratic society. For almost twenty years the healthy creativity of Germany and Italy was carried on only by exiled composers who fled their native lands mainly to the United States. Since the end of the second world war there has been a very active resurgence of creative life in these countries. In the Soviet Union, however, as in most of the countries behind the iron curtain, new tendencies in musical creativity have been more or less successfully repressed. Composition tends to follow traditional lines despite the progressive claims of a revolutionary political ideal. As a result composers of the Soviet and its satellites have continued the traditional nationalistic trends of the nineteenth century. A noticeable break in this traditional trend has been the very productive output of "avant-garde" Polish composers as well as increased performance of contemporary western composers in the Soviet Union and its satellites.

6. The democratization of the educational systems. of most of the world, and the general adoption of compulsory schooling in almost all modern nations, have led to the inclusion of music as an academic discipline. In the European and to some degree in the American universities, the increasing emphasis upon research activities has led to the collection and publication of vast

amounts of music of the past and historical data concerning it. Musicologists in competition with researchers in other branches of the humanities have devoted themselves almost exclusively to the historical aspects of music. The deciphering of old manuscripts, the editing of old treatises concerning all phases of music, the publication of complete editions of composers and large anthologies concerned with various schools, areas of musical performance, or merely geographical location, have given the twentieth century man an available source of music of the past such as never before existed. Research has been extended into the field of recordings making historical editions in notes and sound available to everyone. In great measure this accounts for the active revival of popular interest in music of the past, particularly the Baroque, whose special appeal was to the amateur.

7. A somewhat subtle environmental factor of the twentieth century has also made its influence felt on musical composition. It is obvious that modern man lives in an environment which is much more acoustically disturbing than that of any past era. The noise of modern life has increased many-fold even during this century. Automobiles, tractors, airplanes, mechanical construction machines, office machinery, factory machinery, etc., have brought about a high level of nervous tension which expects and demands a high level of acoustical stimulus in all forms of communication. Whereas speakers less than fifty years ago addressed large audiences without the aid of public address systems, present day speakers find it necessary to address an even limited audience in acoustically adequate halls through loud speaker systems. This raising of the sound level has affected music as well. While orchestras and ensembles are not necessarily larger, the tone level of the individual instruments, and the quality of tone called for, often tend to be strident, piercing and in many respects like that delivered over electric reproducing machines. Composers today are not unmindful of the fact that it is through the medium of recorded sound that they have the greatest opportunity to reach their audience. Consequently they compose with recording in mind. This leads to

the manipulation of the recording devices, microphones, etc., which control and change the original sound to meet the needs of present day acoustical levels.

8. A corollary of the previous phenomenon is the fact that to many listeners recorded music is much more acoustically satisfactory than that of most large concert halls. Moreover recorded music makes it unnecessary for the listener to discommode himself in attending a concert or opera even if within reach. As a result there are many avid music lovers who rarely hear music "in the flesh." Recordings are capable of almost perfect technical performance since all mistakes can be erased and repaired through editing, cutting and splicing of the original tape. What this means to the human factor in music remains to be seen. It undoubtedly leads the composer to expect a "perfect" performance despite all difficulties in the composition.

9. The possession of a high degree of technical proficiency by the performing artist is also the common expectation of both the composer and listener. Since the number of needed performers has declined so drastically in the last thirty years it is to be expected that only the most technically proficient will survive. Performance skill has reached such a high level that composers have no hesitation in writing what seems to be music exclusively for the virtuoso.

II. Function of Music

The commercial aspects of music distribution along with new media of musical communication have led to great changes in the function of music in the twentieth century.

1. The organized concert series in large and small urban centers is a purely twentieth century phenomenon. The availability of any and all performing artists in comparatively remote areas encourages large audiences for a season of "star" performances. The composer is more and more at the mercy of a shrinking number of performers who through managerial pressure feel the necessity of emphasizing the traditional works to satisfy a

large but often undiscriminating audience. Such concerts have their positive value in that they undoubtedly have raised the musical taste of the general public from that of the past century. Programs are likely to contain a great preponderance of highly valuable standard literature. It remains to be seen whether this raising of taste will eventually bring about a desire to hear the compositions of living composers.

2. Music for the twentieth century phenomenon, the motion picture, is an outlet for living composers, particularly since the advent of the sound picture. Nowhere, however, is the effect of mass audience more clearly discernible than in this function. After almost sixty years of motion picture music, thirty of which have been in the form of recorded performance, there have been exceedingly few pieces of music that might be said to be distinguished as artistically noteworthy. Neither incidental motion picture music nor that which is written for a "musical" picture has distinguished itself. Even those films which have won distinction as highly artistic works, and for which competent composers have written very successful scores, indicate that writing music for films is really a task of incidental character. In one sense the ideal of Wagner's thesis that music and drama should be a synthesis is more nearly achieved in the best of motion pictures than in the musical dramas of Wagner where music dominated.

3. A great part of the world's population is constantly bombarded with musical sounds from recordings and radio. Such performances are to be heard in all one's waking surroundings, the home, the market, the office, the factory, the playground, the sports field, etc. These areas, however, afford no outlet to the serious composer. In fact this function of music is largely psychological, affording an antidote for the multifarious sounds that surround humans at all times. The kind of music played has no intent to raise or lower public taste. A negative result is the fact that it induces the hearer to pay little or no direct attention and makes him, therefore, a less discriminating listener.

4. The Church, except in a very few isolated instances, is even more cut off from the contemporary composer than ever before. Composers of stature are rarely commissioned or em-

ployed by the Church. Most choir directors find contemporary religious music too difficult for amateur choirs to perform. While there have been many movements in Catholic and Protestant churches to raise the quality of the music used in the service, these have resulted only in the revival of much of the fine music of the past, especially the sacred repertoire of the Baroque and Renaissance, and even earlier periods.

5. Festivals and concerts sponsored by institutions and societies organized expressly for the purpose of presenting the works of contemporary composers provide one of the most important opportunities for composers to have their works heard. Some of the more important organizations which have sponsored such series or festivals are the International Society for Contemporary Music, the Sessions-Copland Concerts of New York, the annual Donnaueschingen Festival of Contemporary Music, Musica Viva of Munich, Louisville Symphony Association and many others.

6. There has been a continued tendency to employ composers as teachers in the musical institutes and universities in all countries. In many instances such positions are announced as "composers in residence" and parallel the situation in the Renaissance and Baroque periods when the composers were attached to both small and large courts. The functions of the composer and his music in these situations is twofold. He provides instruction through precept and example to those who wish to engage in the creative effort, and he provides musical fare whereby the general university community can experience the idiom of the contemporary composer.

7. While the opera still functions as an important means of reaching a large public, its activity varies greatly from country to country. Whereas central Europe has a tremendously active opera life, the United States is restricted to short seasons in two or three centers. Moreover, the opera houses everywhere tend to function as museums for musical dramatic works rather than as places where the public is introduced to new and vital compositions. A less esoteric but often much more dynamic form of musical theater is that furnished by the Broadway musicale and the ballet. The latter is a modern development of a traditional form.

The former is a descendant of the opéra comique and the operetta, but with a distinctive American flavor that has commanded attention in many world centers, even in the European opera houses of long established tradition. It seems to satisfy the desire for a more sophisticated type of musical dramatic entertainment than that provided by the traditional sentimental operetta of the nineteenth century.

III. Characteristics of Style

The break with the nineteenth century was felt as a compelling necessity by most of the twentieth century composers. Musical techniques employed to achieve the realistic, impressionistic, and nationalistic ends of the previous century had been pushed about as far as possible. The composer felt the necessity of finding new ways to say new things. Musically this meant that melody, harmony, rhythm, and tone quality must be reassessed and studied.

Two answers to the composers' search for new ways to say new things presented themselves: discover more tonal material than the twelve tones of the octave with which to build, or find new principles of construction with the old material. The first answer gives rise to attempts at splitting the octave into smaller intervals than the twelve half steps. This device, called microtonality, was attempted by a few composers but has had no significant adherents. A further attempt to find new material is the use of electronic machines to create tones freed from any tonal relationships as definite as microtonality. The second answer, that of finding new principles of construction, has involved most of the composers of the twentieth century to date.

1. *Formal organization.*
    a. Perhaps the most significant characteristic of twentieth century formal organization is the recognition of the variation principle as basic in musical composition.
    b. One of the most acceptable of the new devices of formal organization is the so-called twelve-tone or

dodecaphonic method of composition. This system, later called serial composition, used the twelve chromatic tones as independent entities without reference to a tonal center. The composition was based on a set pattern of the twelve tones called the tone row, repeated continuously throughout the work in many varied forms. The basic row is subjected to the various forms of contrapuntal treatment traditionally used to secure variety in imitation, inversion, retrograde, retrograde inversion (cancrizans), augmentation, diminution. Moreover the tone row could be transposed to any of the twelve levels of the chromatic scale. In more advanced serial composition the "series" might consist of less than the entire twelve tones, and might even be a rhythmic or tonal pattern. The basic device of the serial technique is, of course, nothing more than a construction of a tonal pattern (of twelve or less notes) and the continuous variation of this construction.

c. There is a tendency toward brevity in all new musical composition. Thematic structures give way to motival elements. Long, spun out themes are displaced by short epigrammatic motives. All musical elements are tightly organized.

d. True repetition and contrast are used less frequently than before. Literal repetition is used for expressive purposes, not for formal organization. Repetition actually becomes variation.

e. The desire for brevity and economy of means tends to eliminate or at least shorten such formal structures as bridge passages, modulatory sections, dissolution of thematic material, closing sections, etc.

2. *Melody.*

a. Melody is completely dominated by the instrumental idiom, whether for voice or instrument. The melodic line is often subjected to wide intervallic skips and a high degree of rhythmic complexity. In addition it is often placed in unusual vocal and instrumental range in order to make use of extreme tonal qaulities.

b. Vocal melody is subjected to contours that are expressive of the text even to the extent of losing specific tonal designation as in the technique of "sprechstimme."

c. Melody loses symmetrical form of phrase and period. There is a tendency to form a melody from short motival fragments.

d. The consecutive notes of a melodic line are often spread over several octaves and given to different instruments rather than contained within the range of a single instrument.

e. The general tendency to write in a contrapuntal style lessens the importance of melody as a dominating vehicle for the musical material. Even in works which use a solo voice or instrument, the solo part becomes one of the lines of the contrapuntal fabric rather than a dominating melodic line.

3. *Rhythm.*

a. Rhythms are characteristically irregular and asymmetrical. Much use is made of odd numbered metric patterns — five, seven, eleven.

b. Rhythmic irregularity also consists in the use of several different rhythms simultaneously (polyrhythms), and in the rapid succession of changing rhythms as for example 5/4 followed by 3/8, 2/4, 7/8, etc.

c. Rhythm is emphasized to the point where a total composition or at least parts of a work are made up of rhythmically exploited sonorities which are lacking in melodic significance and harmonic purpose.

d. Free rhythms such as were found in medieval and Renaissance music are once more used. Bar lines are often omitted.

e. Metric designations are often limited to the designation of only the unit of measure, quarter note, eighth note, half note, etc., without designating the number of notes to a metric unit.

4. *Harmony.*

a. Twentieth century harmony is recognized as being much more dissonant than that of previous eras. Those intervals which were considered dissonant in the harmonic practice of the eighteenth and nineteenth centuries are now used with great freedom.

b. In music which still adheres to the tradition of tonality these dissonant harmonies, while much more freely used, are still recognized as dissonants and are eventually subjected to resolution even if delayed for long periods in the course of a composition.

c. In twentieth century music which does not adhere to the tradition of tonality, music which is often referred to as "atonal," the distinction between dissonance and consonance is purely academic and ceases to exist in actuality. Harmony is recognized as a relationship of all the tones to one another rather than the relationship of all the tones to a single central one. Under such circumstances all relationships are possible and usable. There is no hierarchy of dissonance and consonance.

d. Traditional harmony has extended its use of dissonance through several devices. One is the use of bitonality and eventually polytonality, the use of two or more tonal centers at the same time.

e. Another device is the traditional construction of harmony on nontraditional scale patterns. Such scale patterns derive from medieval modes, folk scales, and arbitrarily constructed ones.

f. A technique midway between "atonal" and tonally dissonant harmony is achieved by the use of nonharmonic tones. Such usage also leads to a greater or less degree of dissonance.

5. *Texture.*

   a. Contrapuntal texture is most often employed by twentieth century composers, especially the twelve tone composers.

   b. With those composers who write in a neo-romantic style the texture, both harmonic and contrapuntal, is inclined to be very thick and heavy. Full, rich, chordal structure derived from the tendency to achieve a "modern" style through the use of dissonance is achieved by contrapuntal and harmonic style.

   c. Twelve tone and serial composers exploit a thin, almost ephemeral, contrapuntal texture in which notated silences tend to play as important a part as the notated sounds.

   d. Contrapuntal practice is not restricted to a counterpoint of individual melodic lines, but often extends in ensemble and orchestral works to a counterpoint of rhythms in which several rhythmic patterns are used simultaneously; a counterpoint of tonal qaulities in which various groupings of instruments and sound sources are pitted against one another; a counterpoint of complete and somewhat independent compositions in which each of several individual groups engage in a simultaneous presentation of individual material.

6. *Media.*

   a. While compositions using large forces are still written, there is a marked tendency to use small ensembles in which unusual combinations are specified. A kind of heterophony of tonal color is achieved by the contrast of widely differing tonal colors in combination.

   b. The revival of instruments which have long been obsolete or infrequently used in art music is common. Such instruments as the harpsichord, the guitar, the mandolin, and a great list of percussion instruments such as the xylophone and tuned drums are often used.

c. Electric devices and electrically constructed instruments have been added to the performing media. These instruments often act as substitutes for existing instruments, but some use has been made of them as new media of sound production.

d. Wind instruments are used more often in solo and choir form.

e. In ensembles there is a tendency to combine wind instruments and string instruments in more nearly equal numbers.

f. The voice is often combined with instruments as an integral part of an ensemble, and is exploited to give a greater variety of tonal color.

g. The percussion instruments receive greater attention with their number and types greatly increased.

h. Traditional tonal qualities of the traditional instruments are distorted in the attempt to gain new color. This has been especially true in jazz music.

IV. Practice and Performance

1. Notational and dynamic directions are increasingly specific. The performer is given very explicit directions as to tempi, dynamics, expression and even tonal quality. Many of the directions are found in the vernacular rather than in traditional Italian, and indicate the attempt to communicate even more clearly than before.

2. The rise of jazz as a vehicle for the creative (improvisatory) expression of the performer is a marked and important phenomenon of the middle of the twentieth century. Such spontaneous creativity varies from the decoration of a cantus firmus taken from the popular song literature to completely original improvisatory performance.

3. In all musical performance including that of old or new music, emphasis on perfection of performance calls for superlative technical proficiency. The possibility of recording a work with near perfection due to the techniques of recording establishes a criteria for all performance that eliminates all but the exceptional virtuosi from the public concert or operatic stage.

4. The criteria established by the high standard of instrumental and vocal performance also makes such technical considerations as purity of tone, intonation, and technical clarity of first rank in the evaluation of musical performance. While virtuosity is no longer a leading element in the musical enjoyment of performance it is a sine qua non of all performers, and as such is taken for granted.

5. Amateur performance is replaced in large measure by perfectionist performances of a recorded nature. Amateur performance has declined in somewhat the same way that letter writing has declined with the widespread use of telephonic and telegraphic communication.

6. The tendency toward perfection and definitiveness leads to the revival of old instruments in the performance of the literature of past eras. Among those instruments which have been most successfully revived are the harpsichord, recorder, baroque organ, classic guitar (lute) and a variety of old string instruments, notably several forms of viols.

V. Instrumental Forms

Two dogmatic statements can be made about the formal construction of twentieth century music. First, it represents a return to classic insistence on formal construction as the central element of musical expression. Second, there is no form which is peculiar or unique to the twentieth century. These statements hold true for the many styles of composition of the past fifty years. As a result composers in the area of instrumental music return to the classic forms of the sonata and sonata-allegro as the central ideal of contemporary instrumental composition. The composite sonata with its sonata-allegro form movement takes on many changes in the hands of modern composers. The old symmetry of phrase, period, and sections gives way to a balance which is based on calculated psychological principles. While composers have retained the traditional terminology of the classic era it must be realized that new schemes of formal organization, melody, harmony, rhythm, texture, and tone quality have given them a new meaning and character.

1. *Sonata and Symphony*. The composite sonata presents the modern composer with the principal vehicle for extended instrumental composition whether these are for solo, chamber ensemble (string quartet) or orchestral (symphony) media. In its most typical contemporary style it is a constructivist piece in which brevity is emphasized. Such brevity is achieved by reducing the recapitulation section of the sonata-allegro form, by use of fragmentary motives rather than extended themes, by avoiding repetition except in extremely varied form, by omitting transition and bridge passages between motival statements, and by reducing the instrumentation to its barest minimum. Often the whole sonata is found in a reduced number of movements if not in a single movement, with several related sections in differing tempos and moods. In some instances the juxtaposition of movements of the composite form and the mixing of the composite movements with sections of the sonata-allegro form are used to achieve new formal constructions.

While the strict harmonic relationship of tonic and dominant which dictated the formal structure of the classic sonata is no longer valid, this principle is still suggested in the modern sonata. This relationship or tension can be realized in a multitude of ways outside the harmonic realm and the twentieth century composers have experimented and continued to experiment with such devices.

Those works labeled as sonatas embrace the many neoclassical instrumental works for piano as well as those for single melodic instrument with keyboard. The idiom and style vary from composer to composer. The technical difficulties posed for the performer also vary greatly from the works which come under the type of "gebrauchsmusik" to those which obviously are meant exclusively for concert performance. The former were written with the amateur and student musician in mind while the latter require proficiency of the highest grade.

Due to its essential classicism, chamber music affords the twentieth century composer one of the prime areas of musical expression. Outside the adoption of the general principles of contemporary music, composers of chamber music have gone far in using newly conceived combinations of instruments and voice in their works. The traditional string quartet is still frequently employed as well as several other classic combinations, but there has been a great amount of writing for groups of from two to fifteen performers in which not only the standard instruments of all families have been combined, but often rarely used instruments have been incorporated. Percussion instruments of all kinds, especially those with tuned bars, are frequently used. Instruments rarely used in recent times have been reinstated in the chamber ensemble. The inclusion of the voice in small ensembles has been especially characteristic of modern chamber music. The use of these instruments is more than mere exploitation of new and unusual media, for the most radical composers have used tone color itself as a means of formal organization.

The symphony continues to be the principal large form for instrumental composition. In the case of some writers, particularly those whose style still favors the Romantic, this form is likely to be of an extended character, with colorful orchestration, and often combining voices with the orchestra. At the other extreme are those symphonic writers who have collapsed the symphony to a mere shadow of its classical self. The serial composers have made the most use of this kind of treatment. A large number of composers lie somewhere between these extremes and use many devices to rejuvenate the classic symphonic form.

Ex: *Sonata for Violin and Piano,* Bartók
       Piano Sonata, Copland
       Sonata for Trombone and Piano, Hindemith
       Sonata for Cello Unaccompanied, Kodály
       Sixth String Quartet, Bartók
       Duo for Violin and Violoncello, Ravel
       Piano Trio, Kirchner
       Ode to Napoleon, Schoenberg (Chamber Music)
       Songs of Anacreon, Dallapiccola (Chamber Music)
       London Symphony, Vaughn Williams
       Symphony in Three Movements, Stravinsky
       Symphony for Small Orchestra, Opus 21, Webern

2. *Concerto.* The frequent return in the twentieth century to ideas of early music is reflected in the revival of the concerto grosso as a prototype. Solo concertos are frequently written, but the orchestral concerto in which many of the instruments act as soloists or in which groups of instruments are pitted one against the other is very typical of the return to early forms within the idiom of the twentieth century. In the case of the solo concerto the composers handle their material in much the same way as in the symphony. The solo instrument is no longer exploited only for virtuoso effects although virtuoso technique is required for performance. The tendency to exhibit the instrument at the expense of the orchestral body is abandoned in favor of a kind of composition in which the soloist and orchestra exploit the musical material in "concert." Cadenzas are employed only if they are appropriate means of developing the musical material.

Ex: *Piano Concerto,* Schoenberg
       Violin Concerto, Berg
       Concerto for Violin No. 2, Prokofiev
       Concerto Grosso No. 1, Bloch
       Concerto for Piano and Woodwinds, Riegger
       Concerto for Orchestra, Bartók

3. *Ballet.* The instrumental theatrical work known as the ballet continues into the twentieth century in a form that is much more concise than its predecessor of the nineteenth cen-

tury, and in a form that is much more abstract than the set of closed dances which made up the so-called classic ballet. Most of the ballets of the twentieth century are one act works, with one or more scenes. The music rarely consists of set dances but is rather in the form of a highly rhythmical symphonic poem which is interpreted by the dancers in appropriate panto-mime and dance gestures. The stylized figures of the dancers of the classic tradition give way to free gestures and movements which symbolize the dramatic libretto in collaboration with the musical symbolism of the orchestral score. The ballet has been one of the most successful vehicles in the presentation of modern music to a receptive public. In the United States it has been the most successful form of dramatic music. Ballet music constitutes one of the most frequently heard forms in orchestral concert programs since the music can be given in its entirety or in suites made up of selected scenes from the score.

> Ex: *El Sombrero de tres picos,* de Falla
> *Le Sacre de printemps,* Stravinsky
> *The Creation of the Earth,* Milhaud
> *The Age of Gold,* Shostakovitch

4. *Overture.* The overture has continued as a single move-ment form quite apart from its original purpose as a prelude to a dramatic work. Most overtures in the twentieth century are really short symphonic poems, often of dramatic expressive quality. Modern dramatic musical works rarely employ an over-ture in the traditional sense so that there are few overtures of this kind in the modern repertory.

> Ex: *Outdoor Overture,* Copland
> *Big Ben Overture,* Toch

5. *Suite.* The twentieth century suite is usually a selection of scenes or sections from a larger work such as a ballet, inci-dental music to a drama or motion picture, or a series of pieces connected rather loosely by thematic relationship, mood, or extramusical idea. Only in some few instances is the suite based

on the tradition of the dance suite. As a consequence it is often the product of the more romantically inclined composers due to its connection with extramusical purpose. The name is used for compositions of this character ranging from orchestral to keyboard suites.

> Ex: *Lyric Suite,* Berg (for string quartet)
> *Appalachian Spring Suite,* Copland (for orchestra)
> *Lieutenant Kije,* Prokofiev (for orchestra)
> *Suite No. 2 for Orchestra,* Bartók
> *Suite, opus 29,* Schoenberg (for piano)

6. *Incidental Music for film, Television and Drama.* A great quantity of music used to accompany dramatic presentations is written in the twentieth century. While the greatest portion of this music is merely "background music," there is some that has achieved independent value, and appears in concert form. This is more generally the case with incidental music to the staged dramas than that for the motion picture. This music, however, when done by very competent composers is so much a part of the film itself that it cannot, and often should not be heard except as a part of the picture. The television is yet too young to have fostered any amount of music for its particular use, and there has been no crystallization of musical dramatic presentations, due, perhaps to economic reasons. As a consequence there are few composers who have been called upon to write music for this media.

> Ex: Motion picture music: *Of Mice and Men,* Copland
> *Quiet City,* Copland
> *Major Barbara,* Walton
> Ex: Incidental music to drama: *Divertissement,* Ibert
> *Oedipus,* Honneger

7. *Short Forms: Dances, Poetic Pieces.* Many short works have been written whose form is usually that of some dance, generally a modern or exotic one, or a simple two- or three-part song structure. Most of these works are written for piano though solo instruments combined with piano and small ensembles or

even orchestral compositions are sometimes cast in these forms. While no new forms evolve out of this genre a great number of experimental pieces are written for standard instruments and electronic production.

Ex: *Mikrokosmos,* Bartók (piano)
Three Pieces in the Shape of a Pear, Satie (piano)
Sarcasms, Prokofiev (piano)
Construction in Metal, Cage (percussion orchestra)
Variations for Orchestra, Schoenberg
Eight Etudes and a Fantasy, Carter (woodwind quartet)

VI. Vocal Forms

In general it might be said that vocal forms used in the twentieth century are the traditional ones found in the preceding periods. Examples of every vocal form found in all the earlier periods since the Romanesque are adapted to the contemporary contrapuntal and harmonic idiom. The voice in solo and choral compositions is now treated more as an instrument than previously. The range is expanded, intervallic skips which are not technically difficult on an instrument are demanded of the voice, vocal dynamic changes are instrumental in character, and even the type of tone quality is dictated by instrumental considerations. In addition the vocalist is confronted with technical demands on vocal production that seem at times unsurmountable. This is particularly true in solo vocal compositions.

1. *Opera.* The opera tends to retain something of the symphonic character of the Wagnerian tradition; however, it has become much more compact and dramatically dynamic. The general tendency towards economy of material makes the dramatic presentation much more concise and intense. There is sometimes a return to closed forms of aria and chorus, with composer reverting to the simplicity of the baroque opera in this respect. Entire texts of dramatic works are often used as operatic librettos without any adaptation for musical setting. In some cases the operas are written in large symphonic forms so that several scenes are treated as movements or sections of abstract music

such as the sonata, variation form, etc. An extreme of the operatic world is the setting of the writings of avant garde literary figures of the twentieth century as, for example, the "stream of consciousness" writers. Such works achieve their dramatic expression through the use of such advanced styles as the twelvetone method of composition as well as highly dissonant chromaticism. The other extreme is the reversion to the ballad opera of the seventeenth century with its simple closed closed forms such as the popular street and folk songs. The Broadway musical comes close to a revival of this kind. Harmonically and melodically it parallels the nineteenth century tradition. Rhythmically it has much of the liberty of twentieth century jazz, and the general mood of the works reflects a certain freedom of expression that is so typically American that several examples of this kind of composition have established themselves in the repertoire of opera houses in many countries.

Despite the degree of extremes represented in the various types of musical dramatic works, an economy of treatment, realism, expressionism, dramatic intensity, a greater or lesser degree of dissonant harmony, and irregularity of rhythm characterize all the twentieth century musical dramas.

> Ex: *Wozzeck,* Berg
> *The Rake's Progress,* Stravinsky
> *The Wise Woman and the King,* Orff
> *Mathis the Painter,* Hindemith
> *Aaron and Moses,* Schoenberg
> *Down in the Valley,* Copland
> *The Three Penny Opera,* Weill
> *Porgy and Bess,* Gershwin

2. *Art Song.* The art song continues to be a popular vehicle for composers. Texts generally tend to be of a more complex nature both in structure and idea than those of the Romantic period, and avoid the sentimentality of the more typical Romantic art song. This is in keeping with the more angular melodic treatment that is given the voice and the added emphasis on the accompaniment, whether this be the traditional

piano or the chamber music ensemble of various kinds which is so often used. The term accompaniment, in fact, is inaccurate in designating the instrumental part of most twentieth century vocal compositions since the voice and whatever instruments used form a total ensemble rather than a vocal line with instrumental background. In many instances composers have turned to folk melodies and given them setting in modern idiom, or at least a setting that is not governed by the lush harmonic texture of Romantic music. Such works have often employed an instrumental chamber group instead of the piano.

A modern phenomenon of song writing has been the disintegration of the melodic line into a highly inflected declamatory part. The device known as "sprechstimme," (speech voice), has been used by a number of the twelve-tone writers as well as other composers in combination with small instrumental groups. In this case the vocal part is almost pure declamation without exact tonal designation, but with rhythmic notation and general inflection indicated.

> Ex: *Songs,* Ives
> *Chansons madécasses,* Ravel
> *Goethe Lieder,* Dallapiccola
> *Marienleben,* Hindemith
> *Pierrot Lunaire,* Schoenberg

3. *Liturgical Music.* Actually there is little music written for purely liturgical purposes by the composers of the twentieth century. Some settings of the mass for the Roman Catholic Church have been done in as extreme style as the twelve-tone system, but these are rare and their performance as liturgical music is even rarer. Likewise some able composers have written music for the Protestant church and the Jewish synagogue. A considerable amount of contemporary liturgical music uses a style that might be called neo-baroque, an adaptation of contrapuntal style to the dissonant idiom of the twentieth century.

> Ex: *Mass,* Stravinsky
> *Sacred Service, "Avodath Hakodesh,"* Bloch
> *Christmas Cantata,* Honneger
> *Choral-Passion,* Distler

4. *Oratorio—Choral Works with Orchestra.* The oratorio in the twentieth century remains almost as dormant as it was in the latter half of the nineteenth century. Only occasionally is a contemporary composer moved to write a work of dramatic expression and length to be performed as a concert presentation. Those that are written generally employ the traditional plan of this form albeit in a style that is in keeping with the twentieth century. The settings of less dramatic forms of texts for chorus, soloists and orchestra are much more common in the twentieth century than oratorio settings. Many composers have used poetic as well as prose texts in works of several movements. Sometimes these are only for chorus and orchestra and sometimes soloists are also called for. Composers have experimented with various types of instrumentation in such works since one of the attributes of contemporary ensemble music is the emphasis on tonal color. In most of these works the instrumental body is again more than a mere accompaniment and the vocalists are something less than soloists. Choral works of this kind tend to be cast in forms dictated by the texts which are usually of the finest literary quality. The complexity of the writing calls for a highly developed choral skill which is unfortunately scarce, so that performances of the finest of twentieth century choral and orchestral scores are indeed rare.

> Ex: *Symphony of Psalms,* Stravinsky
> *Songs of Prisoners,* Dallapiccola
> *Psalmus Hungaricus,* Kodály
> *Belshazzar's Feast,* Walton
> *Laud to the Nativity,* Respighi
> *Carmina Burana,* Orff

5. *Short Choral Works.* A great demand for choral compositions for secondary school and university use as well as for fine amateur and professional choirs has given rise to many shorter choral works usually unaccompanied but often using the piano in support of the voices. These works are usually one movement in length and are settings of significant poems or prose texts of historical or timely interest. The modern treat-

ment of such texts tends to be one of contrapuntal texture with a highly developed independence of line and very free rhythmic treatment. In many cases such treatment is also used in the settings of folk songs. A great wealth of choral material is available in this form ranging from the traditional to very extreme modern style.

Ex: *Peaceable Kingdom*, Randall Thompson
     Mörike Lieder, Distler
     Dirge for Two Veterans, Holst

VII. Important Composers

It is impossible to state with any authority that one or another of the composers of the twentieth century belongs categorically to either of the lists under VII and VIII. Some composers have already established themselves in what seems at the moment to be a permanent historical position because of the value of their works. Others have had or are having marked influence on the musical production of the twentieth century even though there may be doubt as to the intrinsic value of their compositions. Important Composers contains men in both these categories. The authors recognize that perhaps large numbers of those listed under Other Composers may have written works of more intrinsic value than some of those listed under Important Composers. In fact, they are personally strongly of this opinion. They have, however, tried to avoid subjective evaluations as much as possible. Moreover, there is no claim as to the exhaustiveness of these lists. More United States composers are listed than composers from other countries, but this seems understandable in the light of the nature and purpose of the book.

1. Janáček, Leoš (1854-1928) was one of the renowned Czech composers. While he lived the greater portion of his life in the nineteenth century most of his significant works were composed very late, in fact in the last decade of his life. His operas, *Kata Kabanová* (1921) and *From the House of the Dead* (1928); the *Glagolitic Mass* (1926), the *Sinfonietta* (1926), and

the *Concertino for Piano and Chamber Orchestra* (1925), are examples of his late production. His musical expression is terse and economical, based on motivic construction which was derived from a study of speech inflection. While he wrote several chamber music and orchestral works, it his operas which first brought him world-wide recognition and which are finding special favor again some forty years after his death. Besides the works mentioned the operas *Jenufa, Mr. Brouček's Excursion to the Moon,* and *Mr. Brouček's Excursion Into the Fifteenth Century* are among his important works.

2. Satie, Erik (1866-1925) was a French composer whose importance lies more in the personal influence he had on his contemporaries than in his few compositions. He was the counselor, before the First World War, of the group of young composers in France who came to be known as "Les Six," a group which included Darius Milhaud, Arthur Honneger, Francis Poulenc, Georges Auric, Germaine Tailleferre, and Louis Durey.

His style can be characterized as one of complete simplicity. He used the simplest of harmonies, melodies, polyphonic texture, and formal structures. There is no attempt to be profound. This trend toward simplicity was the foreruner of the break with Romanticism and impressionism and the gradual turn toward neoclassicism. His utter disregard for the sentimental and pretentious was reflected in the titles which he attached to many of his works, for example *Cold Pieces, Airs to Make One Flee, Three Pieces in the Shape of a Pear.* These and other piano pieces such as the *Gymnopédies* and *Gnosiennes* are among the best known works of Satie. Two important works among larger forms are the symphonic drama *Sophocles*, based on the dialogues of Plato scored for four sopranos and chamber orchestra, and the ballet, *Parade.*

3. Vaughan Williams, Ralph (1872-1958) was an English composer who very consciously and ardently allied himself with the great folk song revival of England which centered about Cecil Sharp. For a number of years he participated actively in

the search for, and study of, folk songs of the English people. While he seldom quoted folk songs in his works and rarely used actual folk melodies as thematic material, his whole output is infused with the idiom of the English folk song. He never develops a style that is at the same time national and twentieth century, but the idiom of English folk song scarcely allows such a combination. While his works are characterized by modal polyphonic treatment he is essentially a melodist and uses chromaticism and dissonace very sparingly. He wrote in all the many areas of musical composition though his symphonic works and vocal compositions are the more regularly heard. Among the nine symphonies the *London Symphony* (#2), the *Pastoral* (#3) and the *Fourth Symphony* are the best known. *On Wenlock Edge* for tenor, string quartet and piano, and a number of sacred compositions as well as several operas are among his important works. These include the operas *Riders to the Sea,* and *Hugh the Drover; Mass in G Minor,* and a cantata, *The Pilgrim's Progress.*

4. Schoenberg, Arnold (1874-1951) was an Austrian composer most widely known as the founder of the "method of composing with twelve-tones." Schoenberg's earliest compositions were in the romantic tradition of Wagner. His preoccupation with sonorities that avoided the function of tonal harmony placed him, however, in the forefront of the radical composers often referred to as expressionists, before the end of the first decade of the century. Exploitation of a new relationship between tonal material was finally concluded with the publication in 1923 of the *Five Piano Pieces, op. 23.*

In the *Suite for Piano, op. 25,* Schoenberg writes the first composition to be built exclusively on the principle of twelve-tone composition. Schoenberg contended that his new system was not revolutionary but evolutionary, a natural outcome of the tradition of western European music. A considerable group of disciples who had already gathered about him in the early years of the century adopted his techniques and along with Schoenberg himself laid the foundations of the twelve-tone style.

Schoenberg's influence as a practicing teacher continued throughout his long life, from his early years in Vienna where he was ultimately engaged as a professor of compositions at the Vienna Academy, through a professorship at the Prussian Academy of Arts in Berlin, which had to be relinquished with the advent of the Nazi regime in 1933. From 1933 until his death he resided in the United States, where he was a member of one or another university faculty until his seventieth year.

Schoenberg has been influential in the stylistic development of a large number of pupils and followers. Among the most important of these are Berg, Webern, Krenek, Dallapiccola, Skalkottas, Kirchner, and a score of others who have adopted principles of Schoenbergian technique if not the system exclusively. Even Igor Stravinsky in his seventies began to use techniques now called serial composition which stem from Schoenberg.

Among the most widely heard works of Schoenberg are those of his early romantic period, *Verklärte Nacht* (Transfigured Night) originally a string sextet, later transcribed for string orchestra; the *Gurre-Lieder,* for chorus, soloists, and orchestra; and a number of chamber music works such as the *String Quartets Nos. 1 and 2, Pierrot Lunaire,* and a large quantity of songs. The most outstanding of the works in the twelve-tone system are the *Piano Concerto, Violin Concerto op. 36, String Quartets Nos. 3 and 4,* as well as chamber music for unusual instrumental combinations. An incomplete opera, *Moses and Aaron,* first performed posthumously, has had great success.

5. Ives, Charles Edward (1874-1954) was one of the most unusual of American composers. Trained as a musician he hesitated to subject his creative talents to the economic demands that would be made on these talents if he were to devote himself to the career of a composer. As a consequence he entered the business world and became a very successful insurance broker, leaving his composition free from all remunerative considerations. This double life led to a physical breakdown in 1918 that ended his compositional career. The result of his early

decision was that almost all of his works were written in the twenty odd years between 1896 and 1918.

In some respects he foreshadowed many of the practices of later twentieth century composers such as Schoenberg and Stravinsky. His use of polytonality, polyrhythms and the contrapuntal proceedings that are part of the serial composers' techniques, inversion, retrograde, augmentation, and diminution, are all characteristic of his music. While his works are always constructed on a tonal basis he achieved a considerable amount of dissonance, in some cases almost a feeling of atonality with these devices. Despite all the characteristics of modern music, Ives' musical ideas were deeply rooted in New England folk and religious music with themes from folk songs and New England hymnals. Strangely enough almost none of his compositions received performance until the 1940's. The *Third Symphony* was performed in 1947, almost forty years after it was written, and received the Pulitzer Prize. *The Second Symphony* was given its first performance exactly fifty years after it was written. Their influence on American composers was not felt until a few years before Ives' death. His output was devoted mainly to orchestral, chamber, piano, and song literature. Among his most important compositions are the four symphonies, several symphonic poems, *Three Places in New England, Central Park in the Dark, The Unanswered Question,* a large number of songs among which *General Booth Enters Heaven* is thoroughly representative, and many piano pieces including the *Concord Sonata,* and some choral works.

6. Ravel, Maurice (1875-1937) was a French composer whose mixture of impressionistic style with classic clarity would best label him as a post-impressionist. He was not a pupil of Debussy but stood in close relation to him in many aspects. He extended the practice of unresolved dissonances but rarely came to the point of atonality. In many respects he remained closer to the romanticists than to those who came to be considered the radical twentieth century composers. Ravel's love of the exotic in music was revealed not only in his use of rhythms and

scale construction derived from his Basque background but also in his predilection for expression in other exotic idioms. His settings of *Deux Melodies Hebraiques* (Two Hebrew Melodies), *Five Popular Greek Melodies*, and the *Songs of Madagascar* as well as his occupation with Oriental themes in a number of his compositions such as the *Scheherazade* exhibit this love for the exotic. Likewise he was very much influenced by medieval as well as unusual folk tonal systems. His *Rapsodie Espagnole*, *Pavane for a Dead Infanta*, and *Tsigane* represent these interests. Even in those compositions in which he exhibited a decided neoclassic tendency the harmonic idiom, as well as the instrumentation, reflected Ravel's deep interest in old and unusual systems and tonal colors. Among such neoclassic works are *Le Tombeau de Couperin*, the *Mother Goose Suite*, *String Quartet in F*, the *Two Piano Concertos*, and a number of piano works, an area in which Ravel was outstanding; *Gaspard de la nuit*, *Jeux d'eau* (Fountains), *Sonatine*. Ravel also wrote a few stage works among them the operas *L' Heure Espagnole*, *L' Enfant et les Sortileges* (Dreams of a Naughty Boy), and the ballets *Daphnis and Chloe*, *La Valse*, and *Boléro*.

7. de Falla, Manuel (1876-1946) was the most important Spanish composer since the Renaissance. While his style is essentially that of the French impressionists he combined impressionism with a very conscious Spanish nationalism as in *Nights in the Garden of Spain*. He was not unmindful, however, of twentieth century stylistic advances and he combined these with a musical expression that has a real authenticity of Spanish idiom. His love of Spain induced him to exile himself from his native land when it fell to the anti-Republicans, and he lived his last years in the Argentine. His most successful works have been ballets, among which are *El Amor Brujo* (Love the Magician), and *El Sombrero de tres picos* (The Three Cornered Hat). A *Concerto for Harpsichord, Flute, Oboe, Clarinet, Violin, and Cello* is representative of his interest in abstract forms as well.

8. Bloch, Ernest (1880-1959) was a Swiss composer who lived a large portion of his productive life as composer, conductor, and

teacher in the United States. Bloch was an intensely expressive writer, first in a neo-romantic style and later in a somewhat more neoclassic style. His influence as a teacher of twentieth century American composers was widespread, with such men as Roger Sessions, George Antheil and Leon Kirchner, among others, as his students. His major works include a number of symphonic poems among which *Schelomo, Trois Poèmes Juifs* (Three Jewish Poems), and *America* are representative examples. His neoclassicism is expressed in the *Concerti Grossi Nos. 1 and 2.* He wrote a substantial amount of chamber music including five string quartets, some piano music with orchestra and solo works for various instruments. A single choral composition, the *Sacred Service* has been very successful. A single opera, *Macbeth,* has also gained recent attention.

9. Stravinsky, Igor (1882-   ), a Russian by birth, has lived most of his productive career in Paris and Hollywood. While his style has been one of the principal influences on other composers in the twentieth century, particularly the French and those men schooled in France, he has never been attached to any institution or academy and only occasionally has lectured on the general aesthetics of music. He has had no pupils as such. With the composition of his ballet, *Le Sacre du Printemps* (The Rite of Spring) 1913, Stravinsky adopted a dissonant harmonic technique which, however, was not based on any preconceived plan or theory. Earlier compositions already showed dissonant tendencies in the use of such devices as bitonality. Further adoption of polytonality and use of free dissonance, nonharmonic tones, etc., showed an expansion of the complex chromaticism of the nineteenth century, never, however, to the point of complete denial of tonal center. It was not until the middle 1950's that Stravinsky assayed an adoption of the serial technique with its atonal implications.

Stravinsky's style is characterized not only by its harmonic innovations but perhaps even more by its use of primitive and brutal rhythmic patterns, whose complexities are the result of the consecutive use of widely varying metric patterns and a kind of polyphony of widely differing rhythmic strata. The improvisatory freedom of jazz rhythms was often employed. In many instances long passages are almost exclusively rhythmic in nature.

Stravinsky likewise exploits tonal color to its utmost. This is true in both large and small instrumental combinations. Unusual scoring such as the elimination of all the violins, violas and clarinets in the orchestra of the *Symphony of Psalms,* or the accompaniment of four pianos and percussion in *Les Noces,* are typical examples.

Perhaps no other twentieth century composer exhibits so many exclusive uses of diverse styles as Stravinsky who has been a prolific composer over a period of fifty years to date. His rich output of compositions dating from 1908 when he was studying with Rimsky-Korsakov has never abated, and the list of well-known and often heard works makes him the one twentieth century composer whose recognition has been comparatively immediate and universal. This is probably due in part to the great number of stage works, principally ballets, which have made the introduction of his music to the general public somewhat easier than if his compositions had been more predominantly in the form of abstract orchestral or chamber music.

Stravinsky could be classified at various times as a post romantic, a primitivist, a neoclassicist, a neo-romantic, an abstractionist, an expressionist, a constructionist, though withal he has maintained a certain personal idiom that marks all of his compositions.

Some of the important works under various headings are: ballets — *The Firebird, Petrouchka, Rite of Spring, Histoire du Soldat, Jeux de cartes* (Game of Cards); orchestra — several suites taken from the ballets, *Fireworks, Concerto for Piano and Wind Instruments, Symphony in C, Dumbarton Oaks;* chamber music — *Pribautki, Octet for Wind Instruments, Septet for Piano, Wind and String Instruments;* choral — *Sym-*

phony of Psalms, Mass, Canticum Sacrum; piano — *Capriccio for Piano and Orchestra, Sonata for Two Pianos.*

10. Bartók, Béla (1881-1945) was the most distinguished Hungarian composer of the twentieth century. While his harmonic idiom was not based on any preconceived theory, Bartók's music reflected the twentieth century character of freely combined tonal sonorities. His music is essentially tonal in structure but he made extensive use of nonharmonic tones. His harmonic as well as his rhythmic and melodic style was derived from an intense love and study of primitive folk music. The use of exotic scales derived from this source gave rise to melodic and harmonic practices which conformed generally to the twentieth century breakdown of the tonally centered tradition. Bartók also made extensive use of polytonality, a device which results in a kind of controlled dissonance.

Folk music for Bartók was not a means to romantic nationalistic expression, but rather a source of expressive material, universally applicable. His scholarly interest in folk music extended beyond his own national culture and included the music of all the Balkan peoples and even that of North Africa. His music not only reflects his interest in the rhythmic, melodic and harmonic aspects of primitive folk music but he applied the impulse of the primitive to his use of instruments, in particular to the piano, which he treats as a truly percussion instrument.

In his earliest works Bartók was obviously influenced by the impressionism of Debussy. This influence never completely disappeared from his compositions and is to be found in many of the slow movements of later works. The most distinctive design employed by Bartók is the arch form, a symmetrical balance of movements within the composite form of the sonata.

His compositions, which succeeded in finding wide performance and acceptance only after his death in New York in 1945, have since become extremely popular. Among the most distinguished are the three *Piano Concertos,* the *Violin Concerto,* six *String Quartets,* the ballet, *The Miraculous Mandarin,* the opera *The Castle of Duke Bluebeard,* the *Mikrokosmos,* a series of instructional pieces for piano in modern idiom, *Concerto for Orchestra,* and many songs.

11. Webern, Anton (1885-1945) was another of the twentieth century Viennese group of Austrian composers who were pupils and disciples of Arnold Schoenberg. Webern adopted the twelve-tone method to his pointilistic technique, which resulted in an extremely economical use of musical material in which every phase of musical expression is reduced to its barest minimum. Thematic material is often replaced by motives that seem to be compressed. The polyphonic texture is varied by the device of placing the successive notes of the contrapuntal line at different octave levels, and by changing the tonal qualities of each note by using different instruments to perform the individual notes of any one line. The compositions are of extreme brevity, an entire symphony lasting only a few minutes. The performing media consists of very few instruments and these are used only sparingly.

Such techniques give rise to the application of the descriptive term "pointilistic" to the writing of Webern. Webern wrote a rather large number of individual works but their brevity reduces his total output to something less than three or four hours of performance, a remarkable fact when compared with the total output of other composers of the past or even the present.

Mid-century trends tend to indicate that Webern might stand out as one of the most important of twentieth century figures. His influence among the serial and electronic composers is especially significant. The most important works of Webern are *Symphony op. 21, String Quartet op. 28* and the *Cantatas op. 29 and 31.*

12. Berg, Alban (1885-1935) was an Austrian composer, pupil of Schoenberg, and recognized as one of the most expressive composers in the twelve-tone technique. As in the case of Schoenberg, his early compositions show a marked influence of Wagner and Mahler. In his masterpiece, the opera *Wozzeck,* Berg organizes the musical dramatic material into abstract forms

such as a rhapsody, suite, theme and variations (passacaglia) etc. The opera caused great protest when first performed in the 1920's but has since established itself as one of the great repertoire pieces of the twentieth century. Another opera, *Lulu,* only partially finished, and a number of songs as well as some orchestral and chamber music round out a short but productive life. Among the instrumental works the string quartet, *A Lyric Suite,* the *Violin Concerto,* and the *Chamber Concerto for Piano, Violin, and Thirteen Wind Instruments,* are frequently played.

13. Varèse, Edgar (1885-1965), a French composer who lived most of his productive life in America was perhaps the greatest innovator of the twentieth century. His attitude toward music is one of an experimenter. His better known works exhibit an engagement with sounds for the sheer sake of tonal masses, a characteristic that finally led him to exploration in the use of electronic sounds. Although he started his musical career as a romanticist and impressionist all traces of these characteristics, as well as the compositions dating from these periods, disappeared. In his search for tonal depth he exploited the tone qualities of all kinds of unusual instruments and instrumental combinations, being particularly interested in percussion instruments or the percussive effects that can be generated by more conventional instruments. The works which have been most frequently performed are *Hyperism,* scored for two wood winds, seven brass, and sixteen percussion instruments, *Ionisation* written for thirteen performers on thirty different percussion and friction instruments, *Octandre* a chamber work for eight performers, and *Density 21.5* for solo flute.

14. Villa-Lobos, Heitor (1887-1959), one of the foremost South American composers, was a native of Brazil where he was eventually engaged as superintendent of musical and artistic education in Rio de Janeiro. Villa-Lobos' idiom is highly influenced by the folk music of Brazil and sometimes is actually based on folk song themes. He was very interested in fusing the peculiarities of Brazilian music with the tradition of western Europe. An example of this style is to be found in the *Bachianas*

Brasileiras, a set of nine suites in which Brazilian folk music idiom was combined with Bachian counterpoint. A more typically original Brazilian form was the "Choros." In a series of fourteen of these works, Villa-Lobos combines the many elements of Brazilian folk, popular, and Indian music into compositions which use quite unusual instrumental and vocal forces. The most popular among these two groups of compositions are the *Bachianas Brasileiras Nos. 1 and 5* and the *Choros Nos. 1 and 7.*

15. Prokofiev, Sergey Sergeyevitch (1891-1953) was one of Russia's outstanding composers of the twentieth century. He himself listed the following as the four elements of his style: 1. classicism (neoclassicism); 2. innovation which at first was represented in an individual harmonic style, later as an expression of strong emotions; 3. the motoric element, and 4. lyricism. He regarded another element, the grotesque, as an outgrowth of the others. Much of his music, however, is flavored by a certain puckishness or humorous quality.

Prokofiev was widely known as a concert pianist in his early years. He lived in Paris until 1933 when he returned to Russia. His connection with modern practices of western Europe often brought him some criticism, but he remained a highly revered composer and undoubtedly has influenced the younger composers of the Soviet.

His musical output was very extensive. The total number of his works which eventually found concert performance was, perhaps, second only to Stravinsky among the modern composers. His composition extended into every field with the exception of the sacred. Among the best known are his *Seven Symphonies,* the *Third Piano Concerto,* the *Two Violin Concertos,* the symphonic poem, *Peter and the Wolf,* the orchestral suite, *Lieutenant Kije,* ten *Piano Sonatas,* and a great many short piano works among them *Sarcasms.*

16. Milhaud, Darius (1892-   ) is one of the leading French composers of the older twentieth century generation who pioneered the modern idiom in the early part of the century. He is a very prolific composer with works in every area

of music. He has been active as a teacher for many years during which he has taught in the United States extensively. His many experiments have included use of jazz, polytonality, and eventually electronic devices. He has not subscribed to any form of atonality though his use of dissonance in combination with a lively melodic line has given his work a distinct and individual style. His ballets, *The Creation of the World* and *Le Boeuf sur le toit* (The Beef on the Roof), are representative of his concern with jazz idiom. Other works illustrate his preoccupation with the melodies of his native Provence, such as the *Suite Provençale*. Concertos, sonatas, symphonies, and many pieces of chamber music are among the large list of compositions which date from the first decade of the century to the 1960's.

17. Honneger, Arthur (1892-1955), a Swiss composer, was closely allied with the French trends of the twentieth century by his inclusion in the group known as "Les Six." While his early descriptive tone poem, *Pacific 231*, was looked upon as representative of the new machine age Honneger turned from this type of realistic writings to pursue a neoclassic style. His dramatic oratorios, *Joan of Arc at the Stake* and *King David*, are two of the great choral works of the twentieth century. Among a large number of orchestral composition his five *Symphonies* stand out as worthy of note. Honneger also wrote a large amount of chamber and piano music as well as vocal literature.

18. Orff, Carl (1895-   ), a German whose stage works have won him international recognition is, perhaps, one of the most conservative of twentieth century composers. Despite this he represents a number of trends which are typical of this century. In contrast to the nineteenth century musicians who regarded harmony as the principal shaping force, Orff is typical of the twentieth century in placing rhythm in this role. His rhythmic force is drawn from word rhythms, especially from ancient and folk speech, folk dances, and folk songs. He treats these rhythms with a kind of repetitious primitiveness that makes for intense dramatic feeling. Structurally his music is very simple. He avoids contrapuntal practice for the most part, re-

sorting to the simply harmonized melodic line, with rather rare instances of clashing dissonances resulting from the use of non-harmonic tones. Percussion instruments in abundance are in evidence in all his orchestrations. His best known works are the dramatic cantatas *Carmina Burana* and *Catulli Carmina* along with several operas among which *Der Mond* (The Moon), *Die Kluge* (The Wise Woman), and *Antigonae* are the most popular. In addition to these works Orff has written a series of five books called Music for Children which have done much to revolutionize music education in the past ten years.

19. Hindemith, Paul (1895-1963) was a German composer, performer, conductor, teacher, and one of the dominant musical forces in the twentieth century. Hindemith employed several styles of composition. In his earlier works of the 1920's he was openly rebellious toward tradition of all sorts. His music reflected a free contrapuntal character which made much use of dissonance. Hindemith was also very occupied with the idea of general music education at this time in his production of so-called "Gebrauchsmusik" (music for use). This music, vocal and instrumental, was intended to introduce the young and the amateur to the idiom of modern times through school and home performance. A neoclassic turn is evident in much of Hindemith's music of the 1930's. Further study of old music led Hindemith to a polyphonic treatment which, while modern in harmonic idiom, is reminiscent of the thirteenth to sixteenth century practices. Even the lack of bar lines and metric signs, a characteristic of music before 1600, was imitated.

Hindemith was a very prolific composer writing in every conceivable field of musical composition. While he wrote solo works for almost every instrument he was not so much interested in the exploitation of tonal color as most contemporaries. Constructive rather than emotional expression characterizes his works.

The following are his best known works: a song cycle *Das Marienleben* (The Life of Mary), opera, *Mathis der Maler* (Mathis the Painter), *Wir Bauen eine neue Stadt* (We build a

New City) for children's performance, *Ludis Tonalis* for piano, *In Praise of Music*, for chorus and orchestra, *Symphonic Metamorphosis on Themes of Weber*, and *The Four Temperaments* for piano and strings.

20. Sessions, Roger (1896-) is one of the foremost American composers. A pupil of Ernest Bloch, his early works tend toward the Romantic. He soon turned, however, toward a very complex counterpoint which contained much dissonance. While he eventually came under the influence of Schoenberg and has written much music which verges on the twelve-tone system and its atonal results, he has never adopted this style of composition. Sessions defies any label such as neo-romantic, neoclassic or expressionistic though he partakes of each of these in some degree. He has not been a prolific composer, and has made his greatest contribution in the area of orchestral, chamber, and piano music. Among the four symphonies the *First Symphony* represents his early neoclassic style while the *Third Symphony* shows an individual use of twelve-tone technique. Other important works are the *Piano Sonata No. 2, Second String Quartet, Idyll of Theocritus* for soprano and orchestra, and *The Black Maskers*, an early work for orchestra written as incidental music to a play.

21. Gershwin, George (1898-1937) was America's first and most successful composer to incorporate the popular jazz rhythms of the 1920's in classical forms. His success as a composer of popular songs and musicals was already well established when he turned to other types of expression. In these his melodic gift and rhythmic genius gained him success as a serious composer. In addition to numerous Broadway hits such as *Of Thee I Sing, Let 'Em Eat Cake*, and *Girl Crazy*, his more serious and lasting works are *The Rhapsody in Blue, American in Paris, Piano Concerto in F*, and the opera, *Porgy and Bess*.

22. Copland, Aaron (1900-) was a pupil of Nadia Boulanger, and is, perhaps, the most widely known of American composers. He has adopted numerous styles and techniques, jazz, neoclassic constructivism, and modified twelve-tone. His

most successful works have reflected the American scene through symphonic poems, ballets, and operas, as well as a large number of works for radio and motion picture some of which have had the rather unique distinction of being used as concert music. Copland has also written a large quantity of music of a more abstract nature, symphonies, chamber music and piano works. Among his best known compositions are the ballets, *Appalachian Spring, Billy the Kid, Rodeo,* the orchestral works, *El Salon Mexico, Outdoor Overture, Lincoln Portrait, Third Symphony,* and the piano works, *Passacaglia, Piano Variations,* and *Piano Sonata.*

23. Krenek, Ernst (1900-   ) was born in Vienna, but spent a large part of his creative life in the United States. His music has shown the influence of almost all the stylistic experiments of the early twentieth century. An early opera (1927), *Jonny spielt auf!* utilized jazz idioms and had great success both in Europe and America. After many experiments, Krenek finally embraced a modified twelve-tone style. A prolific composer, he has composed eleven operas, three ballets, incidental music for seven plays, a large number of choral works, five symphonies, four piano concertos, six piano sonatas, and eight string quartets. He is also the author of several books including *Music, Here and Now.*

24. Dallapiccola, Luigi (1904-   ) is the foremost of the Italian modern composers. He has combined the dodecaphonic technique with the Italian tradition of vocal line in a very expressive fashion. His masterful adaptation of the twelve-tone system to lyrical expression is best illustrated in his *Canti de prigionia* (Songs of Captivity) a set of choral songs, and in his opera *Il prigioniero* (The Prisoner). A number of chamber music works employing voice and instruments of various kinds are also noteworthy.

25. Shostakovitch, Dmitri Dmitrievitch (1906-   ) is the leading composer of the younger Soviet group. His *First Symphony* written as a graduation piece when he was eighteen years of age brought him immediate fame. He has been under severe official criticism for incorporating the techniques of western

European modern music with its dissonant qualities into his music, as in the case of his opera *Lady Macbeth of Mtzensk.* Obediently he has turned to the traditional forms and styles of the Classic and Romantic periods with tremendous success within the Soviet. With the exception of a small number of works of a few other composers, those of Shostakovitch are the only compositions by living Soviet composers that are heard outside Russia today. Six *String Quartets* and a *Piano Quintet* are the best known of his chamber music. Up to the present he has written eleven symphonies of which the fifth has been the most successful. A large number of ballets and operas, of which only short excerpts have been heard outside Russia, and a great number of film compositions are numbered among his compositions.

26. Carter, Elliott (1908-   ) is an American composer whose music is essentially twentieth century in its contrapuntal texture and its occupation with rhythm and meter as form building elements. Carter's works are infused with modal counterpoint though he has made use of a personal type of twelve-tone technique. In his latest works he has devised a system of "Metric Modulation" whereby he has been able to modulate from one speed to another by changing the rhythmic values of the basic units. Carter is not a prolific composer but his works are of refined techniques. His *Variations for Orchestra, Eight Etudes and a Fantasy* for woodwind quartet, and *String Quartet No. 2* are typical of his output.

27. Cage, John (1912-   ) is an American composer whose radical tendencies in composition have expressed themselves in the derivation of new tonal colors in "preparing" the piano by placing on the strings of the instrument such objects as metal, erasers, screws, etc. He has also experimented in the area of chance or random composition. The latter is accomplished by chance selection of pitch, note values, dynamics, instrumentation, etc., either from notated suggestions or from pure chance as in the case of one of Cage's own works, *Imaginary Landscape,* in which twelve radios, dialed according to predetermined wave lengths, give forth whatever programs or lack of program that

chance to be on the air at the moment. For the prepared piano
Cage has written *Sixteen Sonatas* and *Four Interludes.*

28. Britten, Benjamin (1913-   ) is a prominent British
composer of today. While he has written in many fields of
musical composition it is through his operas and choral works
that he has achieved world-wide recognition. Britten's style is
essentially vocal. He is clearly a classicist in his approach to
musical composition and consequently is not interested in the
Wagnerian idea of "endless melody," but rather stresses the
concept of closed forms in operatic writing. He is not an ad-
herent to any set method or technique of composition, but has
been influenced by a number of widely varying composers in
whose individual styles he has found certain elements of interest.
His operas include: *The Rape of Lucretia, Peter Grimes, Albert
Herring, Billy Budd, The Little Sweep* or *Let's Make an Opera*
and *Midsummer Night's Dream.* In the field of choral works,
The War Requiem and those compositions which are essentially
a cycle of vocal works, *A Ceremony of Carols, Spring Symphony*
and *A Boy Was Born,* are among his most impressive. Not least
illustrative of his love for the variation form is the very popular
The Young Person's Guide to the Orchestra.

29. Kirchner, Leon (1919-   ) is a young American composer, teacher, and brilliant pianist who came under the influence of Schoenberg in his first musical studies. Later he
studied with Ernest Bloch and finally with Roger Sessions. All
of these men influenced him greatly but he never adopted a
system from any one of them. His music fluctuates between a
very highly chromatic idiom and an atonal one. Most characteristic is its motoric drive whether the medium be the orchestra,
the piano or the string quartet. Kirchner's music is imbued with
an intensity of expression that is almost exhausting in its demands on the listener. His importance in the mid-century musical
scene of America is evidenced by the large number of awards
and commissions he has received. His *Concerto for Piano and
Orchestra, Sinfonia,* and *String Quartet No. 1* are representative
of his finest style.

30. Boulez, Pierre (1925-   ), a French composer, is one of the more controversial of the younger twentieth century men who has developed a very complex style of serial composition and has more recently turned to electronic music. The best known work of Boulez is *Le marteau sans maître* (The Hammer Without a Master) written for contralto and a group of six instruments. The unusual instrumentation of flute in G, viola, guitar, vibraphone and "percussion" is indicative of Boulez' concern with tone color, particularly with that of the percussion type instruments. Boulez has been one of the most active participants in the festivals of contemporary music.

31. Stockhausen, Karlheinz (1928-   ) is a young German composer who has given most of his attention to the field of electronic music, although he started his career as a disciple of Webern using the conventional instruments. *Kontra-Punkte* for ten solo instruments is a representative work of this period. Another phase is the *Piano Piece XI* which is a work constructed on the basis of random selection and improvisatory treatment of nineteen notated fragments. The best known of his electronic compositions is *Gesang der Junglinge* (Song of the Youths) which is written for human voice and electronic sound generator. The notation of such music being in graphs and geometric figures precludes any performances other than by those few persons capable of reading such notation. The electronic equipment employed by Stockhausen, and those associated with him at the Northwest German Radio Studio in Cologne, in no way attempts to imitate the sound qualities of conventional instruments. The sounds produced by the signal generators and the electronic synthesizers are exploited for their intrinsic value as "new" sounds.

VIII. Other Composers

Argentina
   Ginastera, Alberto (1916-

Austria
   See Germany

Belgium
　　Poot, Marcel (1901-
　　Pousseur, Henri (1929-

Chile
　　Santa Cruz, Domingo (1899-

Czechoslovakia
　　Martinů, Bohuslav (1890-1959)
　　Habá, Alois (1893-
　　Dobiáš, Václav (1909-
　　Cikker, Jan (1911-
　　Feld, Jindřich (1925-

Denmark
　　Nielson, Carl (1865-1931)
　　Holmboe, Vagn (1909-
　　Bentzon, Niels Viggo (1919-

England
　　Delius, Frederick (1862-1934)
　　Holst, Gustav Theodore (1874-1934)
　　Ireland, John (1879-
　　Bax, Sir Arnold (1883-1953)
　　Berners, Lord (1883-1950)
　　Bliss, Sir Arthur (1891-
　　Rubbra, Edmund (1901-
　　Walton, Sir William (1902-
　　Lambert, Constant (1905-1951)
　　Fricker, Peter Racine (1920-
　　Birtwistle, Harrison (1934-
　　Davies, Peter Maxwell (1934-

France
　　Koechlin, Charles (1867-1950)
　　Roussel, Albert (1869-1937)
　　Schmitt, Florent (1870-1958)
　　Boulanger, Nadia (1887-
　　Durey, Louis (1888-
　　Ibert, Jacques (1890-
　　Tailleferre, Germaine (1892-

Auric, Georges (1899-
Poulenc, Francis (1899-1962)
Messiaen, Olivier (1908-
Martinon, Jean (1910-
Françaix, Jean (1912-

Germany and Austria

Pfitzner, Hans (1869-1949)
Reger, Max (1873-1916)
Schnabel, Arthur (1882-1951)
Toch, Ernst (1887-1964)
Pisk, Paul (1893-
Weill, Kurt (1900-1950)
Apostel, Hans, E. (1901-
Jelinek, Hanns (1901-
Egk, Werner (1901-
Blacher, Boris (1903-
Bialas, Gunther (1907-
Fortner, Wolfgang (1907-
Distler, Hugo (1908-1942)
Schiske, Karl (1916-
Einem, Gottfried von (1918-
Henze, Hans Werner (1926-

Greece

Skalkottas, Nikos (1904-1949)
Xenakis, Yannis (1922-

Hungary

Dohnanyi, Ernst von (1877-1961)
Kodály, Zoltán (1882-

Italy

Busoni, Ferruccio Benvenuto (1866-1924)
Respighi, Ottorino (1879-1936)
Pizzetti, Ildebrando (1880-
Malipiero, Gian Francesco (1882-
Casella, Alfredo (1883-1947)
Zandonai, Riccardo (1883-1944)
Castelnuovo-Tedesco, Mario (1895-
Petrassi, Goffredo (1904-
Peragallo, Mario (1910-

Maderna, Bruno (1920-
Nono, Luigi (1924-
Berio, Luciano (1925-

Mexico

Carrillo, Julian (1875-
Chavez, Carlo (1899-
Revueltas, Silvestre (1899-1940)
Galindo, Blas (1910-

Netherlands

Ruyneman, Daniel (1886-
Pijper, Willem (1894-1947)
Badings, Henk (1907-
Henkemans, Hans (1913-
Ponse, Luctor (1914-
Leeuw, Ton de (1926-
Schat, Peter (1935-

Norway

Valen, Fartein (1887-1952)
Egge, Klaus (1906-
Sostevald, Gunnar (1912-
Mortensen, Finn (1922-

Poland

Szymanowski, Karol (1882-1937)
Bacewicz, Grazyna (1913-
Lutoslawski, Witold (1913-
Serocki, Kazimierz (1922-
Baird, Tadeusz (1928-
Penderecki, Krzysztof (1933-

Russia

Miaskovsky, Nikolai (1881-1950)
Khatchaturian, Aram (1903-
Kabelevsky, Dmitri (1904-
Khrennikov, Tikhon (1913-

Spain

Mompou, Frederico (1893-
Surinach, Carlos (1915-

Switzerland
Schoeck, Othmar (1886-1957)
Martin, Frank (1890-
Burkhard, Willy (1900-1955)
Liebermann, Rolf (1910-

Sweden
Larsson, Lars-Erik (1908-
Blomdahl, Karl-Birger (1916-
Lindholm, Ingvar (1921-
Nilson, Bo (1936-

United States of America
Loeffler, Charles Martin (1861-1935)
Carpenter, John Alden (1876-1951)
Ruggles, Carl (1876-
Powell, John (1882-
Griffes, Charles Tomlinson (1884-1920)
Gruenberg, Louis (1884-
Riegger, Walingford (1885-1961)
Bauer, Marion (1887-1955)
Moore, Douglas (1893-
Rogers, Bernard (1893-
Piston, Walter (1894-
Sowerby, Leo (1895-
Still, William Grant (1895-
Wagenaar, Bernard (1894-
Hanson, Howard (1896-
Thomson, Virgil (1896-
Cowell, Henry (1897-1966)
Porter, Quincy (1897-
Harris, Roy (1898-
Thompson, Randall (1899-
Antheil, George (1900-1961)
Luening, Otto (1900-
Partch, Harry (1901-
Giannini, Vittorio (1903-
Blitzstein, Marc (1905-
Finney, Ross Lee (1906-
Lockwood, Norman (1906-

Barber, Samuel (1910-
Schuman, William (1910-
Hovhaness, Alan (1911-
Menotti, Gian Carlo (1911-
Ussachevsky, Vladimir (1911-
Berger, Arthur (1912-
Dahl, Ingolf (1912-
Weisgall, Hugo (1912-
Brant, Henry (1913-
Dello Joio, Norman (1913-
Fine, Irving (1914-
Goeb, Roger (1914-
Keller, Homer, (1915-
Diamond, David (1915-
Persichetti, Vincent (1915-
Babbitt, Milton (1916-
Harrison, Lou (1917-
Kay, Ulysses (1917-
Bernstein, Leonard (1918-
Bergsma, William (1921-
Imbrie, Andrew (1921-
Foss, Lukas (1922-
Mennin, Peter (1923-
Powell, Mell (1923-
Schuller, Gunther (1925-
Shifrin, Seymour (1926-

IX. and X. Important Writers on Music

The rise of musicological research in the European and American universities has resulted in the publication of a tremendous volume of books dealing with all phases of music by eminent scholars. Many of these works, however, deal not with the twentieth century but with the historical past. The following list has been limited to those books by twentieth century authors who have contributed to the understanding of the music of this century. Lists of scholarly works dealing with research in the historical past are readily available and the most important of these in the English language have been listed in the Introduction.

1. Schoenberg, Arnold (1874-1951) was known as a teacher and theorist as well as a composer. His most important work, *Harmonielehre*, appeared in English as *Theory of Harmony*, (New York 1948). In this work as well as in subsequent English volumes Schoenberg discusses his theory and aesthetics of music. *Style and Idea* (New York, 1950) and *Structural Functions of Harmony* (New York 1954) are two volumes among a large number of articles and monographs that Schoenberg published during his long life.

2. Stravinsky, Igor (1882-   ) while not a teacher nor given to discussion concerning his music did deliver a series of lectures at Harvard which were subsequently published under the title of *Poetics of Music* (Cambridge 1947). He discusses his own musical aesthetics as well as the musical aesthetics of a number of other composers both past and present. A later series of volumes under the title of *Conversations with Igor Stravinsky* were written in collaboration with Robert Craft and discuss all matter of musical questions particularly those concerning modern music.

3. Reti, Rudolf (1885-1957) a Serbian by birth, lived most of his life in the United States and wrote several books the most important of which was published after his death, *Tonality-Atonality-Pantonality* (New York 1958).

4. Toch, Ernst (1887-1964) a Viennese by birth but lived in United States since 1935. He was active as a teacher during much of his career in Europe and America. A German work, *Melodielehre* (Berlin 1923), is one of the few dealing with this subject. An English book, *The Shaping Forces in Music* (New York 1946) deals with general theory and aesthetics of music both past and present.

5. Yasser, Joseph (1893-   ) of Polish birth fled Russia in the 1920's and has lived in the United States since that time. His most important work among many others is *A Theory of Evolving Tonality*. In this work he offers an hypothesis not only for the origin of the pentatonic and heptatonic scales but for a future scale which he envisages as being implied in the work of the twelve-tone composers.

6. Hindemith, Paul (1895-1963) always interested himself in the teaching of music. His composition in the 1920's which he called "Gebrauchsmusik" or "music for use" was evidence of this interest at an early age. From 1940 to 1949 he held the post of professor of the theory of music at Yale University in the United States. Among a large number of books that he wrote, two stand out as particularly pertinent to twentieth century theory and composition. *The Craft of Musical Composition* (New York revised, 1945) and *A Composer's World: Horizons and Limitations,* (Cambridge 1952) state the individual theory of Hindemith's composing technique as well as his aesthetic concepts concerning music of the twentieth century.

7. Sessions, Roger (1896-   ) has been actively engaged in university teaching for the greater part of his life. His very keen and analytical mind has prompted him to write several books which are the result of his long years of experience as composer and teacher. The *Musical Experience of Composer, Performer, Listener* (Princeton 1950) and *Reflections on the Music Life in the United States* are two important works dealing with current problems in music.

8. Hanson, Howard (1896-   ) is a composer, conductor and teacher. His influence on the musical life of the United States has been very great. He has written a great deal in furtherance of the modern composer. His book, *The Harmonic Materials of Modern Music* (New York 1960), gives a mid-century view of the musical theory of the twentieth century.

9. Krenek, Ernst (1900-   ) has been active as a teacher and writer as well as a composer, and writes of the contemporary scene with a large amount of personal knowledge and involvement in his book *Music Here and Now* (New York 1939).

10. Copland, Aaron (1900-   ) is known as a writer and teacher as well as a composer. Three books dealing with music in general but of great importance to the understanding of modern music have come from his pen. *What to Listen for in Music* (New York 1939), *Our New Music* (New York 1941), and *Music and Imagination* (Cambridge 1952) constitute a valuable addition to the writings on contemporary music.

XI. Suggested Readings

XII. Further References

Forte, Allen. *Contemporary Tone Structure*. New York: Columbia University Press, 1955.

Hodier, Andre. *Jazz: Its Evolution and Essence*. New York: Grove Press, 1956.

Leibowitz, Rene. *Schoenberg and His School*. New York: Philosophical Library, 1949.

Modern Music Quarterly (1923-1946) Published by the League of Composers, New York.

Perspectives of New Music (a bi-annual journal). Princeton University Press for the Fromm Music Foundation, 1962.

Pleasants, Henry. *The Agony of Modern Music*. New York: Simon and Schuster, 1955.

Reihe, Die. (An intermittently appearing journal dealing exclusively with serial and electronic music). Bryn Mawr: Presser, 1955.

Salazar, Adolfo. *Music in Our Time*. New York: W. W. Norton, 1946.

Glossary

A CAPPELLA—A term used to designate choral music without accompaniment.

ALEATORY MUSIC—A type of composition based on the element of chance in both the selection of sounds and their performance.

CHORD—A combination of three or more tones sounded simultaneously.

CHROMATIC ALTERATION—Altering a tone of the diatonic scale by means of accidentals.

COMPOSED-THROUGHOUT—The opposite of strophic. A song that has different music for each stanza.

CONSONANCE—In traditional harmony an interval or chord which produces an effect of repose or agreeableness.

CONTRARY MOTION—The movement of two voices in opposite directions.

CONTRATENOR—The third voice in addition to the tenor and discant in fourteenth and fifteenth century vocal compositions. It is sometimes called the male alto voice.

COUNTERPOINT—The combination of two or more distinctive melodic lines into a single musical fabric. It is often used synonomously with polyphony.

DIATONIC—The natural scale made up of five whole tones and two semi-tones. The term is also used to describe melodic motion in the natural scale without alterations.

DISSONANCE—In traditional harmony, an interval or chord which produces an effect of harmonic tension.

DOMINANT—The fifth degree of the diatonic scale or, in harmonic practice, a chord built upon the fifth degree.

DRONE BASS—A sustained bass note that is retained throughout a section or a whole piece. The note is usually the tonic, but it sometimes alternated between the tonic and dominant.

DYNAMICS—Signs, abbreviations and words used to indicate degrees of loudness and volume of sound.

EQUAL TEMPERAMENT—A system of tuning in which the octave is divided into twelve equal semitones (See Apel Dictionary of Music)

FALSETTO—A style of singing by the male voice in which a very high head tone is produced.

HARMONY—A simultaneous sounding of two or more tones. The theory and practice of chord construction and progressions.

HOMOPHONY—Music in which one melodic voice is supported by a chordal accompaniment.

INTERVAL—The difference and distance in pitch between two tones played either successively or simultaneously. Measurement is made by counting the steps of the diatonic scale upwards from the lowest to the highest note. (See Apel Dictionary of Music)

INTONATION—The degree of accuracy of pitch.

INVERSION—(1) An interval or chord is inverted by transferring its lowest tone to the octave below, or vice versa. (2) A melody is inverted by changing each descending interval to the same interval ascending, etc.

LITURGY—The official order of service in the Roman Catholic Church, but the word also applied to authorized services in most Christian Churches.

MELISMA—A flowing, ornamented melody sung on one syllable.

METRIC—The symmetrical grouping of stress and non-stress.

MODULATION—The process of moving from one tonal center to another in the course of a single composition.

MONOPHONY—A single melodic line without accompaniment.

MONO-THEMATIC—A composition based on only one melody or theme.

OSTINATO— A short melodic figure that is repeated in one voice usually the bass, throughout a whole movement or composition.

PARALLEL MOTION—Two or more voices moving in the same direction at the same interval.

PERIOD—A group of measures that makes a natural division of the melody, usually two phrases.

PHRASE—A segment of melody that has a natural pause or ending. It is analogous to a sentence in speech or writing.

PIZZICATO—To pluck the string of a bowed instrument.

POLYPHONY—A musical texture made up two or more simultaneous soundings of independent voices or instruments.

POLY-THEMATIC—A composition based on more than one melody or theme of equal importance.

RANGE—The distance between the highest and lowest pitch of a melody, voice or instrument.

RITORNELLO—(1) An instrumental interlude before or after an aria or scene. (2) The tutti sections of a concerto grosso. (3) The last two lines of the stanza in the fourteenth century madrigal.

SCALE—A series of adjacent tones arranged according to whole and half tones, or any other regular increment of pitch. (See Apel Dictionary of Music)

SEQUENCE—The repetition of a melodic motive in the same part above or below the original.

STROPHIC—A song of which all stanzas are sung to the same music.

SYNCOPATION—A rhythmic device that displaces the accent from a strong beat to a weak beat or a weak portion of a beat.

TABLATURE—Name for the various early systems of notation in which symbols, letters, or figures were used instead of notes on the staff.

TEMPO—The rate of speed by which the music moves. Tempo marks are words and abbreviations used to indicate various degrees of speed.

TETRACHORD—A scale-series of four tones, the highest and lowest of which form the interval of a perfect fourth.

TEXTURE—The density of melodic and harmonic elements designated by such terms as homophonic, polyphonic, chordal etc. (See Apel Dictionary of Music)

THEME—A distinctive melody, or musical idea, that serves as a basis for musical composition.

TONALITY—The quality which is the result of harmonic organization around a central tone, called the tonic or keynote.

TONIC—The first note of the scale, also called keynote.

TRANSCRIPTION—A composition originally written for one media that has been arranged for another voice, instrument, or combination of voices or instruments.

TREMELO—(1) The rapid repetition of a single note a number of times. (2) The rapid alternation between two different notes.

TRI-TONE—The interval made up of three whole tones, also called the augmented fourth.

VIBRATO—A minute fluctuation of pitch both below and above the tone for the purpose of tonal coloring.

VIRTUOSO—A performer with a superior technical facility.

Index